ROUTLEDGE LIBRARY EDITIONS: THE VICTORIAN WORLD

Volume 18

HENRY IRVING

HENRY IRVING

A Re-Evaluation of the Pre-Eminent Victorian Actor-Manager

Edited by
RICHARD FOULKES

LONDON AND NEW YORK

First published in 2008 by Ashgate Publishing Limited

This edition first published in 2016
by Routledge
2 Park Square, Milton Park, Abingdon, Oxon OX14 4RN

and by Routledge
711 Third Avenue, New York, NY 10017

Routledge is an imprint of the Taylor & Francis Group, an informa business

© 2008 Richard Foulkes

All rights reserved. No part of this book may be reprinted or reproduced or utilised in any form or by any electronic, mechanical, or other means, now known or hereafter invented, including photocopying and recording, or in any information storage or retrieval system, without permission in writing from the publishers.

Trademark notice: Product or corporate names may be trademarks or registered trademarks, and are used only for identification and explanation without intent to infringe.

British Library Cataloguing in Publication Data
A catalogue record for this book is available from the British Library

ISBN: 978-1-138-66565-1 (Set)
ISBN: 978-1-315-61965-1 (Set) (ebk)
ISBN: 978-1-138-65793-9 (Volume 18) (hbk)
ISBN: 978-1-138-65795-3 (Volume 18) (pbk)
ISBN: 978-1-315-62105-0 (Volume 18) (ebk)

Publisher's Note
The publisher has gone to great lengths to ensure the quality of this reprint but points out that some imperfections in the original copies may be apparent.

Disclaimer
The publisher has made every effort to trace copyright holders and would welcome correspondence from those they have been unable to trace.

Henry Irving
A Re-Evaluation of the Pre-Eminent Victorian Actor-Manager

Edited by

RICHARD FOULKES

ASHGATE

© Richard Foulkes 2008

All rights reserved. No part of this publication may be reproduced, stored in a retrieval system or transmitted in any form or by any means, electronic, mechanical, photocopying, recording or otherwise without the prior permission of the publisher.

Richard Foulkes has asserted his moral right under the Copyright, Designs and Patents Act, 1988, to be identified as the editor of this work.

Published by
Ashgate Publishing Limited
Gower House
Croft Road
Aldershot
Hampshire GU11 3HR
England

Ashgate Publishing Company
Suite 420
101 Cherry Street
Burlington, VT 05401-4405
USA

www.ashgate.com

British Library Cataloguing in Publication Data
Henry Irving : a re-evaluation of the pre-eminent Victorian actor-manager. – (The nineteenth century series)
1. Irving, Henry, Sir, 1838–1905 2. Actors – Great Britain – Biography 3. Theatrical managers – Great Britain – Biography
I. Foulkes, Richard
792'.028'092

Library of Congress Cataloging-in-Publication Data
Foulkes, Richard.
Henry Irving : a re-evaluation of the pre-eminent Victorian actor-manager / by Richard Foulkes.
   p. cm. – (The nineteenth century series)
   Includes bibliographical references and index.
   ISBN 978-0-7546-5829-0 (alk. paper)
   1. Irving, Henry, Sir, 1838–1905. 2. Actors – Great Britain – Biography. 3. Theatrical managers – Great Britain – Biography. I. Title.

PN2598.I7F68 2007
792.02'8092–dc22
[B]

2007041411

ISBN 978-0-7546-5829-0

Mixed Sources
Product group from well-managed forests and other controlled sources
www.fsc.org Cert no. SA-COC-1565
© 1996 Forest Stewardship Council

Printed and bound in Great Britain by
MPG Books Ltd, Bodmin, Cornwall.

Contents

List of Illustrations and Tables   ix
List of Musical Examples   xi
Acknowledgements   xv

Introduction   1
Richard Foulkes

1. The Chief and his Champion: Irving and J.L. Toole   11
   Michael Read

2. 'He Danced, He Did Not Merely Walk – He Sang, He By No Means Merely Spoke': Irving, Theatricality and the Modernist Theatre   27
   Jim Davis

3. Ellen Terry and Henry Irving: A Working Partnership   37
   Katharine Cockin

4. The Lyceum and the Lord Chamberlain: The Case of Hall Caine's *Mahomet*   49
   Kristan Tetens

5. Embodiment of the King: Henry Irving's *King Arthur*   65
   Doug Kirshen

6. Sins of the Fathers: Dostoevsky and the Murders of Henry and Laurence Irving   87
   Laurence Senelick

7. Irving and his Scenic Artists   99
   Jeffrey Richards

8. 'Henry and 250 Supers': Irving, *Robespierre* and the Staging of the Revolutionary Crowd   117
   Jean Chothia

9. Serenade in a Gondola: Music and Interpolated Action in Irving's Production of *The Merchant of Venice*   135
   Stephen Cockett

10 Arthur Sullivan's Incidental Music to Henry Irving's Production
    of *Macbeth*   149
    Kenneth DeLong

11 The Matter with Irving: Bernard Shaw and Irving Reconsidered   185
    L.W. Conolly

Bibliography   195
Index   205

List of Illustrations and Tables

Illustrations

1	Studio portrait of Henry Irving and J.L. Toole in the 1880s. By permission of V&A Images/Theatre Museum ©	21
2	Sir Henry Irving and J.L. Toole in conversation, Hove Sea Walk, early 1900s. By permission of V&A Images/Theatre Museum ©	23
3	'Meph & Margaret after their holiday', sketch by Ellen Terry. By permission of the National Trust (Smallhythe Place)	40
4	*King Arthur*: The Prologue: Scene – 'The Magic Mere' by Hawes Craven, based on designs by Sir Edward Burne-Jones. *Souvenir of King Arthur*, Doug Kirshen Collection	72
5	*King Arthur*: *The* Prologue – 'Excalibur' (Henry Irving as King Arthur) by Bernard Partridge, based on designs by Sir Edward Burne-Jones. *Souvenir of King Arthur*, Doug Kirshen Collection	73
6	*King Arthur*: Act I: The Great Hall at Camelot, by Hawes Craven, based on designs by Sir Edward Burne-Jones. *Souvenir of King Arthur*, Doug Kirshen Collection	75
7	*King Arthur*: Act II: The Queen's Maying (Ellen Terry as Queen Guinevere), by Hawes Craven, based on designs by Sir Edward Burne-Jones. *Souvenir of King Arthur*, Doug Kirshen Collection	78
8	*King Arthur*: Act III: The Tower Above the River at Camelot (Lena Ashwell as Elaine, Johnston Forbes-Robertson as Lancelot, Ellen Terry as Guinevere and Henry Irving as Arthur), by Hawes Craven, based on designs by Sir Edward Burne-Jones. *Souvenir of King Arthur*, Doug Kirshen Collection	81
9	Laurence Irving as Raskolnikoff with Mabel Hackney in *The Unwritten Law*, Foulsham and Banfield, London, Laurence Senelick Collection	91
10	An artist's impression of Henry Irving in *The Bells*. Raphael Tuck & Co., London, Laurence Senelick Collection	93
11	*King Arthur*: Act II: The Queen's Maying, by Hawes Craven, based on designs by Sir Edward Burne-Jones. Jeffrey Richards Collection	105
12	*Ravenswood*: Act IV Scene 1: Ravenswood – A Room, by Joseph Harker. Jeffrey Richards Collection	106
13	*Faust*: Act IV: Summit of the Brocken, by William Telbin. Jeffrey Richards Collection	106
14	*Macbeth*: Act II: Court of Macbeth's Castle, with Irving as Macbeth and Ellen Terry as Lady Macbeth. Drawing by J[ohn] Jellicoe and Herbert Railton, *Illustrated Sporting and Dramatic News*, 26 January 1889. By permission of the Shakespeare Birthplace Trust	124

15	*Robespierre*: Act V Scene 2: The Convention Scene. Jean Chothia Collection	129
16	Jacques-Louis David, *Le Serment du Jeu de Paume* (*The Tennis Court Oath*). Pen and bistre wash drawing. By permission of the Musée Historique du Château de Versailles (photo: Gérard Blot, RMN ©)	131
17	*The Merchant of Venice*: Act II Scene 3: Shylock's House by a Bridge. Freehand tracing of the sketch in Irving's promptbook	141
18	*The Merchant of Venice*: Act II Scene 3: Shylock Returning Home. Drawing by Cyrus C. Cuneo, *Black and White*, 20 July 1901	145
19	Henry Irving watching a rehearsal. Drawing by J. Bernard Partridge, *Idler*, March 1893, Private Collection	152
20	Henry Irving as Macbeth. Drawing by J. Bernard Partridge, *Souvenir of Macbeth*, Private Collection	154
21	Ellen Terry as Lady Macbeth. Colour photograph by Window & Grove, Private Collection	156
22	Arthur Sullivan: caricature by 'Ape' (Carlo Pellegrini). Watercolour published in *Vanity Fair*, 14 March 1874, Private Collection	159
23	Sullivan's autograph score: *Incidental Music to Macbeth: Introduction* (mm 1–6) Act IV Scene 1. Courtesy of Oriel College, MS, 2, deposited in the Bodleian Library, Oxford	170
24	Sullivan's autograph score: *Incidental Music to Macbeth* (mm 24–31) Act IV Scene 2. Courtesy of Oriel College, MS, 2, deposited in the Bodleian Library, Oxford	171
25	*Macbeth*: Act IV Scene 1: The Weird Sisters and the Third Apparition. *Illustrated Sporting and Dramatic News*, 9 February 1889, Private Collection	172
26	*Macbeth*: Act IV Scene 2: Witches and Spirits in Chorus. Drawing by Bernard Partridge, *Souvenir of Macbeth*, Private Collection	173
27	*Macbeth*: Act VI Scene 6: Macduff and Macbeth. Drawing by J[ohn] Jellicoe and Herbert Railton, *Illustrated London News*, 9 February 1889, Private Collection	174
28	Sullivan's autograph score: *Overture to Macbeth: Opening* (mm 1–7). Courtesy of Oriel College, MS, 2, deposited in the Bodleian Library, Oxford	176

Tables

1	Summary of Sullivan's incidental music to *Macbeth*	164
2	Synotpic analysis of Sullivan's overture to *Macbeth* (1888 autograph score version)	178

List of Musical Examples

1	Sullivan's overture to *Macbeth*: Theme A, mm 1–12 (allegro non troppo vivace)	180
2	Sullivan's overture to *Macbeth*: Theme B, mm 25–31	180
3	Sullivan's overture to *Macbeth*: Theme C, mm 25–27	180
4	Sullivan's overture to *Macbeth*: Theme D, mm 43–48 (horns)	180
5	Sullivan's overture to *Macbeth*: Theme E, mm 51–58 (strings and flute)	180
6	Sullivan's overture to *Macbeth*: Theme F, mm 73–83 (strings, woodwind, harp)	181
7	Sullivan's overture to *Macbeth*: Theme G, mm 91–98 (strings and clarinet)	181
8	Sullivan's overture to *Macbeth*: Theme H, mm 99–108 (strings and clarinet)	181
9	Sullivan's overture to *Macbeth*: Theme J, mm 118–21 (clarinet and trombones)	181
10	Sullivan's overture to *Macbeth*: Coda, mm 232–41	182
11	C.M. Weber's overture to *Der Freischütz*: Coda, mm 281–95	182

Acknowledgements

Acknowledgements are due to all those who, in their different capacities, contributed to the conference 'Henry Irving: A Life in the Victorian Theatre' at the University of Leicester in July 2005.

Professor Joanne Shattock and Professor Vince Newey, as General Editors of The Nineteenth Century Series, have supported the transition from conference to book, as has Ann Donahue at Ashgate.

As editor I owe incalculable thanks (again) to Angie Kendall for her expertise, care and commitment in helping to get this volume ready for publication.

The Central Photographic Unit (in the person of Colin Brooks) of the University of Leicester prepared the illustrations.

Introduction

Richard Foulkes

For the British theatre the concluding decades of the nineteenth century and the first of the twentieth constituted a period of unexampled creativity, diversity and popular appeal. There were various reasons for this. The passage of the Theatre Regulation Act (1843), abolishing the monopoly which, since 1660, had restricted performances of legitimate plays in London to Covent Garden and Drury Lane, led in due course to a boom in theatre-building not only in the capital, but also (indirectly) across the country. This, of course, reflected the shift in population to the metropolis and other expanding, industrial cities. The leisure pursuits of this new urban population were a matter of concern not least to church leaders, who in many cases abandoned long-standing opposition to the theatre, recognising it as potentially far more beneficial (or at least less harmful) than many of the alternatives available. They and others (Gladstone, for instance) could take their cue from the example set by the royal family. From an early age Queen Victoria had been an enthusiast for the theatre (and other entertainments, such as the circus) and, having found in her husband, Prince Albert, a kindred – albeit rather more earnest – spirit, together in 1848 they instituted the Windsor Theatricals while still continuing to patronise public theatres. Following the death of Prince Albert in 1861 his widow no longer considered attendance at theatrical performances to be appropriate, but her eldest son and heir, as Prince of Wales and later King Edward VII, was enthusiastic in his support. Over the years the technical resources of stage management grew with advances in set construction, lighting and so on. On the other side of the curtain, facilities for the audience were greatly improved, especially in theatres that catered for the upper echelons of society. The increasing respectability of the theatre made it an attractive profession for classes which, only a few years earlier, would have regarded it as beyond the pale. At the upper levels of the profession, the financial rewards (especially from long runs in London) were considerable, but, at the other end of the scale, labour was cheap, making large-cast productions economically viable. All this activity created more demand for plays, as well as opportunities for practitioners in related arts such as music and painting.

These propitious circumstances were seized upon at various levels across the land, but the lead being set at the top of the profession was crucial not only for its own achievements, but also for its positive effect on the profession as a whole and public opinion generally. In this respect the theatre was quite extraordinarily well blessed in Henry Irving, who assumed the management of the Lyceum Theatre in 1878, making it, in the popular phrase, a national theatre in all but name and, it might be added, subsidy since that was never regarded as a serious prospect at the time. Irving, like the rest of the British theatre, operated on a simple commercial basis. The fact that Britain, unlike France and most other (continental) European states, did not have an institutional and financial structure for the theatre made Irving's achievements all the more remarkable. In 1895 Irving became the first actor to be knighted and, following his death on 13 October 1905, he was accorded a funeral and burial in Westminster Abbey a week later.

What were the roots of the man who led his profession for more than a quarter of century and who was regarded as their peer by such eminent contemporaries as Gladstone and Tennyson? John Henry Brodribb was born on 6 February 1838 in Keinton Mandeville, near Glastonbury in Somerset, from a long line of sturdy, but unimaginative, Somerset farmers on his father's side. His mother came from strongly Methodist Cornish stock, and much of his upbringing was entrusted to his maternal aunt Sarah Penberthy, a fervent devotee of the sect, who lived at Halsetown above St Ives in Cornwall. His religious upbringing is generally recognised as having a profound and lasting effect on him. In 1848 Irving joined his parents in London and attended the City Commercial School where he excelled in the elocution class. The experience of seeing Samuel Phelps as Hamlet at Sadler's Wells Theatre set Irving on his course as an actor (parental disapproval notwithstanding) and, having adopted the name of Irving partly in honour of the celebrated preacher Edward Irving, he made his professional debut in Sunderland on 29 September 1859 with the prescient words (of Gaston, Duke of Orleans in Bulwer Lytton's *Richelieu*): 'Here's to our enterprise!'

As Laurence Irving demonstrates in his biography of his grandfather[1] Irving served a lengthy provincial apprenticeship before his engagement as leading man for Hezekiah Bateman at the Lyceum Theatre, London in September 1871. It was not until his sensational performance as Mathias in *The Bells* on 25 November that he established himself as a star actor in his own right. By then he had married (in 1869) Florence O'Callaghan, whose legendary question ('Are you going on making a fool of yourself like this all your life?') after his triumph in *The Bells* resulted in their estrangement and separation. The couple had two sons (H.B. and Laurence), both of whom followed their father into the theatrical profession.

In December 1878 Irving took over the management of the Lyceum Theatre, having recruited Ellen Terry as his leading lady. For 20 years the Lyceum was the dramatic centrepiece of London, which was the theatrical capital not only of Britain, but also of its empire and indeed the world. The Lyceum productions of Shakespeare and modern (though usually costume) dramas were the most eagerly awaited and widely discussed cultural events of the day. Yet, however assiduously Irving solicited the support of the royal family, politicians and other prominent public figures, he never forgot the importance of ordinary playgoers of all classes who continued to occupy an important place at the Lyceum and on his regular tours of Britain and America, which he visited eight times. Always ready to take on a public role, as Jeffrey Richards' *Sir Henry Irving Theatre, Culture and Society* (1994) shows, Irving's reward included honorary degrees from the universities of Dublin, Cambridge and Glasgow. Sadly, his later years were clouded by misfortunes: the destruction by fire of much of his scenery in February 1898, the departure of Ellen

---

1 Laurence Irving, *Henry Irving: The Actor and His World*, London, 1951, Appendix B.

Terry from his company in 1902 and his own deteriorating health. As with his debut so with his last appearance, his final words (as Tennyson's Becket) on stage were apt: 'Into Thy hand, O Lord – into Thy hands!' Later on that night of 13 October 1905 Irving collapsed in the entrance hall of the Midland Hotel, Bradford, and at ten minutes to midnight he died.

Though his health had not been good and he had expressed his intention to retire, Irving's death sent what the *Era* described as 'a great thrill of sorrow through all England'.[2] Both the *Era* and the *Stage* published commemorative supplements, but the non-theatrical press also devoted column upon column to the deceased actor. Leading members of the profession eventually prevailed upon the dean of Westminster Abbey for the funeral to take place there, followed by interment. No less than 50,000 applications were received for the 1,200 places at the service. Expressions of sympathy were sent by fellow actors the world over (from the Comédie-Française in Paris to J.C. Williamson in Australia), and 600 wreaths were laid out in the Abbey cloister. Only three rested on the coffin, from the Queen (Alexandra), the Baroness Burdett-Coutts and the Duchess of Fife (Queen Victoria's third child, who was declared the Princess Royal that year). King Edward VII was represented by Sir Digby Probyn and the Prince of Wales by Sir William Carrington. The Lord Mayor of London was present as was the American ambassador (Mr Whitelaw Reed). The pews were filled with distinguished contemporaries, the aristocracy and members of the profession, including Ellen Terry who wrote a touching description of the effect of the rays of 'a splendid tawny sun'.[3] Outside Westminster Abbey crowds stood in respectful silence, and bus and cab drivers had attached black crepe to their whips. In the words of Canon Duckworth, one of many clergy to preach a sermon on Irving's death, 'throughout the English-speaking world' Henry Irving, Britain's first actor-knight, was venerated and mourned.[4]

There can be no doubt about the esteem in which Henry Irving was held at the time of his death – as actor, as manager, as leader of his profession and more besides. Inevitably, the passage of time leads to a re-evaluation of the achievements of great men and women.[5] In the sphere of literature and the arts their novels are reread, their paintings re-examined and their music rediscovered. The process is much more difficult with an actor. An awareness of this permeates an article) that appeared in the *Times Literary Supplement*: 'To-day the dust that was Henry Irving is enshrined at Westminster. Henceforth he is a name, a tradition, a legend. Like all who, in Buffon's phrase, *parlent au corps par le corps*, the stage-player, if our eyes cannot see him nor our ears hear him, is as nothing.' The author goes on to say that this 'eternal commonplace of all acting ... is peculiarly true of such acting as Henry Irving's', the 'finest thing – not seldom the only fine thing – in any stage-character of Irving's was Irving himself'. Thus recollections are 'not of any particular one of his stage

---

2 *Era*, 21 October 1905.
3 Ellen Terry, *The Story of My Life* (London, 1908), pp. 39–40.
4 *Stage*, 20 October 1905.
5 Amongst the events arranged to commemorate the centenary of the death of Sir Henry Irving was a conference at the University of Leicester in July 2005. The chapters in this book originate from papers given then.

impersonations, but of his look and manner and speech at the moment he used to come before the curtain to return thanks to a cheering audience. The dignity and grace and sweetness of it!' Irving's 'secret' was 'this gift of personal domination', which could be 'so great as occasionally to swamp the play':

> He instinctively turned to playing leaders of men because he was a leader of men. As a manager he had a Napoleonic faculty for organization and command; as a *metteur-en-scène* he could not resist doing everything 'In the grand style.' He was not content until he had enlisted the first archaeologists and painters and musicians of the day in the service of the theatre. All he did was done with a certain magnificence. [6]

It is the task of the contributors to this book to engage in a process of rediscovery and re-assessment; to recover, in so far as it is possible, the nature of Irving's achievements, to gauge his importance during his own lifetime and to evaluate his influence in the twentieth and twenty-first centuries. The first two tasks have been undertaken before, though judgements 100 years on from Irving's death may well differ from previous ones, especially in the light of the third task, which assumes a prominence in this volume that it has not done before: Irving's influence on succeeding generations of actors and – in the modern parlance – directors. The book is structured sequentially, dealing in turn with the different elements of performance: acting, the plays, staging and scenery, musical accompaniment and dramatic criticism. Irving's own acting is covered in two contrasting essays by Michael Read and Jim Davis, with Katherine Cockin adding one on his partnership with Ellen Terry. Kristan Tetens, Doug Kirshen and Laurence Senelick all discuss Irving's involvement in the authorship of plays for the Lyceum. Jeffrey Richards and Jean Chothia focus respectively on the scenery and crowd effects in Irving's productions. Stephen Cockett and Kenneth DeLong explore the musical dimension. In conclusion Leonard Conolly examines Irving's relationship with dramatic critic turned dramatist, Bernard Shaw.

Michael Read's account of Irving and Toole makes a fitting starting point. Born in 1830, Toole was eight years Irving's senior and outlived him by nearly a year. Their friendship began in 1857, and thereafter they met every day when they were both in London and corresponded when they were not. Toole consoled Irving on the death of his 'first love', Nellie Moore, and interceded with his estranged wife Florence. He was godfather to Laurence Irving. In many ways – physically, temperamentally, artistically and politically – Irving and Toole were opposites, but they were also complementary and remained mutually dependent, like the Knight of the Sorrowful Countenance and his Sancho Panza. It was Toole who kept faith with Irving during his unpromising apprenticeship in the theatre and it was on tour with Toole's company in 1869 that Irving seized the opportunity to give a solo rendition of Thomas Hood's poem 'The Dream of Eugene Aram' (1824) between two pieces on the bill. Toole's own forte was low comedy, which must have made Irving's intense contribution as the guilt-stricken schoolmaster all the more striking. In due course (1873) Irving appeared in a dramatised version of Eugene Aram by W.G. Wills – one of a number of detailed psychological studies of the effect of conscience on the criminal mind. Thanks to Michael Read's unrivalled knowledge

---

6 'The Drama Henry Irving', *Times Literary Supplement*, 20 October 1905.

of Toole, the roots of Irving's distinctive acting style can be traced back to his days with Toole's comedy company in the decade before his full-scale assumption of the role of Eugene Aram at the Lyceum Theatre.

Whereas Michael Read concentrates on Irving's origins in the mid nineteenth-century theatre, Jim Davis presents a powerful case for the modernity of Irving's acting and its influence on twentieth-century practice. Taking his cue from Edward Gordon Craig's description 'He danced, he did not merely walk – he sang, he by no means merely spoke', Davis argues that, rather than being dismissed – ridiculed even – as some relic of an outdated style, Irving is arguably a prototype for the highly disciplined, physically expressive sort of actor that Craig, Meyerhold, Grotowski and others envisaged and hoped to create in the early twentieth century. Arguably, the most distinctive quality of Irving's acting was his ability to convey his character's thought processes before articulating them verbally, a technique that Davis suggests anticipates the Brechtian *Gest*.

Often dismissed as pictorial acting, Irving's performance style was integral to his detailed attention to *mise en scène* overall, which drew comparisons with the Saxe-Meiningen company and Wagner and the approbation of such a theatrical innovator as André Antoine. Mediated through Craig's memoir and his acknowledged impact on Craig's thinking, Irving can be seen as being much implicated in the new order of theatre (extending to Peter Brook and Peter Hall) as in tradition and the past.

Davis quotes Ellen Terry's single-word answer to the question as to what she remembered most about her years at the Lyceum, 'work' – a motif that Katharine Cockin develops in her chapter on 'Ellen Terry and Henry Irving: A Working Partnership'. As Dr Cockin observes, the relationship was complex with offstage and onstage lives overlapping and drawing in their children – Terry's in particular, whose illegitimacy further complicated their situation and their mother's. The choice of roles for Ellen Terry as the Lyceum's leading lady (some of them especially written for her or at least with her in mind) was not inseparable from her personal circumstances, but Dr Cockin argues that she should be 'envisaged as more of an agent rather than a victim'.

A suitable role for Ellen Terry was clearly an important consideration for Hall Caine who assured Irving that he would develop pathos and 'the noble and contrite aspect of her character' in the play about Muhammad that he was writing for the Lyceum. The authorship of the play was in fact much more complicated than that. The suggestion was Irving's not Caine's, but its origin lay in a play by the French dramatist Henri de Bornier. The successive layers of revision, composition and copyright reflect the practice of the day, with Irving obtaining the text of de Bornier's play, getting it translated into English, asking Hall Caine to revise it, intervening personally in the construction of the script, considering leaving two acts of the original intact, and buying the British rights as an act of courtesy, and all this for a drama that was never performed. Kristan Tetens' detailed exploration of *The Prophet* (as Caine eventually entitled his play) provides compelling evidence of how the planned performance in London of a play on the Islamic prophet Muhammad could send ripples of controversy across the empire. On 26 September 1890 a letter appeared in *The Times* from Raffiüddin Ahmad, vice-president of the Liverpool Moslem Association, referring to news spreading throughout India that 'an English theatrical company intends shortly to represent ... a play called "Mahomet," in which the chief character is the prophet of Arabia'. However such was the level of protest in India that the secretary of state for the subcontinent warned the Lord Chamberlain, as licenser of plays, who intervened, asking Irving to withdraw the play, which he did. Earlier plays on the subject had been performed, but the political situation in 1890 was evidently particularly sensitive and this fascinating collaboration between Irving and Caine never came to fruition.

In contrast, five years later J. Comyns Carr's *King Arthur* was the first major play on the subject to be staged in London for over 200 years and, with its unabashedly jingoistic script and ardent nationalism, it clearly reflected the prevailing *Zeitgeist*. Understandably, Irving had initially attempted to interest Tennyson in the project and, after his refusal, handed the task to W.G. Wills. Characteristically,[7] Irving bought Wills's play although he did not think it would do and turned instead to Carr. Well versed in Arthurian literature (Malory and Tennyson), Carr's particular forte was the fine arts and he scripted each act around one or more breathtaking stage images to be realised by Sir Edward Burne-Jones and the regular Lyceum scenic artists against the strains of a musical score specially composed and conducted by Sir Arthur Sullivan. With Irving as King Arthur and Terry as Guinevere, Carr had a delicate task to perform. As Doug Kirshen observes in Chapter 5, Carr's tactic was to script Guinevere as 'an archetype of feminine beauty and moral weakness' whose 'corrosive sexuality' was the 'proximate cause of her husband's downfall'. Ironically, Carr succeeded where more experienced playwrights had failed in creating 'a complex, multi-faceted character' for Ellen Terry. Though very much a product of its day, Doug Kirshen suggests that, in many respects, *King Arthur* 'anticipates the Hollywood blockbuster', with Irving, like Steven Spielberg and James Cameron, directing a spectacular entertainment whose cultural imperative was commercial viability.

Laurence Senelick describes an intricate, but ultimately circular, pattern in his account of Laurence Irving's adaptation of Dostoevsky's *Crime and Punishment*. Staged in Boston and New York in 1908 under the unwieldy title *The Fool Hath Said in His Heart 'There Is No God'*, when it reappeared at the Garrick Theatre, London as *The Unwritten Law* in November 1910 with Laurence as the guilt-wracked Raskolnikov, comparisons were inevitably made with some of his father's roles. Senelick goes further and demonstrates that Dostoevsky was indebted to *Eugene Aram* (with which, as Read has recorded, Henry Irving was significantly associated in both Hood's and Wills's versions) when he wrote *Crime and Punishment* and that there is a closer relationship between English melodrama and Russian literature than has been suggested hitherto.

At the Lyceum Laurence Irving's contributions included original work (*Peter the Great*) and adaptation (Sardou's *Robespierre*); and, later (1903) at Drury Lane, translation (*Dante*, Sardou again). All these period dramas relied heavily on the scenic resources and skills available at the respective theatres. As Jeffrey Richards points out in Chapter 7, Irving engaged the best scenic designers of the day: Hawes

---

7 See Jeffrey Richards, *Sir Henry Irving: A Victorian Actor and his World* (London, 2005), chapter 6.

Craven, William Telbin and Joseph Harker. However, the fact that none of them had the status of resident scenic artist at the Lyceum is indicative of Irving's all-pervasive control of every aspect of production, as well as a reflection of the practicalities of the play's long run. Richards quotes Bram Stoker's description of how all the elements (in *Faust*) eventually came together to realise Irving's vision. Irving had been able to imagine the effect that his (flaming scarlet) costume as Mephistopheles would create and the difference lighting (gaslight and limelight) would make. If something was not 'right', then out it went regardless of cost, as happened with the inferno cyclorama for *Dante*, which had been painted in Paris. Richards argues that, in his pursuit of harmony between the various elements of production, Irving's approach was the English equivalent of Wagner's *Gesamtkunstwerk*.

Jean Chothia concentrates on the staging of one of Laurence Irving's plays, or rather adaptations – Sardou's *Robespierre*. The centenary of the French Revolution had prompted a number of related plays in London as well as Paris, but – as was often his practice – it was Irving who took the initiative in suggesting a subject to a playwright, in this case Sardou to whom he accorded exceptionally generous terms (£1,000 initially). As usual, the acting script evolved between the author and the actor, with, in this case, the additional intervention of Laurence Irving as translator/ adapter. Although Irving's regular scenic designers were entrusted with most of the scenes, Sardou insisted that the sets for the *Fete* of the Supreme Being (Act II) and the Convention (Act V) were built in Paris so that he could oversee them to ensure their historical accuracy. Dr Chothia narrows her focus to the Convention scene and discusses Irving's intricate, yet apparently spontaneous, staging of the revolutionary crowd ('250 supers') and his management of the visual image, including the role in it of Jean Louis David's *The Tennis Court Oath*. Irving's work at the Lyceum occupied both geographical and temporal crossroads. Just as Irving carefully observed the crowd effects of the Saxe-Meiningen company on their 1881 visit to London, André Antoine long recalled the crowd and lighting effects in Irving's *Macbeth*, which he saw in 1889. Irving toured this huge and complicated production (300 tons of scenery and a company of 87) of *Robespierre* to the United States where successive cohorts of extras were drilled to the same standard as at the Lyceum, impressing at least one reviewer with 'the pauses, the silences' as much as with the roar and hubbub. For all his success in providing customised vehicles for Sarah Bernhardt and Gabrielle Réjane, Sardou failed utterly to do the same for Ellen Terry, who regarded her maternal role as Clarisse du Malucon in *Robespierre* as woefully underwritten.

Music was integral to Irving's holistic view of the stage. Stephen Cockett and Kenneth DeLong provide evocative accounts of Irving's use of music in *The Merchant of Venice* (1879) and *Macbeth* (1888) respectively. Hamilton Clarke's musical score for what turned out to be Irving's most enduring Shakespearian revival offers an overture, entr'acte pieces and settings for songs in the text of *The Merchant of Venice*. It also provides musical accompaniment for the (surviving) Belmont scenes as well as the elopement scene and the interpolated episode. Cockett examines how Irving employed orchestral accompaniment as a strategy to achieve his overall staging intentions. As with scenery, Irving had a clear idea of what music he wanted, but, as he was not a trained musician, it was not easy for him to convey this to his musical director. Nevertheless, as Ellen Terry records, Irving would persist until the music was 'exactly *right*'. The pervasiveness of music in the Victorian theatre anticipated the film score, but, skilfully used, it could also make silence eloquent as evidently happened with Shylock's return to his deserted home. Indeed, as Cockett points out, 'not a single note in the score for *The Merchant of Venice* is associated directly with the Jew'.

Whilst acknowledging the contribution of Hamilton Clarke and others of his ilk, such as Robert Stoepel and Meredith Ball, Kenneth DeLong quotes the exchange between Irving and the music critic Herman Klein to the effect that Arthur Sullivan's agreement to compose the score for Irving's revival of *Macbeth* (1888) promised something on an altogether greater scale, as behoved such an ambitious undertaking (involving 21 scene changes, and over 400 costumes). Arthur Sullivan's incidental music for Irving's revival of *Macbeth* amounted to nigh on 200 pages of orchestral score, the most sustained incidental music for a play that he ever wrote apart from that for *The Tempest*. The music consists of an extended overture and four entr'actes, brief music for stage business, as well as a lengthy piece for the interpolated scene with the witches in Act 4 of Irving's acting version of the play. As with Hamilton Clarke, Irving managed to convey his ideas about the music to Sullivan and, happily, Bram Stoker has left a vivid description of the two great men working together, with Irving expressing 'his inchoate thought' through the 'sway of body and movement of arms and hands'. More conventionally, he suggested the use of particular instruments (the harp, horns). Fascinating in itself, the exploration of Irving's working relationship with Sullivan provides some parallels with his methods with playwrights and scene designers. Comparisons between Irving and Wagner have already been made in previous chapters, but, in this one, DeLong is, of course, concentrating on the specific function of Sullivan's score in Irving's overall concept of *Macbeth* for which he provided a quasi-Wagnerian commentary on the central elements of the play, combining the 'picturesque' with a leitmotif-like conception of the role of incidental music. The partnership between Irving and Sullivan was, of course, renewed for *King Arthur* (1895), the subject of Doug Kirshen's chapter.

Under the alias of Corno di Bassetto, Bernard Shaw served as music critic of the *Star* from 1888 to 1890, but it was as dramatic critic of the *Saturday Review* from 1895 to 1898 that he often discomfited Irving with reviews of his productions and his own performances. Of these, his review of *Richard III* in 1896 was particularly contentious and furthermore overlapped with a lengthy dispute over performance rights for *The Man of Destiny*. Appropriately for the concluding chapter in this book, Leonard Conolly bases his examination of the relationship between the two men on Shaw's article on Irving which was published in the *Neue Freie Presse* (Vienna) on 20 October 1905, just a week after the actor's death and on the day on which his funeral was taking place at Westminster Abbey. The article caused considerable dismay and distress among Irving's friends and admirers. Shaw blamed the poor translation into German and swiftly released his original text. Nevertheless this article – together with his earlier reviews and the dispute over *The Man of Destiny* – helped to create and sustain the impression of the old-fashioned actor-manager versus the radical playwright of the new theatre.

The contributions to this book were prompted by the centenary in 2005 of Irving's death. Cumulatively, they cover all the elements of theatrical production: Irving's performance as an actor; his relationship with Ellen Terry (and her children); his involvement in playwriting, his mastery over every element in the stage picture (sets, lighting, costumes and crowds); his acute sense of the function of music and the power of silence; and his relationship with a leading dramatic critic turned playwright. It is striking that certain strands run through the book: for instance, Eugene Aram (initially in the form of Hood's poem) from 1869 to 1910 (its influence of Laurence Irving's *The Unwritten Law*). Time and time again, Irving's holistic integration of all aspects of theatrical production is manifest. His virtual co-authorship of plays and his close involvement in the composition of the incidental music, the design of scenery and deployment of crowds all serve to reinforce this characteristic of his work. Indeed, the obituary article in the *Times Literary Supplement* proclaimed that 'as a *metteur-en-scène* he could not resist doing everything'. This amounted to doing more than oversee the practicalities of the different aspects of a production; Irving ensured that they all served his own vision of the play, and not least his vision of the character he was playing. In this respect, like Wagner to whom he is compared on several occasions, he was (though he would not have been familiar with the term) a prototype of the twentieth-century director – most obviously, of course, the theatre director (Meyerhold or Brook), but also the Hollywood director, such as Steven Spielberg and James Cameron.

By any measure Henry Irving was an eminent Victorian, as important in his sphere in his own day and as deserving of the attention of posterity as Gladstone, Millais and Tennyson to mention but a few notable contemporaries. However, Irving's reputation, unlike theirs, rests on the notoriously insubstantial evidence of theatrical performance, although this should not, and has not, deterred the contributors to this volume from essaying the task of rediscovering and reassessing this complex, multi-talented and endlessly fascinating man of the theatre. As those fortunate enough to have seen him on the stage –and indeed off – might well have said, we 'shall not look upon his like again'.

Chapter 1

The Chief and his Champion: Irving and J.L. Toole

Michael Read

On the evening of Friday 11 September 1857, Signors Toolerini and Irvingetti, standing together at the front of the stage of the Theatre Royal, Edinburgh, sang a duet of 'Auld Lang Syne'. Their voices, curiously, were less operatic than their body language, but nobody minded, for they were supported by a shrill of actresses and one of the best orchestras a theatre could boast. Under a young maestro, Harry Loveday, it commanded the musical repertoire of one of Britain's finest stock companies in the middle of the nineteenth century. From opera to farce, time after time, all had to be served and supported, including the sort of entertainment in which Signors Toolerini and Irvingetti appeared – opera and farce in bizarre combination. Loveday himself had composed some of the score and had given the rest new settings. Nearby, among the string-players, sat his brother George; and above, across the footlights, stood Toolerini and Irvingetti, to whom he smiled in encouragement as he signalled another cue.

To see them on the stage together made everyone smile. These improbable stars of Italian opera were physical opposites – one of them peculiarly short, the other so tall and bony – and their postures and facial contortions delighted the crowd. Any antics that Toolerini's eyebrows could perform, Irvingetti's were sure to match. The evening was Toolerini's, though. He was taking one of his temporary leaves of the Edinburgh stage.

Loveday turned round and conducted the audience in the familiar refrain. At its close, the ovation for the Italians was immense. Toolerini and Irvingetti bowed low to each other and exchanged a Latin embrace. Irvingetti then retreated from view and, from the side of the stage, as the voices rose for Toolerini alone, studied his partner's way of acknowledging the cheers and marvelled at the easy, off-the-cuff style of his remarks to the house. Just a few words, perfectly judged, and the speaker was taking in the whole auditorium, addressing each person as if he or she was a particular friend. With unforced courtesy he thanked them all and said he would leave for Dublin next day to fulfil an engagement there, and then go to London for another, and 'would do himself the pleasure of making a visit to Edinburgh once every year. That announcement was received with tremendous cheering',[1] and Toolerini, with an elegant bow, walked smartly from the scene. Irvingetti, meanwhile, formed a deep

---

1 *Caledonian Mercury*, 12 September 1857.

impression of the things he was seeing and hearing, and recognized the kind of actor he longed to be.

Signor Toolerini was no Italian. He was J.L. Toole, a Londoner, the comedy sensation of the West End, completing a provincial starring engagement that had begun three months before. That was the length of a season. Usually when London stars came to call, it was just for a week. John Lawrence Toole had been there for 12 weeks, performing a round of his London successes with his visiting co-star Louisa Keeley and the Edinburgh stock company; but Toole was a phenomenon, and Edinburgh hung on to him. Its people had roared at his comic effects since 1853, when the visionary R.H. Wyndham, who ran their theatre, had brought him from Dublin within a year of his professional debut there and made him principal low comedian. While an apprentice at Dublin, Toole had built up a loyalty among the boisterous clientele of the Queen's Theatre and was often preferred to his senior companions, but, once in Edinburgh as the Theatre Royal's chief comic actor, he had a position to lose. Scottish audiences were not renowned for applauding English strangers who presumed to amuse them, but Toole won them over at once. The extraordinary news of his triumph reached London, such that by the autumn of 1854 he was a West End star. Thus it was that, in only his second engagement, J.L. Toole, spectacularly, had turned his opportunities at Edinburgh into a springboard for national fame.

Physiognomy was in his favour. His was a magnificent head – large and well-proportioned, with wavy brown hair sweeping upwards and back from a handsome face, which was square, open and broad, with blue eyes shining with laughter or tears, and lips that seemed ready at any moment to flicker into fun. When distended in horror or indignation, his mouth was so flexible in its exaggerations that it could suddenly alter his whole appearance and amuse the audience all evening. As for his voice, it was deep and juicy, an organ of such versatility and power that it made the ideal instrument for any form of dramatic expression. Perhaps Wyndham had not been taking a risk after all, when he brought him to Edinburgh.

Besides, for all his youth and inexperience, Toole had seen the great actors at work. Right from the start he had been interested in the history of his profession. Samuel Phelps, Charles Mathews the younger, John Baldwin Buckstone and Charles Kean were more than names to him: their performances were familiar in every detail and he could entertain people with imitations. He revered the masters of acting. With hundreds of others he had queued at Drury Lane to get a seat for William Charles Macready's final performance in 1851, and there the decorum of the great tragedian's speech to the audience had impressed him as much as his acting. He never forgot the effect it had upon the silent crowd.

Actors were public figures, he thought. For Toole, making a good speech always seemed as vital as playing a good part. His first one at Edinburgh, naturally, had borne more than a trace of Macready's style. That was in 1854; but back he had come the following spring, staying then for a year and a half; and it was after a second spell in London in the winter of 1856–57 that he returned as a visiting star in his own right 'for a limited engagement' that, by popular demand, soon lost its limits. Toole had expected to act in many places before taking up his London position again towards the end of 1857, but reckoned without his Edinburgh fans, not to mention increasingly attractive terms from Wyndham, intent upon a summer of packed houses.

Edinburgh had known no greater draw than Toole since the glory days of Edmund Kean. Those with long memories could not recall a larger audience than that which, regardless of risk, was jammed in for Toole's farewell benefit on 11 September 1857.[2] First there was a farce, *Honesty is the Best Policy*, with Toole as an eccentric tax inspector, Hector Coco; then the burlesque of Italian opera – *La Somnambula, or The Forty Winks* – with Signor Toolerini as Rodolpho, 'an extremely foreign count', singing solos, duets and choruses with Italian flair. Next came the speech of Toole's that Irvingetti admired so much, followed by more farces: *My Friend from Leatherhead* (Toole as Loophole, his original character) and, finally, *My Poll and My Partner Joe* (Toole as Watchful Waxend, 'a learned cobbler'). Any young actor in the company who envied Toole his hold over the audience or longed for London stardom himself would have noted his methods more closely than usual that last evening before he left.

Signor Irvingetti was Henry Irving, whose real name was John Henry Brodribb, a Cornishman by upbringing, who was then at precisely the same point in his career as Toole had been on *his* first visit to Edinburgh. That city, coincidentally, was *Irving's* second engagement, though, as a tyro juvenile lead, he was given fewer showy roles in which to make his mark than always seemed to be available to principal low comedians. With a slower start and a stonier path, his climb was much tougher than Toole's. Yet there were consolations: he had begun to win the favour of the audience, to enjoy the backstage camaraderie and to make a few friends; and visits by established stars such as the expansive Irish tragedian Barry Sullivan and Macready's former leading lady, Helena Faucit, meant that he could act with people of legendary significance. More than that, their presence had the effect of inspiring new gestures, more varied tones of voice and previously unattempted inflections that sporadically transcended his self-consciousness and drew from the public just a little of the recognition he craved.[3]

But it was the actor who came on 20 June who really opened his eyes. J.L. Toole had all the qualities he wished for himself. True, Toole was no tragedian, as Irving wanted to be, but his method of work and mesmeric control taught Irving more about how to hold the stage than any number of visiting hams. At 27, and brimming with professional maturity, Toole seemed a generation away from the 19-year-old Irving. His social ease contrasted with the awkwardness of the country boy. In addition, he enjoyed the emotional warmth of a settled family life, and lodged with his wife and baby son across the square from the theatre at 23 Union Place, which he made his domestic base whenever he came to the city. Soon, Irving moved from his rented room in Elder Street to another at 17 Union Place, just three doors along the pavement from the Tooles. He may have been hoping to meet Toole socially, for the jealously preserved hierarchies in theatrical companies during the eighteenth and nineteenth centuries (and even for much of the twentieth), where the hard-won status of principal players in relation to supporting ones resembled the distinctions of military rank, discouraged casual conversation between stars and their subordinates.

---

2   See *Caledonian Mercury*, 12 September 1857, and *Era*, 20 September 1857.
3   See Austin Brereton, *The Life of Henry Irving* (London, 1908), Vol. 1, pp. 26–8.

Indeed, it was the custom for rank-and-file players to address their seniors as 'Sir', and the seniors often required it.

Irving saw much of Toole on the stage, at all events, and during those three months was sometimes figuring there as much as he, but longing all the while to exchange, one day, his lanky ungainliness for his companion's polish. In the curtain-raiser on Toole's final night, Irving played Captain Lejoyeux, a poker-backed recruiting officer; then Alessio, 'a very upright fellow', in *La Somnambula*, with a romantic solo, 'Helvetia's Mountain Bowers' to sing; and in the nautical farce that rounded off the bill, a stilted military man, Captain Oakhead. Woodenness of stance and stiffness of limbs were right for each of those parts. Then Toole, having cast all the actors, and having let his young friend play to his limited strengths, was suddenly gone. Irving tracked his course in the newspapers to Dublin and all the way back to London for the winter season – where his idol resumed his place as the star of the Lyceum Theatre.

Irving stayed on in Edinburgh until 1859, and modelled his parting speech of thanks on Toole's. For three years he had tried to earn the same respect. No actor would ever impress him more deeply, either as an artist or as a man, and when the little comedian came back in 1858, again with his wife and son, a comradeship began to develop that would never be broken. Toole maintained that they did not strike up a friendship until Manchester in the early 1860s,[4] but circumstantial evidence suggests that in that summer of 1858 the Toole family moved in with Irving at the theatrical lodging-house owned by Mr and Mrs Grant at 17 Union Place, and on Sunday mornings prayed with him in the church round the corner.[5]

Edinburgh saw nothing of Toole in 1859. The Adelphi Theatre, where now he was, kept him in London too long. In December, though, he bustled some friends into Crosby Hall, Bishopsgate, to hear the now unemployed Irving give a solo reading of Lytton's play *The Lady of Lyons*. Having come to the hall charitably for the sake of a struggling young actor, they went away astonished by his tragic force. Sobs were heard during the climax that Irving worked up towards the end, and Britain's supreme low comedian (a status that few would call into question over the next 35 years) suddenly saw the true potential of his gangling young friend for the kind of sustained tragic acting that he had been given no opportunity to attempt in Edinburgh.

Toole decided to do what he could to promote Irving's career. In the early 1860s he was at the top of his profession, whereas Irving was near the bottom. He introduced him to friends and acquaintances and brought him to lunches and evening parties, sometimes as his guest at the Garrick, where Irving could practise his conversational skills with strangers and meet the leading authors, critics and prospective employers. When their engagements separated them, as they often did, they began their lifelong

---

4 See Joseph Hatton, *Reminiscences of J.L. Toole* (London, 1889), Vol. 1, p. 173.

5 This deduction, though inconclusive, is reasonably suggested by comparison of a letter from Henry Irving to Charles Ford, 8 March 1858, Irving Archive, Theatre Museum, London, reproduced in Laurence Irving, *Henry Irving: The Actor and His World* (London, 1951), pp. 85–6, with an undated letter written from Edinburgh in the summer of the same year: J.L. Toole to Francis F. Toole, University of Rochester, New York.

pleasure of writing to each other. That this habit was well formed at an early stage is evident from a long letter Irving wrote in March 1860 from Dublin, where he had been barracked for weeks.[6] The letter is notable not only for its length, and for the solace he sought from a Dublin favourite who knew how to handle the termagant audience at the Queen's, but also for its friendly tone, sense of humour and patent sincerity. It closed with a benediction: 'God bless.'

For most of the time between 1858 and 1868 letters were the only way they could communicate, since, apart from Toole's visits to the Theatre Royal, Manchester, where Irving was based from 1860 to 1865 and where Toole turned up every year on his annual tour, they did not act together. But they were close, even when apart. In February 1865 Irving wrote and staged a show in Manchester that ingeniously exposed the deceptions of the Davenport brothers, two charlatans from America who, touring Britain, had contrived by cunning stage illusions to draw people into spiritualism. Irving's piece showed up the hoaxers for what they were and drove them out of business, only a few weeks after an Adelphi farce had focused on the same subject, and probably after correspondence with its leading actor.

Toole was forever finding ways to help Irving to his goal. Towards the end of 1867 he was instrumental in bringing him to the Queen's Theatre, Long Acre, which was one of the largest in London and where, from the start of 1868, Irving acted with Toole again, as well as with Charles Wyndham, Lionel Brough, Henrietta Hodson and the 20-year-old Ellen Terry. Toole was by far the principal draw, as the scale of salaries showed. Irving, employed as the 'heavy' man of the company and its stage manager, was paid £3 a week, the same as the resident low comedian, Brough, but Toole got £25. No one else was paid more than Irving and Brough. Charles Wyndham, the 'juvenile lead', got £2 10s, and John Clayton, the 'walking gentleman', £2.[7]

Irving and Toole rapidly made up for their decade apart. Irving, attracted by Toole's fondness for practical joking, enjoyed colluding with him in some elaborate, but harmless, deceptions. Encouraged by their easygoing companionship and the older man's love of the ludicrous, Irving was more at ease with Toole than with anyone else, and found that, perhaps for the first time since boyhood, an impish sense of humour was being tapped and released.[8] He had never been happier than during that season with Toole and his new friends at the Queen's, as they enjoyed together the bohemian life of West End actors and their daily refreshment in the chop-houses of Covent Garden.

Between January 1868 and May 1869 Toole and Irving acted together in 12 plays, first at the Queen's, next at the Standard Theatre in Shoreditch, then at the Surrey Theatre in Lambeth, and on tour together, Toole as the commanding star and Irving as his comic foil or villainous counterweight. Sometimes their business was equal. Toole's and Irving's roles were respectively as follows: Michael Garner and Bob Gassitt in *Dearer than Life*, the Artful Dodger and Bill Sikes in *Oliver Twist*, Moses and Charles Surface in *The School for Scandal*, Bob Acres and Faulkland in

---

6 Much of the letter is reproduced in Irving, *Henry Irving*, pp. 99–101.

7 See H. Chance Newton, *Cues and Curtain Calls* (London, 1927), p. 6.

8 See Bram Stoker, *Personal Reminiscences of Henry Irving* (London, 1906), Vol. 1, pp. 179–80.

The Rivals, Jack Snipe and Robert Arnold in *Not Guilty*, Simmons and Brown in *The Spitalfields Weaver*, Tony Lumpkin and Young Marlow in *She Stoops to Conquer*, Desmarets and De Neuville in *Plot and Passion*, Spriggins and Victor Dubois in *Ici on parle Français*, Paul Pry and Harry Stanley in *Paul Pry*, Tittums and Dr Clipper in *The Steeplechase*, and Caleb Plummer and Tackleton in *Dot*, first at the Standard and then at the Surrey, where Irving was recast as John Peerybingle. Though not as fast work as at Edinburgh, it was lively all the same, bringing back memories of old escapades, of Toolerini and Irvingetti.

Now the two actors were more on a par, and for their summer tour in 1869 Toole wanted Irving to be paid as much as himself and to have prominent billing. But the manager of the Surrey would have none of it. Toole he was glad to book any day, but he did not see why he should take on his accomplice. He wanted Irving's parts for himself. Toole confronted him in his office. No Irving, he insisted, no Toole. The manager, fearing the effect on his business of the loss of the world's favourite comedian, partly relented. Irving could come after all, he said, but would not be paid. For the three weeks that they worked at the Surrey, Toole gave Irving half his money.

> When I was a poor, struggling actor, tramping from town to town in search of engagements, and meeting only with scornful rebuffs and bitter disappointments, and, indeed, in terrible straits to earn my bread, Mr Toole found me, befriended me, gave me work, rescued me from want, and inspired me with hope and courage, and never left me till he saw me well on the road to something like prosperity – and, I may say, something very much like honour.[9]

Mentor and protégé had much in common. Neither had come from a theatrical family, and each was obliged to make his own way in his adopted profession. Both men received a poor but respectable upbringing in Christian principles and faith; both had taken early employment as office clerks in the City of London and abandoned their City offices for the stage. They had also attended (though eight years apart) the evening classes of the City Histrionic Club in George Yard; and each had given amateur performances nearby, at Sussex Hall in Sugarloaf Court. As boys they had haunted the galleries of London playhouses and admired the same actors. As a consequence, they were always proudly aware of their respective places in an honourable tradition, a long line of histrionic succession.

Despite their obvious differences – physically, temperamentally and artistically – Toole and Irving came to recognise a mutual dependence. Of all the managers who might have supported him, it was only the rascally Toole who kept faith with Irving's genius and employed him at a time when no one else would, and gave his talent for classical tragedy its most effective exposure, paving the way for the contract at the Lyceum in 1871, then *The Bells* and all that followed.

The turning-point was Irving's spine-tingling recitation of Thomas Hood's poem of blood and guilt, 'The Dream of Eugene Aram'. In this, a country schoolmaster relives a nightmare in which he committed a murder and strove to hide the evidence, only to find he had not been dreaming at all and that everything was horribly real.

---

9 Henry Irving, as quoted in Newton, *Cues and Curtain Calls*, pp. 51–2.

Toole encouraged Irving to try the poem out between the usual farces while they were touring in the summer of 1869. Croydon, Newcastle, Glasgow, Liverpool, Birmingham, Gloucester, Worcester and Leicester – each thrilled to the novelty; and when, by public insistence, Birmingham and Gloucester were revisited, Irving's monologue had become so great a sensation that no longer was it an experimental interpolation but was advertised with exclamatory anticipation. Irving, his long, pale face picked out eerily by a beam of light, stepped before the curtain:

> ... Methought last night I wrought
> A murder, in a dream!
>
> One that had never done me wrong –
> A feeble man and old;
> I led him to a lonely field,
> The moon shone clear and cold:
> Now here, said I, this man shall die,
> And I will have his gold!

The aspiring young tragedian, motionless and with a haunted gaze, brought everyone under his power. Now it was Toole who watched from the wings as an actor of extraordinary skill took charge of an audience. It seemed to Toole that Irving at last – after so many years of thankless stage villainy and eccentric comedy and farce – was in his proper sphere. The first climax was reached with vocal power in reserve – 'And I saw the Dead in the river bed, / For the faithless stream was dry!' – but the second almost tested its scope – 'And a mighty wind had swept the leaves, / And still the corpse was bare!' All his careful study of Phelps and Sullivan and the hints he had derived from the books he had bought about Edmund Kean underpinned his own genius and shaped it, and helped to bring the audience to their feet in a storm of horror and pleasure. Suddenly, in those towns and cities in the summer of 1869, and in the context of an evening of knockabout farce, audiences realised that they were seeing, as if for the first time, the ideal Hamlet and the perfect Macbeth. All that remained for Toole to do was to release him to managers in the West End, and Irving's course was set.

There the recitation's full impact was felt on 23 March 1871, Irving's benefit night at the Vaudeville Theatre, when the manager of a nearby house, the Lyceum, resolved to make him the leading man of his new company. So, although it would not be right to claim that Toole alone was the making of Irving – the Lyceum's manager chancing to visit the Vaudeville that evening played a decisive part, as did Charles Mathews the younger in spreading good reports of him around the London theatres, and there was also Charles Calvert, stage manager at Manchester, who nurtured Irving's talent when the lessee thought he had none, as well as old Wyndham in Edinburgh, who had gambled as heavily on Irving's abilities as he had, originally, on Toole's, and not forgetting Irving himself, in being himself – it is clear that in 1869 the whole of Irving's future greatness was constructed by J.L. Toole.

In December of that decisive year, and on into the spring of 1870, they had appeared at the Gaiety Theatre in *Uncle Dick's Darling*. Uncle Dick was a good-natured travelling hawker, played by Toole, and his darling was his adopted daughter, who attended a girls' boarding-school and was taught by her headmistress to despise the impoverished fellow who loved her. In contrast, Reginald Chevenix, wealthy, cold and arrogant, was commended as a better match for a girl whose education in mind and manners, so her headmistress went on to explain, had raised her above the common folk with whom she had grown up. The part of Chevenix was small, but, in Irving's hands, acquired strange, unexpected depths. 'Here was a rich original creation', recalled Percy Fitzgerald long afterwards, 'a figure that lingered in the memory, and which you followed, as it moved, with interest and pleasure.'[10] There was, he remembered, 'a surprising finish and reserve. It was agreed that we had now an actor of *genre,* who had the power of creating a character. The impression made was really remarkable, and this specimen of good, pure comedy was set off by the pathetic acting of "friend Toole".' Yet the Gaiety was the home of burlesque, and the play a piece of theatrical hackwork 'made by a good stage carpenter with well seasoned wood'.[11]

The joinery of H.J. Byron, who wrote *Uncle Dick's Darling,* was always slick and well turned, but seldom furnished a play as well as this satire of social class. Byron's design for Chevenix – tall, dark and stern – uncannily hinted at the self-absorption of the future chief of the Lyceum, putting into Irving's mouth some sentiments and attitudes that, for all the repellent qualities of the character he was acting, may also, at that point in his life, have been Irving's own. 'When I have set my mind upon a thing, I generally obtain it,' says Chevenix. 'A man like myself can afford to despise the world's opinion.'[12] For Irving, who had recently married, but who sensed a destiny that was no less demanding or honourable, the following retort of Chevenix's may have been spoken by the ambitious actor with a tremor of acute recognition: 'Can a man in *my* position, with a career of such importance before him – a man with the eyes of the country upon him, waste his time with his *wife*? I am surprised at you.'[13]

The intensity of emotional interplay between the pompous Chevenix and the tender-hearted Uncle Dick was one of the glories of mid-Victorian performance. The premiere, which was attended by the Prince of Wales, inaugurated for Toole a lucrative reign of seven and a half years as the Gaiety's principal comic actor. Irving, though, did not return and, apart from some charity benefits, he and Toole never acted together again.

Only once in his life was Charles Dickens drawn to the Gaiety Theatre, and that was to witness Toole and Irving together in *Uncle Dick's Darling.* Dickens, who 18 years earlier had encouraged Toole to go on the stage, was now enthralled by Irving. 'You may depend upon it, Toole: that man will become a great actor,' he said, as he left the theatre.[14] Dickens died a few weeks later. *Uncle Dick's Darling,* starring Irving and Toole, was the last play he saw.

---

10 Percy Fitzgerald, *Sir Henry Irving: A Biography* (London, 1906), p. 41.
11 John Hollingshead, *Gaiety Chronicles* (London, 1898), p. 106.
12 British Library additional ms 53080R, fol. 15.
13 Ibid., fols 18–19.
14 *Era,* 7 July 1883.

The great actor of Dickens' prediction, like others before and since, was unable to achieve his goal by stagecraft alone. For more than a decade he relied on his mentor to expand his social and professional circles. Toole, who had become a freemason in 1853 and, a decade later, one of the youngest men ever to be elected to the Garrick Club, drew Irving into both those communities. Masonic brotherhood was companionable for the nomadic actors of the nineteenth century, wherever they might find themselves, and socially advantageous for those who wished to associate with local leaders of society and the many influential members of their own profession who were also freemasons. Methodically, Toole was positioning Irving at the intersection of theatrical networks. He was Irving's seconder when his nomination went to the Garrick committee in 1873, only for it to be thrown out. The candidate was too unrefined, it was thought. Undeterred, Toole organised a campaign within the club that ensured Irving's undisputed election the following year.

From the 1870s onwards Toole and Irving enjoyed meeting in various towns whenever their touring routes intersected or drew sufficiently close. When one of them was starring in Edinburgh and the other in Glasgow, they linked up to give readings for local charities, raising enormous sums and taking nothing themselves. To the amusement of both, they competed for favour in the same town during the very first company tour that Irving attempted under his own management. In the first week of September 1878, when Irving's troupe came to the Theatre Royal, Leicester, Toole's was just 200 yards away at the Royal Opera House. The *Leicester Journal* was exultant at the starry conjunction:

Here's success to the good town of Leicester,
The Drama so grandly has bless'd her,
    With Irving and Toole,
    Each head of his school,
Dame Fortune has surely caress'd her.[15]

Staying at the same hotel in Leicester, and as close in spirit as ever, the two actors were now worlds apart in repertoire. Toole brought a gaggle of farces; but Irving had come with *Hamlet* and *The Bells*, for now he was a managing man, with the Lyceum keys in his waistcoat, and the tour that took him to Leicester was a trial for his opening season.

Irving beat Toole into management, beginning on 30 December 1878, compared with 17 November 1879, when Toole, at the other end of the Strand, opened the Folly Theatre, which he refurbished and relaunched as Toole's Theatre in 1882. Both were businessmen now, responsible for the livelihoods of others, with overheads to budget for, as well as plays to choose and perform. Not only did their actors need to be appointed, but also their lieutenants behind the scenes. They consulted each other about staffing. Bram Stoker was brought in to the Lyceum as business manager, a post which, at the Folly, went to George Loveday, who had played his violin in the Edinburgh orchestra pit in the 1850s. For 20 years Irving and Toole had been friends with the Lovedays, whose musicianship had supported some of their earliest performances, and it was to George's brother Harry, former conductor

---

15 *Leicester Journal*, 6 September 1878.

of the orchestra, that Irving now turned for his stage manager. Like many actors before and since, the new rulers of the Lyceum and Folly Theatres were sentimental, superstitious and loyal. With the Loveday brothers at their side again, Toole and Irving felt safe.

Those who complained that Irving's management of the Lyceum neglected new dramatists did not know of the extent to which he unobtrusively assisted them. So well did he and Toole trust each other's judgement that when an actor in Irving's company began to write little comedies that Irving liked but could not always put on, he recommended the author to Toole, who thereupon himself produced three of his plays between 1880 and 1882. The actor-turned-playwright was Arthur Wing Pinero.

With J.M. Barrie it was much the same. In 1891 Barrie, though an accomplished novelist, was untried as a writer of plays. Over supper at the Garrick Club he found Irving sympathetic. If he sent one of his scripts to the Lyceum, he was told, Irving would certainly consider it. The play that arrived was a one-act burlesque, *Ibsen's Ghost*, so Irving referred it to Toole, who gave it a subtitle, *Toole Up To Date,* and staged it immediately, with himself in the leading role. The year after, when Barrie presented Toole with his first full-length play, Toole again produced it, again played the starring part, and enjoyed one of the biggest successes of his entire career. Notching up more than 1,000 performances in the West End and on tour, this play – a farce called *Walker, London* – consolidated Barrie's position as a playwright of note. It was a position that he, like Pinero, owed in large measure to the discerning patronage of the two managers who were often wrongly assumed to have no interest in new dramatists.

From the early 1880s, when Irving's reputation outstripped that of his champion and of every other actor in Britain, Toole referred publicly to him as 'our Leader', whom 'every right-minded actor is proud of'.[16] Irving's leadership qualities set him apart even from the most successful and enterprising of other managers. Theatre workers in the nineteenth century customarily called their boss 'Governor', and so did Irving's; but only at the Lyceum did the workers begin to call their governor 'Chief' (a practice that after 20 years would be aped by some of Beerbohm Tree's company at Her Majesty's Theatre). It was a title that spoke their devotion to Irving, as much as their respect. He had always addressed even the lowliest scene-shifter as 'Sir' and had never been known to tread upon his own stage without first asking for Mr Loveday's permission. By treating his employees with perfect good manners, by advancing the cause of theatrical art in all its forms, in public speeches as well as in practice, by elevating his company above any other in London, and by setting the artistic standards they all strove to match, Irving became, in demonstrable fact, the symbolic head of the British stage, the inspiring leader of all. Toole still championed him, especially in that. When the Chief sailed for America in 1883 on the first of the Lyceum's transcontinental tours, Toole, himself a veteran of American touring, spoke out publicly to wish 'our Leader' God speed and to lament that 'there will

---

16 Undated draft, in Toole's handwriting, of a speech about Irving written in 1883, University of Rochester, New York.

be a great gap in our lives when he goes'.[17] For Toole and for Irving's other friends there would, of course. be a gap of a personal kind, but Toole was here touching on something more – on the sense that the whole theatrical profession in Britain would be separated from its leader, like a ship without its skipper.

At about that time, the Chief and his champion went along to a photographer's studio in London to pose for their portrait together. In it, Irving sits on a low wall and Toole stands beside him (Illustration 1), but the tragedian looks like a light comedian, enjoying himself and looking benign, while the dwarfish comedian frowns, glares heavily towards us, and strikes a tragedian's pose. The image reveals that neither Irving nor Toole conformed to the easy stereotype of his place in art or life. Toole attempted stature by standing on a step, but, even so, his shoulder did not clear the top of the seated man's head. It looks like the picture Max Beerbohm was thinking of when he remembered 'a photograph that used to be in all the shop windows: Irving and Toole together; Toole evidently not quite comfortable in that public juxtaposition, but trying to look very dignified'.[18]

Illustration 1   Studio portrait of Henry Irving (right) and J.L. Toole in the 1880s

---

17 Ibid.
18 Max Beerbohm, *Around Theatres* (London, 1953), p. 441.

Dignity was set aside in 1886 when Toole brought out a burlesque of the Lyceum *Faust*. His unbounded adoration of the Chief did not inhibit his sense of fun: Irving's spectacular production of *Faust* was fair game. The grandeur of his thrilling, supernatural performance of Mephistopheles was transmogrified under the cramped conditions of Toole's Theatre into 'Mephis-Toole-pheles', a zany conjuror all in red, with flashing eyes and wrinkled tights, who kept attempting magic tricks, all of which went wrong. The play, *Faust and Loose*, was the work of F.C. Burnand, and Mephis-Toole-pheles's spells involved much flourishing of an outlandish magic wand and the generation of masses of steam (with consequential jokes about getting into hot water) summoned up by the magic words 'Polly, put the kettle on', which Mephis-Toole-pheles merrily sang. Unlike Irving's other-worldly mist, the great clouds of steam at Toole's Theatre suggested railway platforms and gushed to the accompaniment of locomotive whistles.

> Faust.   Whence come you?
> Meph.   The Lyceum. I thought you knew it.
> Faust.   You're imitating Irving. Please don't do it.
> Meph.   I thought that the resemblance you might see.
> Imitate him? You mean he copies me.[19]

'Henry did not care for burlesques as a rule', wrote Ellen Terry, '... [b]ut everything that Toole did was to him adorable.'[20] Irving never minded his leg being pulled by a true friend and knew that Toole was always the first to protest if anyone said a word against him.

Only once between 1857 and Irving's death 48 years later were differences known to disrupt their friendship – and almost end it for ever – and that was when, in the autumn and winter of 1871–72, Irving was nearing the end of his tether, seeking solace in the bottle, having separated from his wife and two young children. Some of his friends, even Toole, were also becoming estranged from him in their misguided attempts to reconcile him with his wife. The true reconciliation that grew out of it all was not that of Mr and Mrs Irving, but of Irving and Toole. On the single occasion that Irving visited his teenage sons at Marlborough, their boarding-school in Wiltshire, he took Toole along for company, and the four of them went off in the afternoon for a drive through Savernake Forest. According to his grandson, Irving sought the advice of Toole on every personal matter: 'Only his broken marriage had proved too stubborn a calamity for Toole to mend. By unhappy chance, when in 1890 and 1891 he needed his friend's advice as to how best he could further his sons' careers, Toole was on a prolonged tour of Australia.'[21]

The depth of Toole's involvement in Irving's personal life is as remarkable as his contribution to his career. Irving had been an only child, but in Toole, who had grown up with a brother and two sisters, he found a surrogate sibling in whom he could always confide. Toole was the rock when the love of his life, the actress Nellie Moore, died in controversial circumstances in 1869. 'Of his sorrow he never

---

19 British Library additional ms. 53351M, fol. 6.
20 Ellen Terry, *The Story of My Life* (London, 1908), p. 245.
21 Laurence Irving, *The Successors* (London, 1967), p. 172.

spoke except to Toole,' wrote Seymour Hicks, who knew them both well;[22] and, when Irving's finances collapsed towards the end of his Lyceum days, his faithful friend, the little comedian, was the first on the doorstep with a cheque 'running into thousands of pounds'.[23]

Toole could depend no less upon Irving when in need. His son died in 1879 and, a decade later, his daughter and his wife died suddenly and unexpectedly within weeks of each other. Irving, more than anyone else, rescued him from despair, as he would continue to do until the end of his life, when Toole could no longer walk and had to be wheeled about the streets like a child in a pushchair. A promenade photographer at Hove, close to Brighton where Toole made a second home in his last years, caught them in his lens as they made their way along. The subjects of the photographer's scrutiny were as unaware of his presence as was he to the significance of his achievement in having chanced to record, in the early twentieth century, a startling and significant image of two of the most conspicuous personalities of the nineteenth. The men are muffled against the chill (Illustration 2), and the invalid in his Bath chair is holding forth to his friend, who trudges along at his side, attentive to the last.

Illustration 2   Sir Henry Irving (centre) and J.L. Toole in conversation, Hove Sea Walk, early 1900s

---

22 Seymour Hicks, *Between Ourselves* (London, 1930), p. 118.
23 Newton, *Cues and Curtain Calls*, p. 72.

Irving frequently visited the feeble old man during his long decline, and they were always writing to each other. Toole, who in Edinburgh in 1857 had drawn Irving into his family life, was now as lonely as he. Both, in the end, were parted from their children and wives: Toole a bereaved father twice over, and a widower for 17 years; Irving, a husband and father, but living alone, separated for 34 years from his wife and denied the upbringing and companionship of his two boys, whose mother systematically steered their thoughts and affections against him and all he stood for. Irving ministered to Toole in the spring and summer of 1889 when others believed that nothing could be done to relieve his suffering after the deaths of his closest relatives, and drew him back into public life. The Lyceum Theatre and Toole's Theatre companies united on 22 June that year to present all the entertainments at the Actors' Benevolent Fund benefit, donating their services and raising a large sum for other distressed actors and actresses. The bill included *The Bells* for Irving and an old farce for Toole; and four days later Irving escorted him to a place of honour on the Lyceum stage at a special supper for Irving's company and the Prince of Wales. The tour of Australia and New Zealand, which at that time made Toole one of the relatively few English actors ever to have ventured so far afield, was also Irving's idea, to set him before appreciative crowds once again and to distract him from the sights and sounds of home and all familiar places where, day and night, his dead family haunted him.

So they both had their fill of adversity. Through it all, mutual dependency grew. Toole counselled Irving's younger son after he had attempted suicide in 1892 and gave him work, as he had done for his father, when no one else wanted him. Toole was the boy's godfather. Irving's firstborn in 1870 was named Henry Brodribb after his father; but the second, the following year, was called Lawrence after his father's best friend, John Lawrence Toole, the 'w' somehow or other becoming 'u' in the register.[24] In 1897 Irving's grandson, the child of H.B. Irving and the actress Dorothea Baird, was named after his Uncle Laurence. Despite the misspelling, the Irving family had Toole inscribed within it for two generations.

In an extreme contrast of fortunes, at about the time the Chief was knighted in 1895, his champion had the first of several strokes. Then, before the year was out, his theatre was condemned and closed down. On 19 December 1896, while touring in Lancashire, Toole's homeless company disbanded for ever. That very night, by a strange coincidence of blows, Irving fell and injured his knee so badly that he was laid up for two months. Five days later, on Christmas Eve, grunting and struggling up the narrow staircase to Irving's first-floor rooms in Grafton Street, where the Chief was propped up in bed, came Toole with his humour and his colourful parcels of presents. The scene was a curious one, at once pathetic and merry. The redundant comedian and other friends entertained the invalid with stories and songs and sat with him throughout the night and into Christmas morning.

In time, Sir Henry Irving recovered enough strength to carry on, but not Toole. Three weeks later, in Brighton, he, too, had a fall and became bedridden. Subsequently, his spinal cord degenerated, and he never expected to outlive the younger man. When he heard of Irving's sudden death in October 1905, he cried

---

24 Private letter, Laurence Irving (1897–1988) to the author, 19 January 1978.

out in terrible pain: 'Then let me die too!' No one recognised the wheelchair-bound old man at the funeral, sobbing unendingly into his chest, his head unable to support its own weight, and his body shrunken to the size of a small boy's. Toole was never brought to London again, the place of his birth, his childhood and, for 40 years, his work. He and Irving had been regarded for most of that time as the complementary joint figureheads of the British stage. 'Extremes meet; they always do and always will,' wrote Sir Squire Bancroft.[25] 'The closest friend Henry Irving had was J.L. Toole.' Not even Loveday or Stoker was as close.[26] Stoker understood the situation fully. He sent him a lock of Irving's hair, and 'to the memory of John Lawrence Toole, loving comrade and true friend of Henry Irving' dedicated his published reminiscences of his master.

Toole died within a year of Irving. He had planned to leave him his mansion in London and much of his wealth. Always he had been his guardian angel and a lucky charm, observing Lyceum dress rehearsals from a place of concealment at the Chief's particular request; and there, as he watched the great man at work, his thoughts were often of Edinburgh days, of Toolerini and Irvingetti, and a tall, unfinished youth with the future in his eyes.

---

25 Squire Bancroft, *Empty Chairs* (London, 1925), p. 192.
26 Personal knowledge from a conversation with Laurence Irving (1897–1988), 7 February 1978.

Chapter 2

'He Danced, He Did Not Merely Walk – He Sang, He By No Means Merely Spoke': Irving, Theatricality and the Modernist Theatre

Jim Davis

What if, instead of considering Sir Henry Irving as the last of the great Victorian actors, we considered him as one of the harbingers of modernist theatre? What if we took our cue from Edward Gordon Craig, who tells us of the new movement in theatre with which he identified himself in the early twentieth century, claiming: 'It was the eternal old and good movement coming once more to life: it was the attempt to revitalize our European Theatre from within. To put it in a sentence, it was to wake up ourselves, and so wake up our house. It was doing in our way what Irving had done in his.'[1]

And, within Europe at large, Craig identifies Isadora Duncan, Appia, Stanislavski, Reinhardt, Meyerhold, Diaghileff, Copeau, Tairov and Piscator, among others, as contributing to the new movement and eager to express things in a new way. Irving, too, says Craig, 'had expressed in a new way – in his way – and I, his pupil, followed his lead. A new way of looking at an old thing – this was our principal idea.' Indeed, for Craig, 'it is this new movement – the English section of it – that gives its salute to Irving as having inspired it, and will remain at that salute'.[2]

According to W.D. King, Craig saw Irving as 'his model for the Supreme Creator'[3] and his 'writings on Irving tend to construct his memory as a prophetic embodiment of Craig's own theories about the artist of the theatre'.[4] There is, of course, a certain degree of idolatry in Craig's estimate of Irving, and it is important to recognise that Craig's Irving is a construct just as any other biographical subject becomes the construct of the biographer. But this should not be an excuse for ignoring the implications of Craig's statements. And we should accept the implicit challenge in Craig's assessment of Irving to rethink the ways in which we periodise theatre history and Irving's place within it. There are perfectly good reasons to see Irving as the last of the great nineteenth-century English actors, triumphantly drawing to

---

1   Edward Gordon Craig, *Henry Irving* (London, 1930), p. 198.
2   Ibid., pp. 200–1.
3   W.D. King, *Henry Irving's Waterloo* (Berkeley, 1993), p. 31.
4   Ibid., p. 53.

a close the theatre of the Victorian period and even lending his name to a distinct era, 'the age of Irving'. Yet there is also a case for linking Irving's name with those of Saxe-Meiningen, Antoine and Stanislavski when we consider new developments in staging. And, while Irving never formulated a system of acting, his views on acting as an art, on the discipline and ethics involved in the actor's calling and on the importance of rehearsal, anticipate many of the concerns later expressed by Stanislavski. Moreover, Craig's Irving is an actor whose combination of theatricality and physical precision and control anticipates not only the ubermarionette, but also the theatres of Meyerhold and even Grotowski. The theatre of Irving, far from being a contained and unified segment of theatre history, should be viewed as a transitional force with a certain degree of seepage into the theatrical thinking that informed the modernist movement. Craig certainly recognises that Irving was 'the end of a great line of actors',[5] one who gathered together the old traditions, used only what was of use to him and exploited what he had taken to the limit. But, to Craig, he could not be periodised as a mere Victorian.

Craig has been portrayed as a man torn between two sorts of theatre. Peter Brook identifies one part of him with Irving's theatre, but:

> ... [i]n complete contradiction to this is the other Gordon Craig, the man who wrote that actors should be abolished and marionettes put in their place, the man who said there should be no more scenery, only folding screens. Craig loved Irving's theatre – its painted forests, its thunder sheets, its naïve melodramas – but at the same time he dreamed of another theatre where all the elements would be harmonious and where art would be a religion.[6]

In so situating Craig, Brook perpetuates two common misconceptions; first, that Craig wished to replace actors with puppets; second, that his later thinking represents a complete break with Irving's influence. For one of Irving's legacies to Craig was the notion of a theatre where all the arts were harmonious and where art was a religion. Craig was to reformulate these values in new and idiosyncratic ways, but Irving's example continued to hover in the background.

Craig, who had seen so much of avant-garde European theatre by 1930, the year his memoir of Irving was published, commences his book thus: 'Let me state at once, in clearest unmistakable terms, that I have never known of, or seen, a greater actor than was Irving.'[7] And he later refers to Irving as 'the greatest actor of his time'.[8] Craig had developed his notion of the perfect actor, the ubermarionette, the actor whose skills are almost superhuman in their precision and technical accomplishment. For Craig, Irving was the quintessential ubermarionette – he 'was the nearest thing ever known to what I have called the ubermarionette' – 'from Irving the whole notion receives corroboration',[9] a view to which he adhered long after Irving's death. As

---

5 Craig, *Henry Irving*, p. 18.
6 Peter Brook, *The Shifting Point: Forty Years of Theatrical Exploration 1946–1987* (London, 1988), p. 24. Brook's view of the two Craigs also surfaces in *The Empty Space*.
7 Craig, *Henry Irving*, p. 1.
8 Ibid., p. 21.
9 Ibid., p. 32.

well as achieving precision in voice and movement, says Craig, Irving also achieved a control of feature that 'constituted a mask'.[10] His face was an expressive instrument – a mask which eschewed spontaneity, but which instead became part of the overall 'design' of his role:

> And so it was that each syllable and each pause, each step and each look, was as nearly perfectly designed and of a piece with the whole as could possibly be.
> I believe that this is what the great actors of Japan did – design their parts.[11]

In Craig's view, Irving was artificial, even slightly stylised in the way he achieved his effects – he astonished, he was expressive, he was dramatic, says Craig – but he was never commonplace. And he eschewed inspiration, preferring calculation. Through unceasing rehearsal of his actors he tried to make good marionettes of them – meaning, in Craig's sense, that he attempted to inculcate the greatest possible degree of control and expressiveness into their performances.

There is no doubt that views about Irving's physical and vocal skills were mixed. Henry James, who was not impressed by Irving, considered:

> Mr Irving's peculiarities and eccentricities of speech are so strange, so numerous, so personal to himself, his views of pronunciation, of modulation, of elocution so highly developed, the tricks he plays with the divine mother-tongue so audacious and fantastic, that the spectator who desires to be in sympathy with him finds himself confronted with a bristling hedge of difficulties.[12]

Henry Arthur Jones acknowledged Irving's vocal limitations, but found his voice 'tremendously effective, searching, withering, forbidding, exclusive, dominating, unanswerable ... like a jet of carbolic acid'.[13] Yet, when Clement Scott heard Irving speak Tennyson's lines in *Becket*, he praised the actor's 'good balance, accent, music and discretion in elocution'.[14] Irving's physical abilities and facial expression also drew mixed responses, and he was a frequent object of caricature, as in APE's (Pellegrini's) famous *Vanity Fair* portrayal of him as Mathias in *The Bells*. 'I never thought "Ape" so poor as when on December 19th, 1874, he gave us *The Bells* in that week's *Vanity Fair*', wrote Edward Gordon Craig. 'Better by far were A B's caricatures, and best of all, though less comic, Sargent's one parody. All the caricaturists attributed to Irving bent knees, bent back, or a dragging leg – like the aesthete in *Iolanthe* – which if not particularly funny, was anyhow quite untrue.'[15] One of the most extreme critiques of Irving appeared in *The Fashionable Tragedian*, a pamphlet co-authored by William Archer in 1877, which ridiculed him on all counts. It criticised Lyceum audiences for applauding 'every jerk, every spasm, every hysteric scream – we had almost said every convulsion – in which he

---

10 Ibid., p. 78.
11 Ibid., p. 79.
12 Quoted in Alan Wade, ed., *The Scenic Art* (London, 1949), p. 139.
13 Henry A. Jones, *The Shadow of Henry Irving* (London, 1931), quoted in Jeffrey Richards, *Sir Henry Irving: A Victorian Actor and His World* (London, 2005), p. 318.
14 Clement Scott, *From 'The Bells' to 'King Arthur'* (London, 1896), p. 358.
15 Craig, *Henry Irving*, p. 73.

chose to indulge'. It considered that 'his figure utterly precludes the possibility of dignity, grace, or even ease: some of his most effective attitudes might well be taken for a representation of the last stage of Asian cholera – total collapse'.[16] Six years later Archer again criticised Irving's skills as an actor, particularly his speech and movement, in *Henry Irving: Actor and Manager: A Critical Study*.

Defending Irving against William Archer's criticisms of his physical and vocal idiosyncrasies as a performer, Craig wrote: 'He danced, he did not merely walk – he sang, he by no means merely spoke. He was essentially artificial in distinction to being merely natural.'[17] Craig describes Irving's performance as Mathias as a 'dance', as an exquisitely choreographed and calculated piece of performance. Even Irving's walk, says Craig, 'was a whole language'.[18] In effect, Irving was a 'theatrical' rather than a 'naturalistic' actor, an actor who embraced and embodied the artifice of the theatre, although not an actor who therefore discarded nature. He told an audience at Harvard University that '[t]o be natural on stage is most difficult, and yet a grain of nature is worth a bushel of artifice'.[19] However, he acknowledged that exaggeration applied to everything on the stage. 'To appear to be natural, you must in reality be much broader than nature. To act on the stage as one really would in a room, would be ineffective and colourless.'[20]

Irving's views on acting are expressed in a number of publications as well as in his speeches. Even if he used others to write some of these speeches for him, we can assume that they broadly represent his position on the topic he discusses.[21] His preface to Talma's 'On the Actor's Art' states: 'There must be no suggestion of effort. The essence of acting is its apparent spontaneity. Perfect illusion is obtained when every effect seems to be an accident.'[22] But 'acting, like every other art, has a mechanism' and 'no actor [says Irving] can make progress till he has mastered a certain mechanism which is within the scope of patient intelligence'. While great acting cannot be taught, it can only be brought forth when the 'actor is a master of the methods of his craft'.[23] Such a statement clearly aligns Irving with Stanislavski, in some respects, and even with Diderot. Yet we know that Irving was not convinced by Diderot's arguments, which championed the need for the actor's head to be in control of his or her heart, since he believed the actor must also possess genuine emotion. In a study of Victorian acting George Taylor suggests that Irving's belief that sensibility and technical control could be exercised at the same time, that the mind of the actor should have 'a double consciousness', concurs, however unintentionally, with developments in psychology in the late nineteenth century, particularly the

---

16 William Archer and R.W. Lowe, *The Fashionable Tragedian* (London, 1877), quoted in Austin Brereton, *The Life of Henry Irving* (London, 1908), Vol. 1, pp. 230–1.

17 Craig, *Henry Irving*, p. 74.

18 Ibid., p. 71.

19 Henry Irving, 'The Art of Acting (1885)', in Jeffrey Richards ed., *Sir Henry Irving, Theatre, Culture and Society: Essays, Addresses and Lectures* (Keele, 1994), p. 41.

20 Ibid., p. 42.

21 See Richards, ed., *Sir Henry Irving, Theatre, Culture and Society*, pp. 24–5 for a discussion of this issue.

22 Ibid., p. 30.

23 Ibid.

work of Ribot and Freud.[24] In countering Diderot's views on acting, Irving made the following comment, to which Taylor draws our attention: 'It is necessary to this art [of acting] that the mind should have a double consciousness, in which all the emotions proper to the occasion may have full swing, while the actor is all the time on the alert for every detail of his method.'[25] Taylor realises that undue emphasis can be placed on a single remark, but concludes that 'the concept that feelings, behaviour and even personality are formed and controlled by unconscious layers of "motivation" was to be crucial in twentieth-century theories of acting, particularly those of Stanislavski and the American method'.[26] Christopher Innes also argues that Irving anticipates Stanislavski through his synthesis of emotional expression and technique, although Innes suggests that Irving's ability to attain alternately dynamism and stasis in performance was almost a prototype for the expressionist style of acting.[27]

Something of a contradiction begins to emerge in discussions of Irving's prowess as an actor. Within the pictorial style of performance that Irving advocated the actor became absorbed within the stage environment, in effect excluding awareness of the audience. This in itself contributed to change and innovation in the theatre, fulfilling Diderot's requirement for the actor's absorption in the business of the stage.[28] In effect, Irving was championing a more realistic style of performance, despite the inherent artifice of pictorialism. For all its alleged eccentricity his own acting, often enhanced by precise and detailed observation, innovatively engaged with the inner and outer man. His skill in representing guilt and repression, to which so many commentators have drawn attention, also contributed to a more realistic mode of acting.[29] Yet Craig's Irving is praised for qualities that were inherently theatrical, almost as if he was as opposed to verisimilitude as Craig was. While there was nothing distinctively avant-garde about Irving, the very traditions he represented in Craig's view – and Craig is at pains to attest that, while discarding traditions not worth preserving, Irving did not completely eschew tradition – were also those that twentieth-century practitioners and theorists such as Craig and Meyerhold sought to retrieve for the stage. Meyerhold's early interest in stylisation and his later development of biomechanics as a form of actor training, inspired by a diversity of theatrical forms including classical Japanese theatre, aim at the discipline, control and precision that Craig sought in the ubermarionette and had discovered to be at the heart of Irving's technique as an actor. Meyerhold, like Craig, used the metaphor of puppetry to indicate what he wished to achieve,[30] while his notion of pre-acting[31]

---

24 George Taylor, *Players and Performances in the Victorian Theatre* (Manchester, 1989), p. 152.

25 Ibid., quoting Henry Irving, *The Drama: Addresses* (London, 1893), pp. 55–6.

26 Ibid., p. 152.

27 Christopher Innes, *Edward Gordon Craig* (Cambridge, 1983), p. 12.

28 See John Osborne, *The Meiningen Court Theatre 1866–1890* (Cambridge, 1988), pp. 50–1.

29 See, for example, Peter Thomson, 'Irving and the Lyceum: Volcano and Cathedral', in *On Actors and Acting* (Exeter, 2000), pp. 148–63.

30 Edward Braun, ed., *Meyerhold on Theatre* (London, 1968), pp. 128–9.

31 Ibid., pp. 205–6.

(also derived from Japanese and Chinese theatre) is uncannily encapsulated in the following description of Irving by Craig:

> While every sentence of a role was to him of the utmost importance, he was ever mindful to act before he spoke, and then to follow up the words by acting again.
>
> Before a phrase or a word, Irving would always do something, so that the spectator should never be in doubt as to what the phrase or word was intended to mean; and he gave words special meanings ...[32]

Admittedly, Irving himself believed that 'the most natural, the most seemingly accidental effects are obtained when the working of the mind is visible before the tongue gives it words',[33] a notion not dissimilar to Stanislavski's idea of 'adaptation', while Meyerhold sees pre-acting as part of the function of the post-revolutionary 'actor-tribune', a demonstration of attitude that anticipates the Brechtian *Gest*. But perhaps we can see in Craig's claim that Irving's pre-acting gave his words an 'Irving significance',[34] a function not altogether dissimilar from that identified by Meyerhold. And, at the risk of overstating the case, even the later emphasis of Grotowski on physical control and emotional intensity, and on the face as mask, for example, may indicate that actors such as Richard Cieslak were the true heirs of Craig's Irving within modernist theatre.

The case for Irving's significance in a continuum – rather than a rigidly compartmentalised version – of the history of acting and staging may seem strange in the light of criticism levelled against him by Archer and Shaw. While Shaw's dismissal of Shakespeare as an intellectual inferior has been taken as eccentricity, his many attacks on Irving and on Irving's inability to play any role other than Irving – 'There was no question then of a bad Shylock or a good Shylock; he was simply not Shylock at all, and when his own creation came into conflict with Shakespeare's, ... [he] positively acted Shakespeare off the stage'[35] – have arguably affected Irving's posthumous reputation, as has Archer's critique of Irving's vocal and physical abilities. Of course, Shaw's and Archer's Irving is as much a creation as Craig's Irving. And Craig and Shaw were clearly embattled over Irving – a conflict that is particularly well articulated in W.D. King's book.[36] Yet even the comments of Craig's mother, Ellen Terry, on Irving's extreme egotism and apparent lack of interest in the work of other major European actors, further help to create the image of the blinkered, conceited and parochial actor-manager,[37] while Clement Scott anchors him firmly as an exemplar of good old Victorian values almost by default, given his admiration for Irving and cantankerous rejection of Ibsen and the new drama.[38]

---

32 Craig, *Henry Irving*, p. 202.
33 Quoted in Bram Stoker, *Personal Reminiscences of Henry Irving* (London, 1906), Vol. 2, p. 11.
34 Craig, *Henry Irving*, p. 202.
35 George Bernard Shaw, 'Blaming the Bard', *Our Theatres in the Nineties* (London, 1932, reprinted 1948), Vol. 2, p. 198.
36 See King, *Henry Irving's Waterloo*, pp. 215–19.
37 Ellen Terry, *The Story of My Life* (London, 1908), p. 95.
38 See Scott, *From 'The Bells' to 'King Arthur'* for Scott's assessment of Irving.

There is, of course, the difficulty of Irving's aversion to Ibsen, or at least to Shaw's Ibsen. In 1891 Irving implicitly referred to Shaw in a speech made in Glasgow:

> Ibsen, it is said, is in the future to be our dramatic teacher, and I learn from one of his prophets that his plays have abolished God, duty, the devotion of a mother to her children, and the obligation of man to his fellow man ... Is any English playwright going to expound this philosophy to the public? The English drama must be an exposition of English life and character, and I fail to recognise in these new notions any resemblance to the sentiments which prevail amongst the great mass of our countrymen.[39]

Irving's dismissal of Ibsen as intrinsically antithetical to English values is perhaps on a par with his denunciation of the moral excesses of some French plays. Yet we need to put against this Irving's very necessary task of advocacy for the moral and social role of theatre. Paradoxically, this very advocacy contributed to a climate where the theatre's moral and social value was gradually taken more seriously and in which Ibsen's plays eventually earned due recognition. But the significant point is that the construction of Irving as an enemy to modernist dramatic literature, in particular to the plays of Ibsen and Shaw, should not blind us to the qualities and example he represented for those who wished to assert the continuing place of theatricality, stylisation, physicality and image in the theatre.

Craig's Irving is particularly notable for his skills not only as an actor, but also as a stage manager. In 1881 the Duke of Saxe-Meiningen's company visited London, demonstrating through productions such as *Julius Caesar* not only detailed attention to the *mise en scène*, but also an emphasis on pictorial effect and the interpretative potential of the human body in space. The Meiningen theatre was particularly noted for its crowd scenes, for which a large number of extras were carefully drilled to create as realistic an effect as possible. After exposure to the work of the Saxe-Meiningen company, Irving soon demonstrated that he could achieve equally realistic crowd scenes, while his attention to rehearsal and to how the play looked and his considerable interest in the social, ethical and aesthetic value of theatre suggest points of comparison not only with Saxe-Meiningen, but also with Stanislavski. Under the Meiningen influence Irving even restructured the Lyceum stage, using steps and platforms to vary the levels of action in productions such as *Macbeth*. Christopher Innes, however, makes the distinction between the realism of the Saxe-Meiningen productions and Irving's emphasis on the aesthetic quality of the Saxe-Meiningen techniques.[40] In effect, Irving emphasised a unified production concept and a sustained sense of atmosphere over the significance of verisimilitude in the Saxe-Meiningen sense. In 1889 André Antoine, whose Théâtre Libre was to have a lasting impact on European theatre through its advocacy of naturalistic drama and stage realism, visited the Lyceum. While dismissive of Irving as an actor, Antoine admired Irving's stage management:

> But what was incomparable was his stagecraft, which is something we can hardly conceive of in France. The scene [in *Macbeth*] where the castle wakes up, and above all that of the

---

39 Richards, ed., *Sir Henry Irving, Theatre, Culture and Society*, p. 134.
40 Innes, *Edward Gordon Craig*, p. 10.

banquet, with the appearance of the ghost, are masterpieces, with lighting effects of which we have no idea as yet.[41]

Subsequently, Antoine wrote that 'every Frenchman who has visited Irving's theatre in London has come home in a state of excitement, having seen things there that he never suspected to exist', adding that 'Irving manipulated his crowds with patient care and achieved an ensemble that astonishes our travellers'.[42]

It has long been acknowledged that the revivals of Charles Kean, a rather spineless actor but brilliant stage manager, influenced the work of Saxe-Meiningen. It has also become something of a truism that the rise of modernism was in reaction to the type of theatre that Irving, among others, represented. But what if we were to place Irving with Saxe-Meiningen, Antoine and Stanislavski, for example, and analyse his achievements alongside theirs? Why do we dwell on the differences, indoctrinated as we are by Archer and Shaw, rather than consider the parallel forms of theatre in existence – the points of comparison as well as contrast? Why not acknowledge the history of late nineteenth-century European theatre as a series of intersections as much as a process of cause and effect or of reaction and innovation? Admittedly, Irving was no supporter of new writing: he was critical of 'the moral squalor'[43] of Zola and, as we have seen, of Ibsen. Yet his ability to synthesise different art forms in productions such as *King Arthur* (1895), which drew not only on his own talents and those of his company, but also on those of Sir Arthur Sullivan and Sir Edward Burne-Jones, brought him close to realising Wagner's notion of the *Gesamtkunstwerk* or total artwork. For Irving, the dramatic text was at times a subsidiary part of the theatrical whole. While he was aware that costumes and scenery were not absolutely essential to the interpretation and impact of a play in performance, especially in the case of Shakespeare, he believed in meeting the expectations of contemporary audiences by providing a suitable environment for the plays he presented, 'seeking aids for the imagination amongst the scientific appliances, the inventions and discoveries of the time'.[44]

Irving believed in sustained rehearsal and, as a result, created something extraordinary, surpassing even the theatres of Stanislavski and Reinhardt in the excitement generated, according to Craig. Like Stanislavski, Irving advocated self-discipline and the centrality of the work ethic in the creation of good theatre. Craig felt that Irving had broken with many a tradition, but not with that of working untiringly. Ellen Terry remembered her first experience of performing with Irving:

> From the first I noticed that Mr Irving worked more concentratedly than all the other actors put together, and the most important lesson of my working life I learnt from him, that to do one's work well one must work continually, live a life of constant self-denial for that purpose and, in short, keep one's nose upon the grindstone.[45]

---

41 Quoted in Denis Bablet, *The Theatre of Edward Gordon Craig* (London, 1981), p. 15.
42 Ibid.
43 'Some Misconceptions about the Stage', in Richards, ed., *Sir Henry Irving Theatre, Culture and Society*, p. 141.
44 Ibid., p. 140.
45 Quoted in T. Edgar Pemberton, *Sir Charles Wyndham: A Biography* (London, 1904), pp. 52–3.

In her memoirs she entitles the first chapter on the Lyceum 'Work at the Lyceum', commenting, '[w]hen I am asked what I remember about the first ten years at the Lyceum, I can answer in one word: *Work*'.[46] And Irving himself declared: 'If our art is worth anything at all, it is worth the honest, conscientious self-devotion of men and women who, while they may not achieve fame, may have the satisfaction of being workers in a calling which does credit to many degrees of talent.'[47] Excellence in any art – and to Irving, like Stanislavski, acting was an art – 'is attained [says Irving] only by arduous labour, unswerving purpose and unfailing discipline'.[48] Moreover this dedication to hard work is enhanced by the subordination of the actor's individuality to the harmonious impact of the whole. This really could be Stanislavski talking, as could Irving's subsequent comment that the actor's art 'must be something to hold in reverence if he wishes others to hold it in esteem'.[49] Indeed, although not credited with it sufficiently, Irving's example and proselytising help to prepare the way for a revised and more professionally-based understanding of the art of acting and its ethical responsibilities. And, like Stanislavski, Irving advocated the social, moral and educational function of the theatre and the importance of these to contemporary society.

Craig did not believe that acting should be called an art or the actor an artist since too much depended on accident. Craig's Irving, however, fulfilled many of those criteria that would have elevated the actor's craft to the level of art in Craig's terms. Moreover, Craig's Irving, unlike Shaw's and Archer's Irving, cannot be simply compartmentalised as a traditionalist or an enemy to modernism. Irving, too, contributed to, or at least anticipated, some of those non-literary features of modernist theatre that came after him. Paradoxically, he sought to create credible environments for his productions, while sacrificing verisimilitude for the sake of atmosphere and the artifice of pictorial effect. His acting was detailed, based on careful observation, psychologically credible, and seeking truth to nature, but it was also perceived as stylised and artificial. Irving was hardly a modernist himself, nor could he be described as a stage director in the way we use the term today. Yet Craig's description of Irving – 'He danced, he did not merely walk – he sang, he by no means merely spoke. He was essentially artificial in distinction to being merely natural'[50] – is a fitting epithet not only for Irving, but also for all those actors and directors who have aspired beyond the mundane and the everyday in realising their vision of the world around them. We must stop treating Irving as a Victorian curiosity and recognise that he, too, contributed to innovation and change in the European theatre of the late nineteenth and early-twentieth centuries.

---

46 Terry, *The Story of My Life*, p. 102.

47 Henry Irving, 'The Art of Acting (1885)', in Richards, ed., *Sir Henry Irving, Theatre, Culture and Society*, p. 49.

48 Ibid., p. 50.

49 Ibid., 'The Art of Acting (1891)', p. 82.

50 Craig, *Henry Irving*, p. 72.

Chapter 3

Ellen Terry and Henry Irving: A Working Partnership

Katharine Cockin

Ellen Terry and Henry Irving had a long and financially successful working relationship at the Lyceum Theatre, most memorably, perhaps, as partners in crime in *Macbeth*. Irving was known as the 'Vicar', the 'Chief' and the 'Governor'. These patriarchal titles emphasised with every utterance that Irving, the actor-manager, was in charge. The tendency to blur the boundaries between stage and wings, to presume that an embrace on stage might linger after the lights have been extinguished, is still the staple of popular journalism, but George Bernard Shaw made an authoritative public statement about Ellen Terry's relationships after her death. In the very long preface he had the privilege to write to the controversial Shaw–Terry correspondence, he claimed:

> One may say that her marriages were adventures and her friendships enduring. And all these friendships had the character of innocent love affairs: her friends were her lovers in every sense except the technical one; and she was incapable of returning their regard coolly: she felt either warmly or not at all.[1]

In enumerating the unorthodox relationships in Terry's life, Shaw appears to have included Henry Irving, along with Edward Godwin, as potential husbands:

> Ellen Terry could be a woman of very exceptional virtue without having the smallest respect for the law. She did not care enough about it to have even a prejudice against it. If the man of her choice was free, she married him. If the marriage was not a success, she left him. She had many enduring friendships, some transient fancies, and five domestic partnerships of which two were not legalized, though they would have been if the English marriage law had been decently reasonable.[2]

Shaw's characterisation of Terry as an outlaw demands more attention than space will allow for here, but the idea that Irving constituted one of her 'domestic partnerships' prompts some scrutiny of archival evidence.

---

1 Ellen Terry and George Bernard Shaw, *Ellen Terry and Bernard Shaw: A Correspondence*, ed. Christopher St John (London, 1931), p. xvii.
2 Ibid., p. xvii.

As Laurence Irving noted, there are unexpectedly few extant letters between Henry Irving and Ellen Terry.[3] Rather than Irving playing a surprisingly minor role in Terry's correspondence, it is likely that, after her death, many private papers were destroyed by family.[4] James Carew, Terry's third husband, says in a letter to Terry's daughter, Edith Craig, that he has letters of her mother's but cannot bring himself to destroy them,[5] possibly implying that the destruction of such letters was to be expected.[6] Two letters from Edward Gordon Craig to James Carew indicate that Carew chose to dispose of some other personal letters in a different way. On 30 November 1929 Edward Gordon Craig wrote from Genoa, thanking Carew for the present of Henry Irving's letters to Ellen Terry and the book of his roles.[7] Gordon Craig[8] had, in fact, tried to get hold of these letters from his mother, 11 years earlier, using his wife as an intermediary. Elena Meo then wrote on his behalf to Ellen Terry asking for letters written to her from Irving and from Shaw:

> Now for something important. Ted wants you to make him a present of the letters of Sir Henry – even letters that don't appear important – for he thinks much of them – & says there was much in even a few words of Henrys to those that understood him & them. he wants to write a book he says he does not want them to fall into the wrong hands & the wrong thing & someone write a book on them & the wrong thing written. also Mr Mr Bernard Shaws for he thinks they must be so immensely interesting & both should be well preserved he wants you so much to give them to him & does not like to ask you himself as I tell him I am sure that you will if you knew he wanted them & would preserve them??[9]

This casts in a different light the moral objections Gordon Craig was to express very publicly after the publication of the Shaw–Terry correspondence. On 17 May 1931 Gordon Craig wrote to James Carew, asking for copies of the 16 letters from

---

3   Laurence Irving, *Henry Irving: The Actor and His World* (London, 1951 [1989]), p. 480. There are four items of correspondence from Irving to Ellen Terry in the archive at Smallhythe Place: a Christmas card in 1885 (ET 1.233); a telegram on 10 July 1892 (ET 1.235); a letter begging her not to return to the theatre until she recovered her health (7 June, ET 1.234); and a fragment of a letter from Dublin proclaiming 'Your own till death' (n.d., ET 1.232). All correspondence hereafter is held at the National Trust's Smallhythe Place. I am grateful to the National Trust for permission to quote from this material.

4   At Smallhythe Place, a small number of letters and documents present with burnt edges, supporting the evidence provided by Sir Donald Sinden that Olive Chaplin admitted that she had destroyed Ellen Terry's private papers. See Donald Sinden, *A Touch of the Memoirs* (London, 1982). For further discussion of this, see John H.B. Irving, 'Quest For Missing Ellen Terry Letters', *First Knight: The Journal of the Irving Society*, **2**, December 2001, pp. 44–51.

5   Letter from Jim [James Carew] to Edy [Edith Craig], Sunday, SC22-B198.

6   After Mrs Rumball's death, Ellen Terry wrote to Rumball's daughter, Bo: 'I hope you will please send any letters or papers of mine to me. So they ought not to fall into others hands': letter from Nelly [Ellen Terry] to Bo, 7 April, ET 5.204.

7   Letter from Ted [Edward Gordon Craig] to Jim [James Carew], 30 November 1929, ET 4.063.

8   In this chapter I refer to Edward Gordon Craig as Gordon Craig in order to make a clear distinction between him and his sister, Edith Craig.

9   Letter from Elena Meo to Ellen Terry, 11 October 1918, ET Z1.725/57a.

George Bernard Shaw to Ellen Terry, which Carew had sold to Adams but which Gordon Craig wanted to use in his forthcoming book, *Ellen Terry and Her Secret Self*.[10]

The available evidence suggests that the Terry–Irving relationship was intimate, but the nature of the intimacy was complex. With reference to the surviving traces of a frustratingly ephemeral Irving in the archives at Smallhythe Place, I will be exploring some new insights into their working relationship during the Lyceum days. I will also consider Irving's impact on Terry and her children and Irving's place in the memorialisation of Terry at Smallhythe Place. Although there has been some questions about the extent to which Ellen Terry had the opportunity to develop the roles she was given and the impact on her career of the kinds of roles she played during her employment at the Lyceum Theatre, at the turn of the century she was extremely wealthy and able to act as a patron to others. Some of the questions about Terry's life take on a different light if she is foregrounded – envisaged as more of an agent than a victim of circumstances.

When Laurence Irving described the relationship between Henry Irving and Ellen Terry in familial terms – 'They were at once each other's parent and child'[11] – he was speaking with the authority of kinship with one half of the famous couple. The idea that the intimacy they shared is intelligible within the discourse of family is persuasive and was applicable to her relationship with others: Edward Gordon Craig infantilised her, while Bernard Shaw tried to be mothered by her. Terry's correspondence suggests that Irving *was* one of the family: he featured in family news in her letters to friends, and he joined her on holiday with and without her children. In looking forward to her holiday, Ellen Terry conveyed her emotional intensity by writing about herself in the third person: 'I think to have 3 people she cares for very very much & 3 such real Ducks, is a real lovely holiday'.[12] Irving appears to have been involved in childcare, looking after Edward Gordon Craig while Terry was away. She was delighted to report that Irving 'says he's a perfect love of a boy & gives him the best of characters'.[13] As her letter written in Lucerne shows, she has the freedom to joke about their rest from the stage: 'I've no news except that Henry is getting fat!! & I'm getting fatter – when our holiday is ended we shall only be fit for Barnum's Show! – or as an advertisement for Thorley's food for cattle –'.[14] In illustrating her report with a cartoon, captioned 'Meph = & Margaret, after their holiday!' (Illustration 3), Terry makes her joke depend on the allusion to their current roles in *Faust* where Irving is elsewhere depicted in considerably leaner terms. The fabric of theatre and life was inseparable for Terry and Irving during this period. When on tour in Chicago during the World's Fair, her accommodation was at a distance from Irving, as she wrote to her sister Marion: 'This is the 1st time Henry & I are staying in different Hotels & we are both dull for that but I cd not stay in

---

10 Letter from Edward Gordon Craig to James Carew, 17 May 1931, ET 4.070.
11 Irving, *Henry Irving*, p. 480.
12 Letter from Nellen T. [Ellen Terry] to [Bertha Bramley] 11 August, ET 2.030.
13 Letter from Nellen T. [Ellen Terry] to [Bertha Bramley] 12 August, ET 2.066.
14 Letter from [Ellen Terry] to Marie, Thursday 9 August, ET 2.064. The sketch appears on p. 4, which is catalogued as ET 2.024.

the middle of the City, & he took his rooms 2 months ago'.[15] Although this is not necessarily evidence of their being lovers, it does suggest a great depth of feeling and that they needed to be near to each other in their daily existence: the postscript reads 'Henry never was so sweet & kind & unselfish as he is now to me long may it last!'[16]

Illustration 3   'Meph & Margaret after their holiday', sketch by Ellen Terry

Concerned about Irving's health, Terry tried to persuade him to take more fresh air, have a break from work and join her for a regular drive.[17] At a time when they were both unwell, Terry wrote in emergency to Honi Stanford from Irving's home at Grafton Street: 'Do you take other Patients than Ladies & Babies? If so wd you

---

15 Letter from Nell [Ellen Terry] to 'Old Girl' [Marion Terry] 29 September [1893], ET 2.257.

16 Nina Auerbach, *Ellen Terry: Player in Her Time* (London, 1987), p. 205. See also Frances Hughes, 'The End of a Quest: Letters of Stephen Coleridge and E.T.', *First Knight: The Journal of the Irving Society*, **IX**(1), June 2005, pp. 13–26.

17 Letter from Nell [Ellen Terry] to Bertha [Bramley] 30 October, ET 2.041.

or wd you not be induced to nurse a man! Our dearest Mr Irving – I'd give you up (much as I want you) for him = Dr Farr brings this. Answer him'.[18]

Terry's housekeeper, Mrs Rumball, is the addressee of the few extant letters from Irving in the Ellen Terry archive. Using the family's term of endearment for Mrs Rumball, 'with my best love my dear old Boo', Irving conveys brief reports on the health and happiness of 'Nell' and sends an invitation to Boo for dinner on Christmas Eve at the Lyceum in 1882.[19] And Ellen Terry kept Boo informed about Irving's health, even at second-hand, when Dorothea Baird reported that he was 'terribly short of breath – which is not a good sign='.[20]

With the absence of Edward Godwin, their biological father, Terry's children, Edith Craig and Edward Gordon Craig, may have regarded Irving as a father figure. He was also, at various times, their employer. They both benefited from training at the Lyceum. Edith Craig acted in a number of small parts in Lyceum productions, even in *Macbeth*. Her performance in *The Lyons Mail* was praised by Eleanora Duse, and her work as a costumier, memorably designing the jewelled scarf for Irving as Shylock, was consolidated with Irving's employment of her to design the costumes for *Robespierre*.[21] Irving's influence surfaced later in her work with the London-based theatre society, the Pioneer Players, which produced the ill-fated *The Man of Destiny*.[22] Craig had gained valuable experience as a performer and costume designer at the Lyceum Theatre, inevitably learning much about theatrical production generally. She features in the intriguing sketches made of a Lyceum trip to the United States by the artist, Pamela Colman Smith, who depicts Irving as an aetiolated figure, authoritatively dominating from the background.[23] Colman Smith collaborated with Craig on scene designs for W.B. Yeats who acknowledged Craig's assistance in stage technique.[24]

Irving was an available, visibly dominant, male figure. To what extent Terry's children were influenced by Irving will be of relevance when theatre historians reassess the place they both had in the development of twentieth-century theatre. Edith Craig is becoming known for her work in women's suffrage theatre, but she should also receive proper credit for her experimental productions with the Pioneer Players, the Leeds Art Theatre and other groups.[25] While Art Theatre is assumed to have bypassed England for decades, in London Edith Craig directed numerous ground-breaking productions, including a Russian expressionist play in 1915. The idea that Edward Gordon or Edith Craig was modernist in contrast to Irving's orthodoxy does not stand up to close inspection. A newly discovered letter from

---

18 Letter from ET [Ellen Terry] to Honi [Stanford] n.d., ET 2.246.

19 Letter from Henry Irving to Boo [Mrs Rumball], ET 7.002; invitation from Henry Irving to Mrs Rumball, ET 7.004.

20 Letter from N [Ellen Terry] to [Mrs Rumball], Tuesday 25 April, ET 5.056.

21 Katharine Cockin, *Edith Craig (1869–1947): Dramatic Lives* (London, 1998), p. 40.

22 Ibid., p. 109.

23 Colman Smith decorated a small wooden box with an image of a ship at sea, reminiscent of the transatlantic journey of the Lyceum company (held at Smallhythe Place).

24 Cockin, *Edith Craig*, p. 73.

25 Katharine Cockin, *Women and Theatre in the Age of Suffrage: The Pioneer Players 1911–25* (London, 2001).

Henry Irving to Edith Craig shows that he was encouraging about her work with the independent theatre.[26]

Christopher St John, in a position close enough to be an authoritative observer and to bear witness to the Irving–Terry extended family, was Terry's 'literary henchman' and Irving's elegist in her tribute to Irving in 1905, the 26-page hand-coloured booklet in Colman Smith's imprint, *The Green Sheaf*.[27]

If Irving was involved in a mutual parenting role towards Ellen Terry, as suggested by Laurence Irving, it might be assumed that their relationship was not sexual and that the asymmetrical power relationship of parent–child flowed between them. This postulates a dynamic exchange which was mutually supportive, nurturing and disciplinary. However, the familial relationship may not be specific to Irving and Terry. Terry's son, Edward Gordon Craig, described the actor-manager in patriarchal terms: 'The actor manager was head of his own house and family – that is to say theatre and company – and that, in a sense, was all very much to the good.'[28] Gordon Craig makes much of Irving's control of his actors. Set against the possibility that Irving held Terry back to some extent in her work as a performer at the Lyceum is the private disclosure Terry made to May Webster, which indicates a productive tension between them which others might misinterpret: 'I see the papers say he & I have "quarrelled" – the blithering idiots! Ain't they clever? – It takes 2 to quarrel – & he wont!! I've tried for 19 years & he just won't! Unberufen!!!'[29] Irving maintained composure in the face of provocation. According to Edward Gordon Craig, 'no person was better controlled … It is the discipline of the body.'[30] Whether the lack of engagement Terry noted in Irving was of a piece with the aesthetic self-control identified by her son or related to the intimate bantering she demanded and he eschewed is not clear. However, in this one letter at least, Terry expresses dissatisfaction with the lack of response she found in Irving as a combatant, or perhaps as a player of games.

As a performer and producer, Irving is said to have provided little critical feedback to Terry on her performance. The Ellen Terry archive presents some provisional answers to this question. Was it, as Jeffrey Richards has suggested, '[p]robably because she was doing, and he knew she would do, what he wanted in terms of imparting to the roles her distinctive qualities'?[31] Terry's preparations for performance were rigorous, and the annotations to her acting copies of plays demonstrate the scholarly engagement she had with the material in considering possibilities of plot development and characterisation. Notably, her marginalia in her copy of *Macbeth* to 'ask Henry' suggests that her preparations were directed towards a dialogue with the actor-manager rather than an egocentric pursuit of her work in isolation.[32] It might be

---

26 Letter from Henry Irving to Edie [? Edith Craig] dated 1902, Smallhythe Place, HIL-B2.

27 Christopher St John, *Henry Irving* (London, 1905).

28 Edward Gordon Craig, *Henry Irving* (London, 1930), p. 138.

29 Unpublished handwritten signed letter from Nellen Terry [Ellen Terry] to May [Webster] Friday [postmarked March 1897], ET Z2.266.

30 Craig, *Henry Irving*, p. 179.

31 Jeffrey Richards, *Sir Henry Irving: A Victorian Actor and His World* (London, 2005), p. 55.

32 Annotation on one of Ellen Terry's copies of *Macbeth* (Smallhythe Place).

that Irving refrained from giving her public direction about her performance because he knew that her studies were thorough and he trusted her judgement. He would not have been alone: other artists and writers, such as George Bernard Shaw, respected her opinion. It is possible that Irving withdrew from passionate engagement with her about the performance because a relatively public display of emotion in rehearsal could be misinterpreted by others, to her detriment.

Rather than manifesting a basic insecurity, Terry's concern about her performance on occasions could be recast as a conscientious, self-reflective practice. She could have been frustrated by the different treatment she received as signalling her difference from the other actors. If Irving was not treating her as an equal at work and instead treating her primarily with gender in mind, she would be baffled and frustrated if she felt that their emotional intimacy placed them on an equal footing. In response to her playfulness and wit, Irving maintained a reserve which she could not unsettle. There were elements of their lives offstage which needed management: their relationship; their failed marriages to other people; her illegitimate children. These issues are not easily separable,[33] and the emotional discharge spilt over into the workplace. This may have contributed to Ellen Terry's extreme reaction to the critics' charges of 'indelicacy' in her performance in *The Merchant of Venice*.[34] The associations she had for the general public with womanliness and choosing 'love',[35] positioned her uneasily in relation to the facts of her family life. And this did not go unnoticed by the radicals who claimed her as one of their own – a 'New Woman' who dared to be free.[36] Nowadays Terry's choices in life would position her as a mother of children outside marriage, but during her lifetime these signs of a fallen woman were, to some extent, overlooked in the slippery world of the theatre. Nevertheless, Terry's public life exposed her to potential criticism, and it is possible, therefore, that Irving's behaviour towards her, especially his distance, may have been intended as a protective measure. This would not necessarily have been a symbolic, chivalric act; the protection of her reputation would also have helped safeguard her livelihood.

Terry depended on her work at the Lyceum. This becomes most apparent in her correspondence with friends where she reveals the rigours of her work and the toll it takes on her health. In the United States she was unwell, but reported that she was 'just continuing however to get through with my work for Dutys sake & Mr Irvings'.[37] The relentlessness of work is reported in her correspondence when she notes that 'for the next month I'm as bad as buried – always inside the Theatre walls at least from 12 to 12 – It's really dreadful – but a month will end it for then we produce our play.'[38] Feminist critics have explored the gendered discourse of illness and the

---

33 Richards, *Sir Henry Irving*, p. 40.
34 Ibid., p. 54.
35 Christopher St John, *Henry Irving*, quoted in Richards, *Sir Henry Irving*, p. 46.
36 Cockin, *Women and Theatre*, p. 49. Ellen Terry was president of the Pioneer Players theatre society.
37 Letter from Margaret E.T. [Ellen Terry] to Elise [Ennions] [postmarked 26 January 1886], ET. 2.193.
38 Letter from Nell [Ellen Terry] to Bertha [Bramley], 19 November, ET. 2.193.

readiness to attribute illness, instability and even madness to women.[39] Developments in medical and scientific knowledge, and symptoms which might have hormonal, gynaecological or psychological causes, need to be noted when interpreting some of Terry's correspondence. Within the theatre as a field of employment illness produces further meanings. Theatrical productions in the commercial sector, without the protection of a patron, required audiences to make them successful. Ill-health could kill a play or a career. Terry was aware of this, and her private confessions of illness or fatigue while working, and these episodes exhibited various symptoms, would no doubt be concealed from others since she would not wish to jeopardise her position at work. In one letter to someone staying at the Three Arts Club, she instructs: '<u>On no account</u> do I want <u>anyone at the Club to know I am ill</u> – All the Profession wd know it then & it wd do me harm – I'm only taking a rest cure.'[40] Although out of action for four nights, and unable to perform in Brighton, she ultimately resumed work before she had fully recovered: 'My vocal chords are <u>that</u> red! & I'm obliged to act in spite of the torture.'[41] Edward Gordon Craig noted that Irving 'too often credited others with his own power of endurance',[42] glossing this with a quotation from his mother that 'were I to be run over by a steam-roller to-morrow, Henry would be deeply grieved; would say quietly; "What a pity!" – and would add, after two minutes' reflection: "Who is there – er – to go on for her to-night?"'.[43] Nevertheless, Irving's management of the Lyceum apparently did allow for the equivalent of sick leave *in extremis*, as one of Terry's letters shows: 'I'm rather ill & may not be able to join the Lyceum Co on tour for the 1st month – they begin on the 17th Sep, at Bristol. I've written to "the dear man" (Henry) & "begged off" & if I get leave I shall hope to run over for a day to West Drayton before I again begin work.'[44] Terry was allowed time off again when Edward Godwin died and bereavement struck her down for three months. She reflected: 'I didn't know how terribly it would alter me – I went on at my work for a time but broke down at last.'[45]

Irving's public presentation of Terry is worth considering. On at least one occasion, at the end of a tour of *The Merchant of Venice* in New York, Irving appears to have spoken from the stage to the audience on behalf of Terry, while she was present: 'I speak for Miss Terry, who has shared in the hopes and aspirations which were inspired by your welcome when first we touched the shores of your great country. We are ever your respectful, loyal, and affectionate servants.'[46] To what extent this amounts to his

---

39 See Elaine Showalter, *The Female Malady* (London, 1987); Lucy Bland, *Banishing the Beast* (London, 1995).

40 Letter from The Owl [Ellen Terry] to [Nella Powell], 24 April, ET 5.215.

41 Letter from Bertha [Bramley] to Nell [Ellen Terry] midnight, Wednesday, ET 2.022. Nina Auerbach has analysed the impact of hysteria on Terry's acting; see Auerbach, *Ellen Terry*, p. 132.

42 Craig, *Henry Irving*, p. 98.

43 Ibid.

44 Letter from Nell [Ellen Terry] annotated '1894', ET 2.025.

45 Letter from Nell [Ellen Terry] 23 December [18]86, ET 2.023.

46 Unidentified press cutting, HIL-G367.

silencing of her, an interpretation implied in a recent dramatisation,[47] would require more investigation into the customary practice of actor-managers in relation to their leading ladies and whether or not, psychically or physiologically, she had possession of her voice at that time. On another occasion a specific announcement, the most devastating perhaps for a performer, was made from the stage on her behalf: 'This week the Doctor Mackenzie forbids me speaking, & an apology for loss of voice is given for me each night in front of curtain at the Lyceum'.[48]

Terry often wrote to her close female friends expressing anxiety about her health and managing to keep up the pace at work: 'not being able to do my work makes me anxious & fearful – Suppose my voice never comes back!'[49] At another point, she confided again in her friend Bertha Bramley about her 'melancholy' but summoned energy for an enthusiastic invitation at the end of the letter to see *Faust* on Saturday, as 'Saturdays the play goes best = Now this "Faust" is out – launched – floating – the part of Margaret is not particularly exacting'.[50] She was not happy with her part in *Peter the Great*: 'Unfortunately I have a horrid part – a vulgar very short part – I've promised Laurence to play it, but I'm almost sorry I've done so.'[51] At busy times she was comforted by correspondence with friends: 'Oh! It's lovely to see the handwriting of so many I care very much for! How to send a sign back to them all? That's the difficulty, seeing as how time flies & I have a good six months work to do in 6 weeks – !! ... not a word do I know of Viola (my next work).'[52] The freedom of such confession, the intimacy of the correspondence and the relationship between correspondent and addressee must be considered in any interpretation of the extent of her anxiety. To Arthur Bright she is negative about her performance, but expresses her love of *Romeo and Juliet*.[53]

Terry often invited friends to the theatre, sending tickets and recommending which performance to see. *The Amber Heart* was 'a pretty play' and *The Merchant of Venice* 'the perfectest play for chicks'.[54] She suggested that her friend Bertha Bramley come to see *Ravenswood* 'in bits from the little corner = Mr Gladstone was there the other night, wrapped up from the draughts in my white shawl – his great head was as white as the shawl in the dark corner',[55] and, on another occasion, to *The Lyons Mail*: 'H.I. – is splendid in it – I enclose a ticket',[56] and had urged her 'and anyone you know with money to take tickets' for a charity matinee. 'No scenery – but it will look beautiful with curtains – flowers – lights – & ladies!'[57] She was

---

47 Barrie Wheatley, *The Man Who Made Dracula*, produced by the Northern Theatre Company at the Northern Academy for Performing Arts, Hull, England, 31 March 2006.
48 Letter from Nell [Ellen Terry] 23 July [18]84, ET 2.103.
49 Letter from Nell [Ellen Terry] to Bertha [Bramley] 23 February [18]86, ET 2.020.
50 Letter from Nell [Ellen Terry] to Bertha [Bramley] Saturday, ET 2.014.
51 Letter from Nell [Ellen Terry] to Bertha [Bramley] 30 October, ET 2.041.
52 Letter from Nell [Ellen Terry] to Bertha [Bramley] Monday, ET 2.016.
53 Letter from ET [Ellen Terry] to Arthur J.G. Bright, ET 2.061a.
54 Letter from Nell [Ellen Terry] Thursday 2 June, ET.2.054.
55 Letter from Nell [Ellen Terry] to Bertha B. [Bramley] 11 December [18]90, ET 2.024.
56 Letter from Ellen T. [Ellen Terry] to Bertha [Bramley] 3 June [18]98; ET 2.026.
57 Ibid.

forthcoming about her opinions of a production, including the performances of her colleagues. To May Webster, she declared: 'I hope you like Sans Gene the second visit as well as the first = It is not a good play is it? & to my amazement I find it is a very hard working part!!! – but I like the woman – she is so unusual – '.[58] She reported, 'Mr Irving is superb as the Archbishop – Poor Rosa Mundi is a faintest sketch & most difficult, but I work hard at it – & my frocks are very pretty'.[59] To her friend Albert Fleming, she recommended:

> Go & see 'Much Ado' – it is a good entertainment – & Miss Emery is very funny – The change of scene from the church ruins the play I think – the passion is all checked – Viola Tree is quite remarkable it seems to me – & my eyes are moist when ever I watch her on the stage. The scene where she sits amongst her brides maids is beautiful.[60]

Terry wrote that Sully's performance in Paris of *Hamlet* was 'most interesting' but 'more earthy than H.I's – Henry's even seemed to me to be already more than half in Heaven with – "the King my father" – On the whole I much prefer our English Hamlet.'[61]

Terry was aware of the overfamiliarity of the general public and conscious of her public image generally. She wrote to her friend about a death threat from an anonymous female correspondent signing herself 'an American Gentleman'; Terry described the complaint that she was 'far too old & fat to be acting, & that no one wants to see me any more on the stage, & warning me not to go to America or I shall be shot!'[62] But this response was unusual; the audience was usually appreciative. When on tour, reading *Macbeth*, she wrote that 'it was quite marvellous to see the Great Halls full of people, crowds of working people too, some quite rough & to note how they hung on to the words, & how enthusiastic they all were'.[63] Some impression of the relationship between Irving and the audience is provided from a press cutting entitled 'The Colonials at the Lyceum'.[64] Irving had invited the colonial troops, who were in London for the Diamond Jubilee, to see *A Story of Waterloo* and *The Bells* at the Lyceum Theatre: 'Grey and turbaned veterans from the Indian Army, broad-hatted Australians, and Negroes in buff and white shoulder belts were especially noticeable.' Irving was called three times, and the speech attributed to him suggests that he empathised with these soldiers:

> 'Ladies and gentlemen – no, I won't say ladies and gentlemen; if you will let me, I will say my dear comrades, for our meeting to-day proves we are comrades one and all – I cannot tell you how much I value the delight, and honour, and privilege, and pride of making you welcome here to-day. I hope that, centuries hence, our children will hold very dear to them the spirit which gives us the opportunity of meeting here – that spirit of love to our Queen

---

58 Letter from ET [Ellen Terry] to May [Webster] Sunday morning, ET 2.270.

59 Letter from ET [Ellen Terry] to [Albert Fleming] Wednesday 22 February [?1893], ET 2.305.

60 Letter from ET [Ellen Terry] to Daffy [Albert Fleming] 17 February, ET 2.311.

61 Fragment of letter [from Ellen Terry] n.d.; ET 2.057.

62 Letter from Nell [Ellen Terry] Saturday, ET 2.027.

63 Letter from Nell [Ellen Terry] 20 June, ET 2.046.

64 'The Colonials at the Lyceum', unidentified press cutting, n.d., HIL-G478.

and our country, to that great nation which you typify as the strength, and glory, and power of it, and to that sweet, and gracious, and kindly Queen for whom your swords will flash and our hearts will pray.'[65]

Because the troops were united in patriotism and a colonial identity, Irving chose the word 'comrades' to embrace them all.

Some of the extant documents in Terry's archive are manifestly annotated for the record. From these ephemeral and intriguing traces can be reconstructed various fragmented narratives: opinions of Irving's legacy to the acting profession; the private lives of Irving, Terry and her family. Ellen Terry appears to have agreed with an unidentified review. She underlined the correspondent's judgement that '[u]ntil you have seen M. Coquelin you do not know how admirable is the "Mathias" of Mr Irving' and added her own comment, 'Bravo'.[66] Another press cutting, concerning Lord Houghton's speech at Dulwich College, is annotated in Irving's hand. A journalist's reference to Irving's idiosyncratic pronunciation is challenged for posterity by Edith Craig, but recorded on her behalf: 'Edy remarks that these phonetic signs for Irving's pronunciation give no idea of it under stress of emotion.'[67]

While some documents appear to preserve the authorised line on Henry Irving's memory, others contribute curiously to a picture of Ellen Terry's devotion and admiration. Terry had made a note of quotations she had seen on display in Irving's study: 'The greatest truths are the simplest & so are the greatest of men' and 'Victor Hugo says: "Never to be understood is a reason for being always obeyed"'.[68] In noting this detail of his most intimate environment, she may have been trying to get closer to him, retaining, through the words he chose for inspiration, an insight into his inner perspective and values. Marked 'private', her instructions for the preparation of a wreath to remember his death conveys, in its specific detail, the reverence with which she treated his memory: 'Please prepare for me the usual (delicate) Rosemary wreath for the grave at Westminster of Sir Henry Irving ... Please attach the enclosed paper – tying it loosely on the wreath – with very narrow white soft silk ribbon ...'.[69] The impact of Irving's death reveals itself in the ritual, the specified texture of the materials – sensuous, rich and slight – as well as in the manner of the gesture, the securing of the paper 'loosely'. Catalogues of various sales of Ellen Terry's property are annotated, sometimes in an irritated spirit, indicating the inadequacy of the description of the object. But the annotation and personalisation of the catalogue indicates that the owner was reluctant to part with her possessions and memories. Occasionally, items relating to Irving are mentioned. In the catalogue of the 'Sale of jewels of Miss Ellen Terry on Wednesday 21 July 1920 at Christie, Manson & Woods, 8 King Street, St James' is listed a gold ring worn by Sir Henry Irving in *The Belle's Stratagem*. A year later, the remaining contents of 215 King's Road, Chelsea, were sold on Tuesday 31 May 1921. Against 'lot 69 Old Japanese large bronze vase', Ellen Terry poignantly recorded its biography: 'I have grown spring flowers in it

---

65 Ibid.
66 HIL-G582.
67 *Ayrshire Post*, 11 February 1938, HIL-G542.
68 Document, n.d., Smallhythe Place.
69 Instructions marked 'private', n.d, ET 2.389.

each year outside in my small garden – it is a very fine bronze from Japan – via New York to London – 3 hundred years old – H.I. gave it to me.'[70] While the passing of time inevitably brings with it periods of mourning for those close to us, Terry also faced the loss of precious mementoes. The physical connection with the past through familiar objects had to be relinquished, but it was not easy.

The intimacy and emotional depth of the relationship between Ellen Terry and Henry Irving is sustained even in such apparently innocuous documents that survived the posthumous censorship by those protecting her privacy.[71] After Terry's death, Edith Craig worked hard to ensure that a lasting memorial was established to her mother. Terry's house in Kent was established as the Ellen Terry Memorial Museum and was given to the National Trust in 1939; it is now known as Smallhythe Place. Craig also advertised in the national press for Ellen Terry's letters to be donated to the museum. Some press cuttings document the memorialisation of Terry and Irving in the 1930s, when a call was put out for 'relics' for an exhibition. The cataloguing of this extensive archive, which includes photographs, playbills, play programmes, plays and a large collection of press cuttings, will provide the resource for historians and students of the theatre that Edith Craig always envisaged and also help to develop an understanding of the workings of Terry, Irving and many other figures in nineteenth- and twentieth-century theatre.

Acknowledgement

I am grateful to the AHRC Resource Enhancement Award 2006–8 for the financial support for the Ellen Terry and Edith Craig database project, which will facilitate the completion of the recording of the vast collection of documents at Smallhythe Place.

---

70 Sale catalogue, SCB23A-C2.

71 A number of other intriguing documents have surfaced. A detailed family tree for Irving has been sketched out, probably by Edith Craig, traced back to 1608, with the introduction of the name 'Morgan' into the family; the Clutton branch goes back to 1702, and the Australian branch of the family is also identified (HIL-M6). Some of Henry Irving's printed Christmas cards for 1885, signed but never sent, were put into an envelope addressed in his hand to 'Madame Sans Gene from her Lieutenant 27 Feb 1897', possibly used on stage as a prop (HIL-B1). Speeches by Irving are extant, relating the meeting of the Actors' Association onstage at the Lyceum on 22 November 1892 and an undated speech to the mayor, and guests of Marlowe (HIL-H1 and HIL-H2).

Chapter 4

The Lyceum and the Lord Chamberlain: The Case of Hall Caine's *Mahomet*

Kristan Tetens

Bram Stoker notes in his *Personal Reminiscences of Henry Irving* that Irving had long wanted to produce a play based on the life of Muhammad, the prophet of Islam. The explorer Sir Richard Burton had been among the first to suggest an 'Eastern' topic to Irving; at a supper party in London in September 1886 he told his friend how much might be done with a play taken from some story, or group of stories, in the *Arabian Nights*, an unexpurgated translation of which Burton had published the year before. 'Burton had a most vivid way of putting things – especially of the East,' Stoker recalled. 'Burton *knew* the East ... its romances; its beauty; its horrors. Irving grew fired as the night wore on, and it became evident that he had it in his mind from that time to produce some such play as [Burton] suggested, should occasion serve.'[1]

Irving had caught a glimpse of the East in 1879 during a cruise taken with his patroness, the Baroness Angela Burdett-Coutts, which included Morocco, Algeria, Tunisia and the eastern Mediterranean from Turkey to Egypt. This voyage is often credited with providing Irving with his conception of Shylock, thought to be based on his observations of Levantine Jews, but it also provided him with first-hand knowledge of Islamic cultures.[2] When a new play on the life of Muhammad was published in Paris by Henri de Bornier and accepted for production by the Comédie-Française in 1888, an English production on the topic seemed timely. Irving obtained a copy of de Bornier's five-act verse drama, which was called *Mahomet*, had it translated into English, and asked the novelist and playwright Hall Caine to revise it for production at the Lyceum.[3]

---

1 Bram Stoker, *Personal Reminiscences of Henry Irving* (London, 1906), Vol. 1, pp. 360–1 and Vol. 2, p. 118. Irving and Stoker each owned a set of Burton's *The Book of The Thousand Nights and a Night: A Plain and Literal Translation of the Arabian Nights' Entertainments*, which had been published by the Kama Shastra Society in ten volumes for private subscribers (London and Benares, 1885), and its six-volume sequel, which appeared between 1886 and 1888. Burton had travelled to Mecca and Medina in 1853, disguised as a Muslim pilgrim.

2 The cruise in the steam yacht *Walrus*, which followed Irving's first season as sole lessee and manager of the Lyceum, is described in Laurence Irving, *Henry Irving: The Actor and His World* (London, 1951), pp. 330–4.

3 A charge of £8 10s in the Lyceum account book for the 1889–90 season is the only expense clearly related to Irving's *Mahomet* recorded by Stoker. It seems unlikely that this

Irving first met Caine in Liverpool in the summer of 1874 while on tour under the management of Hezekiah Bateman and his wife, Sidney. The actor's performances thrilled Caine, who was then just 21 years old and working as a draughtsman in a firm of Liverpool builders while he tried to launch a literary career. Later that year, when Caine was preparing the first issue of a new monthly magazine, he contacted Irving to request a photograph that could be used to illustrate an essay on the actor's influence on the contemporary theatre. Irving, touched by the young man's interest and well aware of the benefits of being on good terms with up-and-coming writers, complied and then invited him to the London premiere of *Hamlet* on 31 October, which Caine attended in his capacity as theatrical critic for the Liverpool *Town Crier*. His enthusiastic review of the production, with Irving as Hamlet and Isabel Bateman as Ophelia, was reprinted and distributed widely as a broadsheet pamphlet. Caine followed this with a number of lectures and essays on Irving's art.[4] 'Caine seemed to intuitively understand not only Irving's work but his aim and method,' Stoker later wrote. 'Irving felt this and had a high opinion of Caine's powers. I do not know anyone whose opinions interested him more.'[5] In 1876, when Edward Aveling claimed to be Irving's brother, prompting Aveling's non-conformist minister father to rage against the theatre and all those associated with it, Caine wrote a rebuttal at Irving's behest that was published in the Liverpool *Argus*, a service that earned him the actor's lasting gratitude. In September 1878, at Caine's invitation, Irving presided at a meeting of the Liverpool Notes and Queries Society. Three months later, on 30 December, Caine attended one of the most brilliant nights in British theatrical history: Irving's first performance at the Lyceum under his own management, when he presented a new production of *Hamlet* with Ellen Terry as Ophelia. It was at this time that Caine met Stoker, Irving's business manager, who was to become one of his closest friends.[6] In 1881 Caine left Liverpool and moved to

---

tiny figure represented the purchase of performance rights from de Bornier, as Tracy C. Davis implies in her brief sketch of the planned production in *The Economics of the British Stage, 1800–1914* (Cambridge, 2000), pp. 148–50. More probably, it was the fee paid to a typist. Irving typically paid a flat fee of several hundred pounds to purchase a play outright; in the 1890s, he generally paid a fixed royalty per performance. See Jeffrey Richards, *Sir Henry Irving: A Victorian Actor and His World* (London and New York, 2005), pp. 190–5. Since de Bornier's play was completed and in circulation among French theatre managers in 1888 (a year that Irving visited Paris), it is possible that payment for the English rights to de Bornier's play was included as part of a £755 line item for authors' fees recorded in an account book that summarizes Irving's income and expenses between December 1888 and February 1890. The Lyceum account books are part of the Laurence Irving Collection, Theatre Museum, London (hereafter Laurence Irving Collection).

4 See Stoker, *Personal Reminiscences*, Vol. 2, pp. 115–30. Vivien Allen provides a detailed account of Caine's relationship with Irving, which lasted until the actor's death in 1905, in *Hall Caine: Portrait of a Victorian Romancer* (Sheffield, 1997). For an example of Caine's writings on Irving, see *Richard III and Macbeth: The Spirit of Romantic Play in Relationship to the Principles of Greek and of Gothic Art, and to the Picturesque Interpretations of Mr. Henry Irving: A Dramatic Study* (London and Liverpool, 1877).

5 Stoker, *Personal Reminiscences*, Vol. 2, p. 116.

6 Stoker occasionally acted as Caine's literary agent, introducing him to publishers, drafting his contracts, handling various legal matters, and editing his novels. Caine sometimes

London to serve as amanuensis to the painter and poet Dante Gabriel Rossetti. After Rossetti's death in 1882, Caine turned his attention to writing fiction. He was by this time on friendly terms with the leaders of London's literary and artistic circles and a regular at Irving's Beefsteak Room gatherings at the Lyceum.

The actor had hoped to produce a play based on Caine's third book, *The Deemster*, a novel of Manx life published in 1887, but discovered, when he returned in April 1888 from his third American tour, that the stage rights had been bought by Wilson Barrett.[7] From that time, according to Stoker, Irving 'had a strong desire that Caine should write some play that he could act'.[8] The actor repeatedly suggested subjects, themes and characters; Caine spent considerable time and energy 'in an effort to fit Irving with a part, and the pigeon-holes of my study are still heavy with sketches and drafts and scenarios of dramas which either he or I or our constant friend and colleague Bram Stoker (to whose loyal comradeship we both owed so much), thought possible for the Lyceum Theatre'. Many of the ideas discussed had weird or supernaturally tinged religious themes. Two of them, the Wandering Jew and the Flying Dutchman, featured a main character that is made to wander the face of the earth until Judgement Day, by land and sea, respectively, after spurning or challenging God. In another, the Demon Lover, based on an old Scottish ballad, the main character is the Devil disguised as a sailor who lures the wife of another man to her death. Yet, 'in spite of the utmost sincerity on both sides', according to Caine, these efforts came to nothing.[9]

By 1889, when the idea of a Lyceum *Mahomet* arose, Caine was enjoying a growing reputation as a novelist and playwright. He had found popular success with the novel and stage versions of *The Deemster*. His fourth novel, *The Bondman*, appeared in serial form between June and November and would become an instant bestseller upon its publication as a book in January 1890. A new play, *Good Old*

---

critiqued drafts of Stoker's novels. Stoker dedicated *Dracula* to Caine in 1897; in 1908 he edited Caine's autobiography, which Caine dedicated to him. See Paul Murray, *From the Shadow of Dracula: A Life of Bram Stoker* (London, 2004), pp. 126–9.

7   The stage version of *The Deemster*, called *Ben-my-Chree* (Manx for 'Girl of My Heart') was written jointly by Caine and Barrett and opened at the Princess's Theatre in May 1888. It was a commercial, if not critical, success and was revived regularly over the next several decades. See Allen, *Hall Caine*, pp. 188–9.

8   Stoker, *Personal Reminiscences*, Vol. 2, p. 118.

9   Hall Caine, *My Story* (New York, 1909), p. 341. Irving had already essayed the part of the Flying Dutchman in *Vanderdecken*, a blank-verse drama by Percy Fitzgerald and W.G. Wills produced at the Lyceum by Mrs Bateman in June 1878. After the *Mahomet* affair, Irving and Caine revisited these ideas many times but always without result. In 1891 Irving was 'hugely interested' in producing a play based on a novel Caine was then planning on the subject of Jewish oppression in Poland, but the book never materialised. (Twenty years earlier Irving had made his first major London success with a play centred on the murder of a Polish Jew in Leopold Lewis's *The Bells*.) In 1894 Caine wrote a narrative poem based on the Demon Lover idea that he believed could be turned into a play for Irving but the actor rejected it, saying he was too old for the part. Irving and Caine were still discussing a play on the Flying Dutchman theme as late as 1896, the same year Irving rejected Caine's new play *Home, Sweet Home*. See Stoker, *Personal Reminiscences*, Vol. 2, pp. 122–4, and Allen, *Hall Caine*, pp. 217ff and pp. 238–9.

Times, had been produced by Barrett at the Princess's Theatre in February. Thus, when Irving brought to his rooms a typewritten translation of de Bornier's *Mahomet*, Caine was a rising man of letters with some experience in writing for the stage. Of de Bornier's play Irving told him: 'It's not right, but it's the right subject. See if you can do it over again.'[10] Perhaps to inspire Caine, the actor lent him several volumes of Burton's *Arabian Nights*, which included copious annotations on Muslim manners and customs.

On 29 November 1889 Caine sent his initial thoughts on de Bornier's play to Irving. 'I have read Mahomet, and am profoundly impressed by the potentialities of the subject, but deeply disappointed with the play as a creation,' he said. Caine found the first, second and third acts 'quite valueless'. The fourth and fifth acts, however, he thought were (or could be) 'as fine & stirring as anything in drama. The scene of Mahomet's return after saving the life of the lover of his wife is really thrilling. But it could be enormously heightened ... the catastrophe ought to be fine, & yet it is not. You want the thing worked up to from the opening lines.' Despite the inadequacies of the French play, Caine urged Irving not to reject it until they had an opportunity to discuss it further: 'The subject is too fine, the atmosphere too rich & new to be lightly set aside. But the changes (as you thought) would have to be very great. Indeed the whole fabric ought to be built up again.' Caine was already thinking of ways in which that might be done: 'I have one leading idea, which stirs my blood to think of. It centres in the Jewish mistress, who is completely thrown away in this play. I see a very stirring & picturesque first act, too.'[11] Caine asked Irving if he thought de Bornier would permit him to use the subject as well as the entire fourth act and half of the fifth act, but otherwise to rewrite the play.

The following month, Caine wrote to Irving again: 'I have thought much on Mahomet, & the subject grows larger & yet more impressive. There is a great play in it.' Caine regretted that de Bornier had been the first in the field with a new treatment of the subject. While he and Irving waited to hear whether the playwright would allow extensive changes to be made to the play, Caine told the actor he had developed an alternative plan in case such permission were denied. Muhammad would be dropped as the play's central character: 'I would call it The Prophet & the scene only would be similar. In all other particulars the play would be different.' In a postscript, and perhaps in response to a request that he not discuss his work on the play with others, Caine assured Irving that he had not mentioned *Mahomet* to anyone except Stoker.[12]

By the beginning of 1890 Caine had discarded de Bornier's play as a starting-point and instead was preparing an original scenario for Irving's consideration. In the late afternoon of 26 January he presented his idea of the play to Stoker and his wife, Florence, at their Chelsea home, where Caine was staying. 'His image rises now before me,' Stoker recalled:

---

10 Hall Caine, *My Story*, p. 343. A copy of the translation, prepared for Irving by Stoker's wife, Florence, is among the documents in the Sir Thomas Henry Hall Caine Papers, Manx National Heritage Library and Archives, ref. no. 09542, box 21.

11 Hall Caine to Henry Irving, 29 November 1889, Laurence Irving Collection.

12 Hall Caine to Henry Irving, 21 December 1889, Laurence Irving Collection.

He sits on a low chair in front of the fire; his face is pale something waxen-looking ... His red hair, fine and long, and pushed back from his high forehead, is so thin that through it as the flames leap we can see the white line of the head so like to Shakespeare's. He is himself all aflame. His hands have a natural eloquence – something like Irving's; they foretell and emphasise the coming thoughts. His large eyes shine like jewels as the firelight flashes ... As he goes on he gets more and more afire till at last he is like a living flame. We sit quite still; we fear to interrupt him. The end of his story leaves us fired and exalted too.[13]

The next day the two men went to see Irving in his office at the Lyceum. Caine told him the story of the play, which Irving enthusiastically approved. Caine set to work. In March he spent three weeks in Morocco to gather details of Muslim life for the play and for a new novel.[14] In April, a surprise: the French government announced that it was halting the Comédie-Française production of de Bornier's play. The public was told that because the production of the play would create serious diplomatic difficulties, the Council of Ministers had decided that it could not be produced by a state-supported theatre like the Comédie-Française. This decision had been prompted in part by the intervention of Abdülhamid II, the Ottoman sultan, who perceived in the play an insult to Muslim traditions (particularly Sunni traditions) of aniconism, which hold that the representation or impersonation of the prophet is a form of idol worship prohibited by the Qur'an and several Hadith.[15]

To a modern reader, de Bornier's play is breathtakingly arrogant in its treatment of Islam. It is, in part, a duel between Islam and Christianity, with Christianity triumphant at the end as the character of Muhammad, declaring that Jesus was the greater prophet, commits suicide by drinking poison so that his unfaithful wife can be reunited with her lover.[16] Caine, who had been wise to drop the play as a model, called its plot 'false to history, untrue to character, Western in thought, and Parisian in sentiment'.[17] The *Spectator*, however, one of several English journals that followed the affair, wondered what all the fuss was about. Noting that the play would be very effective on the stage, it attributed the play's suppression to the French government's dislike of nobility – de Bornier was a viscount – and its anti-Christian bias.[18] Little did anyone know that the elements for a similar showdown between government authority and dramatic art were coming together at Irving's theatre in Wellington Street.

---

13 Stoker, *Personal Reminiscences*, Vol. 2, pp. 119–20.

14 The novel, *The Scapegoat,* was serialized in the *Graphic* beginning in April 1890 and published in book form in 1892.

15 On traditions of Islamic aniconism and prohibitions on figuration, see Alain Besançon, *The Forbidden Image: An Intellectual History of Iconoclasm,* trans. Jane Marie Todd (Chicago, 2000), pp. 77–81, and Jean-François Clément, 'L'image dans le monde arabe: interdits et possibilitiés,' in Gilbert Beaugé and Jean-François Clément, *L'image dans le monde arabe* (Paris, 1995), pp. 11–42. The vitality of these traditions in our own time was demonstrated by the reaction of Muslims all over the world to caricatures of Muhammad published by the Danish newspaper *Jyllands-Posten* in September 2005.

16 Henri de Bornier, *Mahomet, drame en cinq actes, en vers* (Paris, 1890).

17 Hall Caine, 'A Literary Causerie', *Speaker,* 4 October 1890.

18 'M. de Bornier's "Mahomet"', *Spectator,* 21 June 1890.

With Paris in a frenzy over the banning of de Bornier's play, Caine quietly continued work on his own version of the prophet's story, which would centre on Muhammad's flight from Mecca (the Hijra of 622 CE) and his triumphant return there from Medina some years later. On 17 May Caine wrote to Irving to tell him that he had completed the first three acts of *Mahomet*: 'They seem to me to justify our expectations of the subject. They possess me. I can scarcely put my hand to anything else.' He worried that Ellen Terry would be unhappy with her part and asked Irving to reassure her that he would soften 'the one act of great treachery which she would have to do' with additional passages of pathos and also that the final two acts would show the noble and contrite aspect of her character: 'You will see that acting on your hint I have given her one pretty, playful scene (with the boy) ... if I could at some time have a chat with her I might much enhance the charm of it.' Caine noted that he had added a situation for her at the end of the third act that seemed to him to 'afford scope for acting such as hardly anything in modern drama ... I must not weaken the effect of it by saying in advance what it is. What I've said already will sound vain enough, but the subject possesses me, & you will forgive the vanity.' Caine seemed even more pleased with the character of Muhammad: 'The prophet himself I must leave you to judge of. I love him.' Caine cited the character's nobility, simplicity, unselfishness, wisdom, humour and passion. 'Naturally he is least operative in the 3rd Act, where he is the victim of a base plot, & only when in the 4th & 5th Acts the evil is laid bare before him will all his greatness appear,' Caine told Irving. 'But I have no doubt of him even in the 3rd Act, & in the 1st & 2nd he is without equal.' Caine sent his handwritten manuscript to Stoker for typing and asked for a meeting with Irving after he had had an opportunity to review the partially completed play.[19]

The tenor of this exchange between author and actor was typical of their relationship. 'There was to both men a natural expression of intellectual frankness, as if they held the purpose as well as the facts of ideas in common,' Stoker recalled later. 'The two men were very much alike in certain intellectual ways. To both was given an almost abnormal faculty of self-abstraction and of concentrating all their powers on a given subject for any length of time. To both was illimitable patience in the doing of their work.' Stoker noted that the two men also shared 'a faculty of getting up and ultimately applying to the work in hand an amazing amount of information'.[20]

On 31 May Irving and Terry completed their twelfth Lyceum season, which had featured *The Dead Heart*, *The Bells*, *Louis XI* and *Olivia*. Beginning on 3 June they toured the provinces for nearly a month, giving readings from *Macbeth*. Irving then played *The Bells* and *Louis XI* for two weeks at the Grand Theatre, Islington. After that, Irving and Terry went their separate ways on holiday, reuniting in Winchelsea before returning to London to prepare for the new season, which would include Herman Merivale's *Ravenswood*, an adaptation of Sir Walter Scott's *The Bride of Lammermoor*.

While Irving was away from London, rumours that he intended to portray the prophet of Islam began to spread. 'The very fact of approaching de Bornier regarding

---

19 Hall Caine to Henry Irving, 17 May 1890, Laurence Irving Collection.
20 Stoker, *Personal Reminiscences*, Vol. 2. pp. 116–7.

his play had somehow leaked out,' Stoker recalled.[21] On 20 June a brief item in the French *Journal des débats* asserted that de Bornier's *Mahomet* had inspired the English production. Although this was true, a longer paragraph in the *Pall Mall Gazette*, one week later, went to great lengths to clarify the connection: 'We are in a position to state that, though Mr. Irving had never the very slightest intention of producing M. Henri de Bornier's play at the Lyceum, or any play founded upon it, he bought the English rights of it, partly as an act of courtesy, and partly to hold control of the subject.' The paper noted that Irving had commissioned an Eastern play from a well-known English novelist and dramatist: 'This play, which is not in any sense whatever an adaptation of M. de Bornier's play, but an entirely original work, in all its essentials quite different, is now nearly written and ready, and report speaks of it in very warm terms.'[22] Such highly detailed information could only have come from someone intimately involved with the planned production; almost certainly it was provided by Caine himself, who throughout his career was known for his brazen self-promotion, or by one of his literary friends on his behalf. It could also have come from Stoker. If the goal had been to distance the Lyceum production from the banned French play, it was an ill-conceived strategy that backfired terribly, serving only to bring Irving's plans to the notice of Muslim communities at home and abroad.

The play – in four acts, not five, as Caine had told Irving in May – does in fact owe little to de Bornier. It begins in Mecca just before the return of Mahomet – 'this son of the desert, this man of the book, this brand new Prophet' – from the Jabal al-Nour mountain.[23] Among those waiting for him is Rachel, a Jewess, who has persuaded her lover, Omar, to kill Mahomet in revenge for the murder of her father. When Mahomet arrives in the city (he is described as 'a man of forty years, bare-headed, his hood fallen back, dressed in the pilgrim's garb of sheepskin, and walking with a staff'), he proclaims that his doctrine is 'to worship one God and to serve no false gods'. When the jeering crowd threatens him, Rachel takes him into her house and later lulls him to sleep with a song and a slow 'Egyptian' dance. Omar raises a knife to kill Mahomet, but his courage fails and instead he provides the prophet with a password that will allow him to escape enemies waiting outside. As Act II begins, Mahomet and his followers, including Omar, approach Medina after several days on the open desert. 'Twelve midnights past [Islam] was driven out of Mecca in disgrace, with derision, before the assassin's knife,' says Mahomet, 'yet the day is coming when it will return in honour, with triumph and before bended knees.' Rachel arrives and tells Mahomet that she wishes to join him. Privately, Rachel tells Omar that her conversion was insincere and that she has come to be with him, not with Mahomet. Omar tells her to return to Mecca, but she refuses. He begins to tell Mahomet of

---

21 Stoker, *Personal Reminiscences*, Vol. 2, p. 120.
22 'Théâtres et Concerts', *Journal des débats*, 20 June 1890; 'Mr. Irving as "Mahomet": New Schemes at the Lyceum', *Pall Mall Gazette*, 27 June 1890. Strangely, the French journal reported that Irving's production of *Mahomet* had been banned months before it was dropped at the request of the Lord Chamberlain.
23 A typewritten copy of the play and annotated drafts of individual acts survive in the Sir Thomas Henry Hall Caine Papers, Manx National Heritage Library and Archives, ref. no. 09542, box 21. A critical edition of the play is being prepared for publication.

Rachel's involvement in the plot to murder him in Mecca, but Mahomet refuses to listen. Act III takes place in Medina two years later. Mahomet, now married to Rachel, has brought peace and order to the city. He sends a mission to the leaders of Mecca, demanding that they adopt Islam. When they refuse, Mahomet vows that Mecca will fall. Rachel learns of Mahomet's plans and plays at marching into Mecca with Mahomet's young grandson, using fans for swords (this is the 'one pretty, playful scene [with the boy]' that Caine added for Terry and described to Irving in May 1890). Rachel sees her chance for revenge at last. She persuades Mahomet to lead the advance party into Mecca and then writes a letter to the city's leaders, warning them of the impending attack. As Mahomet addresses the people of Medina from the *minbar* of the mosque, he decides that Omar will lead the advance party instead. Rachel, still in love with Omar, falls to the ground with a scream. The final act begins with Mahomet and his followers encamped at night on the plain outside Mecca. A messenger brings the news that the advance party has been captured. Rachel confesses her treachery to Mahomet, who now suspects she is having an adulterous relationship with Omar. Intending to kill Omar, Mahomet arranges to have him returned to the camp. Omar denies Mahomet's charges of adultery and tells him that he gladly led the advance party, knowing that it would save the prophet's life at the probable cost of his own. Mahomet begs Omar's forgiveness. In Mecca, the jailer in charge of Mahomet's imprisoned advance party is ordered to find 4,000 Bedouins to attack Mahomet's camp; instead, he arranges to open the city gates to Mahomet, who enters Mecca peacefully and forgives those who had persecuted him. The prophet announces that he will return to the desert to rest and pray: 'The faith of Islam is founded, its empire begun ... Mahomet's task is finished, his life's work is done.' He then turns to the crowd: 'Farewell, everyone who has followed me in hunger and thirst and the want of all things. I must leave you now. But God has been more merciful to me than to Moses, for he has suffered me to see the day of my people's glory. The face of Allah shine on you forever! He rides upon the heavens; his excellence is in the sky. Truth has come and falsehood has fled before the sword. The night is gone, and look, the day has dawned! Farewell! Farewell!' At the very moment the sun rises over the horizon, Mahomet climbs the hill outside the city and then descends behind it, going out at the place he was first seen.

One of Caine's friends, the novelist Robert Leighton, had read *Mahomet* in manuscript and noted that 'without an inartistic adherence to the strict lines of history', the play follows 'with reverent fidelity the great landmarks of the prophet's life'.[24] Caine himself asserted that 'the dramatic grit of Mahomet's story lies ... in his struggles with the Coreish [Quraysh]'.[25] Onto this historical armature Caine layered the fictional intrigue of a love triangle, a highly sentimental plot device that figures prominently in his other works, and comic relief in the form of teasing scenes between a pair of young lovers and the antics of a jester. It is not difficult to imagine the extravagant romantic realism with which Irving would have staged the play, which provides significant scope for exotic display: the swirling sights and sounds of the Meccan marketplace; the approach of Mahomet from the rocky red hills surrounding

---

24 Robert Leighton, Letter to the Editor, *Speaker*, 1 November 1890.
25 Caine, 'A Literary Causerie'.

the city; the entrapment of Mahomet by Rachel as she sings and performs a sensual harem dance, a scene lit by spirit lamps; Omar poised above the sleeping Mahomet with knife in hand; the heat- and wind-blasted desert between Mecca and Medina; Mahomet's weary caravan of followers, their meagre worldly possessions strapped to the backs of camels; the prosperous city of Medina, with its massive gate, high stone battlements and graceful minarets; Mahomet's address to the people of Medina in the spacious mosque, its enormous columns, intricately patterned walls and high dome illuminated by flickering flambeaux as his followers make offerings of gold and silver; Rachel's collapse in the mosque as she is forced to prepare her lover for a mission she knows he is unlikely to survive; Mahomet's camp on the plain outside Mecca, with tents extending to the horizon and the lights of the city glittering in the distance; and the prophet's exit in a blaze of rising sun, symbolic of the dawn of a new day for humanity. Much of the action is accompanied by multi-racial throngs of men, women and children, including Arabs, Jews, Bedouins and Egyptian slaves. Hundreds of supernumeraries and dozens of live animals would have been required. Without question, the production would have been a thrilling theatrical realisation of Richard Burton's East, brought to vivid life by Irving and his designers.[26]

Within weeks of the appearance of the paragraph in the *Pall Mall Gazette*, however, newspapers across India had published notices on the subject, and Muslims both there and in England began to organise protests that took the form of public meetings, petitions and letter-writing campaigns. In Delhi several Muslim leaders told Deputy Commissioner Robert Clarke that they were 'unwilling to give unnecessary publicity' to newspaper reports of the Lyceum production; Clarke thanked them for taking the 'quieter and probably more effective course of representing their anxiety' directly to him. In a letter to the Delhi superintendent, Clarke noted that 'the mere fact of Muhammad being represented by an actor on the stage could not be other than painful to every believing Mahommedan'.[27] Among the prominent Indian Muslims who led protests was Abdul Luteef (or Latif), founder of the Mohammedan Literary Society in Calcutta and a leading advocate for the social, cultural and intellectual progress of Muslims in Bengal. Luteef had taken an active role in protesting the proposed Comédie-Française production of de Bornier's play; now he was incredulous that a similar sacrilege might happen in London. He wrote to Lord Lansdowne, the viceroy of India, and to several former viceroys, including Northbrook and Ripon, whom he urged to 'exercise all legal powers as well as moral

---

26 In its staging the play would have fallen squarely into the tradition of orientalist spectacle described by Edward Ziter in *The Orient on the Victorian Stage* (Cambridge, 2003) and John M. MacKenzie in *Orientalism: History, Theory, and the Arts* (Manchester, 1995). However, as I argue below, it would be wrong to characterise Caine's *Mahomet* as a straightforward example of orientalist appropriation, given his personal views on the British presence in the Arab world.

27 See Robert Clarke to Colonel Leopold John Herbert Grey, 27 November 1890, LC1/547, National Archives. For related documents, see Department of Asia, Pacific, and Africa Collection, British Library, India Office records, L/P&J/6/291: 2237 (1890).

persuasion to prevent such an outrage to Mohammedan feeling'.[28] On 2 September he sent an impassioned letter to several English-language newspapers in India:

> Little did I think that the evil which we Mohammedans so much dreaded would raise its head in England itself. I can assure you that this news has been received by the Indian Musselmans with the greatest regret and surprise ... Ordinarily, the matter might not have any importance attached to it in the eyes of the British public, but the French incident, the Turkish protest, and the agitation which even then spread up to India, should open the eyes of all thinking men to the inadvisability of allowing such representations to take place.[29]

Luteef was a trusted broker between the British administrators of India and the Muslim community there; in 1883 he had been made a Companion of The Most Eminent Order of the Indian Empire in recognition of his services. The high esteem in which he was held is reflected in the speed with which his concerns about the Lyceum production were addressed. One week after Luteef's letter was published, Richard Assheton Cross, the secretary of state for India, requested that the Lord Chamberlain's Office and the Home Office investigate whether the production was rumour or fact.[30]

On 26 September a letter from the vice-president of the Liverpool Moslem Association, Raffiüddin Ahmad, appeared in *The Times*. 'The Indian Mussulmans are deeply irritated to learn of the proposed mockery of the prophet on the stage of a country which has pledged itself to respect their religious feelings, and the Queen of which has been destined by Providence to reign over a greater number of Moslems than any single ruler, Mahomedan or Christian, on the surface of the globe,' he wrote, asking the newspaper's readers, 'Is it right and proper to hurt the religious feelings of so many of your fellow-subjects in the East, to satisfy the whims or fill the coffers of a theatrical company, however influential it may be?'[31] Ahmad's letter prompted immediate action on the part of Edward Frederick Smyth Pigott, the Examiner of Plays, who sent a copy of it to Sir Spencer Ponsonby-Fane, comptroller of the Lord Chamberlain's Office and Pigott's immediate superior. 'With respect to the enclosed', he wrote, 'pray assure all whom it may concern, whether Mahomedans or Managers, that I shall never dream of submitting to you, for the LC's licence, any piece calculated to offend the religious feelings of any portion of Her Majesty's subjects of whatever creed.' Muslims, he asserted, had 'the same right to be respected as Christians, and we do not permit Jesus Christ to be represented on the stage'. He observed that he had, however, 'never heard a whisper of any such

---

28 See Abdul Luteef to the Earl of Northbrook, 2 September 1890, forwarded by Northbrook to the Lord Chamberlain's Office, LC1/547/118, National Archives. Northbrook requested that the Lord Chamberlain consider the demands of Luteef, whom he described as a 'prominent Mahomedan gentleman of Calcutta'.

29 Abdul Luteef, Letter to the Editor written on 2 September 1890 in Calcutta and published on 22 September in the *Overland Mail* and the *Homeland Mail*; reprinted in the *Indian Mirror*, 21 October, and the *Indian Daily News*, 23 October.

30 Richard Assheton Cross to Sir Spencer Ponsonby-Fane, 29 September 1890, LC1/547/119, National Archives.

31 Raffiüddin Ahmad, Letter to the Editor, *The Times*, 26 September 1890.

intention on the part of any manager ... and I make it my business to know all that is going on in theatrical affairs'.³² Clearly, he had missed the announcement of Irving's plans in the *Pall Mall Gazette* three months before.

Official communications warning of dire consequences should the Lyceum production go forward poured into Whitehall. Abdülhamid II, through Rustem Paşa, the Turkish ambassador to Britain, expressed his deep concern to Salisbury, the prime minister.³³ The India Office received numerous letters from civil servants throughout India, describing the probable effect of the production on the ability of Britain to maintain peace in key regions of the subcontinent. Lord Lathom, the Lord Chamberlain, recognizing the political exigencies involved, wrote privately to Irving, requesting that further work on *Mahomet* be halted and informing him that such a play would not be licensed. He told Irving that Britain was obliged to consider the religious sensibilities of India's 50 million Muslims and the tens of millions located elsewhere in the Empire. Despite the example of what had happened to de Bornier's play in France, which he must certainly have been aware of, Stoker called this a 'bolt from the blue' and seems to have been genuinely surprised that anyone could object to the Lyceum *Mahomet*. 'None of us had the slightest idea', he wrote, 'that there *could* be any objection in a professedly Christian nation to a play on the subject.' He noted that 'the Lord Chamberlain's department does its spiriting very gently; all that those in contact with it are made aware of is the velvet glove. But the steel hand works all the same – perhaps better than if stark. It is an understood thing that the Lord Chamberlain's request is a command in matters under his jurisdiction.'³⁴ Irving complied at once with the Lord Chamberlain's wishes and then sent a telegraph to Caine apprising him of the situation. Caine recalled that it was 'a deep disappointment to Irving himself, for the dusky son of the desert was a part that might have suited him to the ground, and to me it looked like an overwhelming disaster, slamming the door on the efforts of years'. The Lyceum *Mahomet* was, he claimed, 'by much the best of my dramatic efforts'.³⁵ Irving offered to compensate Caine for his labour, but Caine refused to accept any payment.

Although life at the Lyceum went on – Irving and Terry had opened their thirteenth Lyceum season on 20 September with *Ravenswood* – Caine found it difficult to get

---

32 Edward F. Pigott to Sir Spencer Ponsonby-Fane, 28 September 1890, LC1/547, National Archives, London. Pigott was not, as Tracy C. Davis states in *The Economics of the British Stage*, p. 150, 'initially indifferent to depiction of the Prophet' – quite the opposite, in fact. For a sketch of Pigott's career and an overview of official objection to the stage representation of religious themes, see John Russell Stephens, *The Censorship of English Drama, 1824–1901* (Cambridge, 1980). Richard Foulkes provides essential context in *Church and Stage in Victorian England* (Cambridge, 1997).

33 One result of the Lyceum *Mahomet* contretemps was that Salisbury promised Abdülhamid II that the Lord Chamberlain would, in future, alert the Foreign Office to any plans by a theatre manager to produce a play on similar themes (Philip Currie to Sir Spencer Ponsonby-Fane, 28 October 1893, LC1/601, National Archives). In the autumn of 1890, the Liverpool Moslem Association sent a letter of thanks to the sultan for his intervention.

34 Stoker, *Personal Reminiscences*, Vol. 2, pp. 120–1.

35 Caine, *My Story*, p. 343.

over the loss.³⁶ In October he wrote an angry article for the *Speaker* that allowed him, he later said, to relieve his feelings 'by spitting on my antagonists'.³⁷ What Caine most resented was the Lord Chamberlain's interference with his prerogative as an artist to depict a subject of his own choosing:

> I claim the right ... to protest in the name of literary liberty against the blind bigotry and silly superstition that would cry "Hands off!" whenever a sacred subject comes within the province of imaginative art ... I hold that the only right a man wants to touch any subject, however sacred, in any art, no matter what, is the right of an honest intention to do it well ... To pay court to all religious feelings, as such, is either to narrow all art by the exclusion of the highest themes, or to reduce it to child's play.

Pointing out the thousands of Christians who had travelled that very year to see the passion play at Oberammergau, Caine asserted that:

> Christianity has recognised what Islam has never seen – that art may be a help towards spiritual life, and that the divinity of its Founder is not obscured, but vivified, by truthful representations of His humanity.³⁸

Many agreed with Caine, including Robert Leighton, who had read *Mahomet* in manuscript. 'So far from doing any possible wrong to the faith of Mohammedans ... the play is calculated to be of the greatest service,' Leighton wrote in a letter to the editor of the *Speaker*, adding, 'It appears to me a grievous thing that a dramatic censorship which allows the performance of farces such as *The Pink Dominoes* and burlesques such as *Venus* should set its face rigidly against a serious subject treated with the seriousness, the good taste, and the learning which Mr. Caine has devoted to the dramatic delineation of the grand figure of the prophet.'³⁹ Another person who claimed to have read the play told the *Graphic* that 'in the opinion of competent judges, this play is in entire sympathy with Islam'.⁴⁰ Muslim leaders declared that such justifications were beside the point. Jahan Kader Mirza, a member

---

36 Perhaps, as has been suggested by Mary Hammond, Caine was so upset because 'he was in effect seeing the last of his chances for performance by an actor/manager with a reputation for creating "art" theatre'. The majority of Caine's plays were staged by managers – including Wilson Barrett at the Princess's Theatre, John M. East at the Lyric Opera House, Hammersmith, and Arthur Collins at Drury Lane – all known for their popular, often spectacular, productions. See Mary Hammond, 'Hall Caine and the Melodrama on Page, Stage, and Screen', *Nineteenth Century Theatre and Film*, 31, June 2004.

37 Robert Harborough Sherard, 'Hall Caine: Story of His Life and Work, Derived from Conversations', *McClure's Magazine*, 6, December 1895.

38 Caine, 'A Literary Causerie'.

39 Robert Leighton, Letter to the Editor, *Speaker*, 1 November 1890. Leighton's low opinion of the dramatic censorship was widely shared. Pigott was the target of particular abuse from the beginning of his term as Examiner of Plays in 1874 until his death in 1895. Opposing views of Pigott and his office are provided in obituaries by Clement Scott, 'Death of Mr. Pigott, Examiner of Stage Plays', *Daily Telegraph*, 25 February 1895, and George Bernard Shaw, 'Down with the Censorship!', *Saturday Review*, 2 March 1895.

40 Letter to the Editor, *Graphic*, 3 October 1890, reprinted in the *Indian Daily News*, 4 November 1890.

of the royal family of the Indian princely state of Oudh and a vice-president of Luteef's Mohammedan Literary Society, observed that 'the real objection of my co-religionists was based not on the particular tone and language of the play, but upon the repugnance which they feel to any human beings personating the character of the Holy Prophet and revered members of his family, and their being dragged down into a spectacle for public amusement'.[41]

It may be argued that Caine's failure to fully appreciate Muslim objections to the physical depiction of Muhammad means that his interest in the life of the prophet was largely mercenary. This would be incorrect. Over the course of his career, Caine wrote richly textured stories set in Africa and the Middle East that were based on his personal observation of Islamic cultures during extended visits to Morocco, Egypt, the Sudan and Palestine. Displaying an obvious empathy for those fighting to preserve their political and cultural autonomy, he wrote with urgency about the forces reshaping traditional Arab ways of life and with unflinching directness about religious bigotry and racial tension. He supported the nationalist aspirations of Arabs in Egypt, outraging Britain's imperial administrators and earning the admiration of George Bernard Shaw.[42] A committed Christian Socialist who had substantial contacts in the British Muslim and Jewish communities, he dared to imagine a reconciliation of the world's great religions. Although Irving's production of *Mahomet* would undoubtedly have shared certain tropes of orientalist discourse with other late-Victorian depictions of Eastern subjects, it would have been unique during this period in its attempt to show a fully rounded and sympathetic portrait of Muhammad to non-Muslim audiences.

By the time Caine's article appeared in the *Speaker*, he had finished the play, changed its name to *The Prophet*, and sold it to the actor E.S. Willard for production in the United States, although there is no evidence that Willard or anyone else ever staged it.[43] Caine's efforts were not entirely wasted, however: Stoker notes that he 'preserved his work by privately printing, three years later, the scenario of the story

---

41 Jahan Kader Mirza, Letter to the Editor, *Graphic*, written on 27 October 1890 and reprinted in the *Indian Mirror*, 3 January 1891.

42 Caine's novel, *The White Prophet* (London, 1909), for example, which is set in Egypt, was based in part on the Denshawai incident of 13 June 1906, in which a pigeon-shooting party turned into a confrontation between the British army of occupation and the residents of Denshawai, a small village in the Nile delta. When one soldier died, the British retaliated by hanging four residents, flogging eight and imposing lengthy prison sentences on several others. The incident sparked widespread opposition to the occupation and eventually led to the resignation of Lord Cromer, the British administrator of Egypt. As Vivien Allen notes in *Hall Caine*, p. 339, "In *The White Prophet* Caine set out to put the Nationalist point of view and expose what lay behind the Denshawai affair. The result was to infuriate the authorities concerned and lay him open to attacks by people who considered him little better than a traitor." Caine responded to his critics in a privately printed pamphlet called 'Why I Wrote *The White Prophet*' (London, 1909); Shaw came to Caine's defence with a pamphlet of his own called 'The Critics of *The White Prophet*' (Heinemann, 1909).

43 Sherard, 'Hall Caine: Story of His Life and Work, Derived from Conversations'.

in dramatic form' after altering some characters and changing its setting to modern Morocco.⁴⁴

In December 1890, just over a year after he began work on *Mahomet*, a dejected Caine wrote to Irving: 'I return at last the 9 vols of Burton's Arabian Nights which you were so good as to lend me when we were considering the Mahomet which began so hopefully & ended so disastrously. I am going to publish the thing, so many of my literary friends have urged me to do so after reading it, but there is no great public for printed plays.' In this letter he mentions he is working on a new play that might appeal to Irving, one that seems to him to 'possess very great possibilities indeed, & to present one character of great strength. It is called The Lord Chief Justice.'⁴⁵ Apparently, hope sprang eternal. Like Caine's other efforts to 'fit Irving with a part', however, this one also was doomed to failure. Still, those who study Irving and his circle today owe much to Caine who, from his earliest acquaintance with the actor, was one of his most perceptive observers. In describing the *Mahomet* episode in his autobiography, Caine provides a shrewd assessment of Irving's temperament:

> The truth is that, great actor as Irving was, the dominating element of his personality was for many years a hampering difficulty in the way of popular success. When in my boyhood I knew him first, he was a young fellow of thirty, very bright, very joyous, not very studious, not very intellectual, full of animal vigour, never resting, never pausing, always rushing about, and hardly ever seen to go upstairs at less than three steps at a time. At the end of his life he was a grave and rather sad old man, very solemn, distinctly intellectual, and with a never-failing sense of personal dignity. Between his earlier and his later days he had done something which I have never known to be done by anybody else – he had created a character and assumed it for himself ... It was a character of singular nobility and distinction, but a difficult character, too, not easy to put on, and having little in common with the outstanding traits of his original self – a silent, reposeful, rather subtle, slightly humorous, detached, and almost isolated personality, with a sharp tongue but a sunny smile and certain gleams of the deepest tenderness ... There was nothing artificial or theatrical in Irving's assumption of this character, which grew on him and became his own and gave value to every act of his later life; but all the same it stood in the way of his success in a profession wherein the first necessity is that the actor should be able to sink his own individuality and get into the skin of somebody else ... Toward the end of his life, with the ever-increasing domination of his own character and the limitation of choice which always come with advancing years, it was only possible for him to play parts that contained something of himself.⁴⁶

Small wonder, then, that Irving had been intrigued by the opportunity to add another theatrical portrait of a grand charismatic figure to his gallery of characters.

---

44 Stoker, *Personal Reminiscences*, Vol. 2, p. 121. This novella, *The Mahdi; or, Love and Race: A Drama in Story*, was published on 1 December 1894 by James Clarke & Co. in a private edition of 100 copies. Caine's three-act dramatic version of the novella was given a copyright performance at the Haymarket Theatre on 3 December, one day before the story was published in the Christmas number of *The Christian World*.

45 Hall Caine to Henry Irving, 23 December 1890, Laurence Irving Collection. Burton had died in October; Caine's plans to publish *Mahomet* fell through.

46 Caine, *My Story*, pp. 341–3.

Acknowledgements

My thanks to those who participated in the 'Henry Irving: A Life in the Victorian Theatre' centenary conference (University of Leicester, 2005) for their helpful comments, especially Jeffrey Richards, Michael Holroyd and Laurence Senelick. My appreciation also to the ever-resourceful staffs of the National Archives of England, Wales, and the United Kingdom; the Department of Asia, Pacific, and Africa Collections at the British Library; and the Theatre Museum, London. For assistance on the Isle of Man I am grateful to Roger Sims, librarian/archivist at Manx National Heritage, to Christopher Gawne and to Alison Foster. Alokananda Dutta and Sharba Roy Chowdhury provided invaluable research assistance in India.

Chapter 5

Embodiment of the King: Henry Irving's *King Arthur*

Doug Kirshen

Henry Irving's much-anticipated production of *King Arthur; a Drama in a Prologue and Four Acts* arrived at a watershed moment in Victorian cultural history. This dramatic hit of London's 1895 season combined mainstream social, sexual and political values with a canny distillation of Victorian Arthurania – a prolific genre that had flourished for decades in poetry and painting, but had been slow to reach the legitimate stage. Irving and his collaborators extracted tales, characters and images from other media and crystallised them in the immanent physicality of the theatre. With an expert blend of textual, visual and aural elements, they crafted a theatrical experience that refracted Victorian ideals through the ostensibly medieval lens of Arthurian chivalry. In an era of geopolitical anxiety and patriotic imperialism, the heroic chivalry of *King Arthur* provided a reassuring nexus of national pride. In a West End season bracketed by the stunning rise and fall of Oscar Wilde,[1] *King Arthur* offered a welcome affirmation of normative masculinity. With its conservative patriotism and gender politics, its artful amalgamation of cultural precedents and its skilful anticipation of audience expectations, Irving's *King Arthur* is a striking example of the cultural logic of late-Victorian England.

Although the play and its playwright, J. Comyns Carr, are now all-but forgotten, *King Arthur* was a major cultural event in its day – a critically acclaimed and commercially lucrative event that assembled an impressive array of talent both on and off the stage. The production set the standard of performative Arthurania for decades to come. The play opened Irving's seventeenth season as actor-manager of the Lyceum Theatre on 12 January 1895, with the soon-to-be knighted Sir Henry as the king, Ellen Terry as Guinevere and Johnston Forbes-Robertson as Lancelot. According to *The Times*, the elaborate staging, with music written and conducted by Sir Arthur Sullivan, and sets and costumes designed by Sir Edward Burne-Jones,

---

1 The first four months of 1895 saw Wilde fall from the pinnacle of West End success to the depths of social disgrace and criminal conviction. *An Ideal Husband* opened a week before *King Arthur* on 5 January at the Haymarket and was still running when *The Importance of Being Earnest* premiered on Valentine's Day at the St James's. Two months later, as *King Arthur* was nearing the end of its run at the Lyceum, Wilde was facing sodomy charges at the Old Bailey, and his name was being removed from advertisements and publicity for both plays. See Richard Ellmann, *Oscar Wilde* (New York, 1988).

'held a large audience enthralled for the space of four hours'.² Although George Bernard Shaw would ridicule Irving and his dream-team of Victorian knights as 'amateur King Arthurs' enacting a childish game of chivalry,³ for the most part the production impressed the critics. William Archer called it '[a] splendid pageant and a well-built folk-play ... a genuine success'.⁴ The *Theatre* praised it as 'a play which touches the emotions, a play of human nature, a play of heart and feeling'.⁵ And although *The Times* critic declared the stage 'a medium unfavourable to the exhibition of the loftier virtues', he acknowledged Irving's 'success' in doing so, recognising *King Arthur* as 'one of his most characteristic' achievements. Irving's business manager, Bram Stoker, noted that it was 'one of the certain draws' of the Lyceum repertory, recording 105 performances in London, 12 elsewhere in Britain, and 74 on tour in North America.⁶ Undoubtedly, Sir Henry's 'once and future king'⁷ would have returned many more times had the scenery not been destroyed by fire in 1898.

King Arthur's West End triumph was a long time coming. Although a major revival of Arthurian themes had been underway for more than 60 years in English arts and letters, no major Victorian drama about the legendary king had premiered prior to the Lyceum production. Carr's script, which was published by Macmillan shortly after its debut,⁸ was the first major English play focusing on Arthur to premiere in over 200 years, since the Henry Purcell–John Dryden opera, *King Arthur, or, the British Worthy*, débuted in 1691.⁹ In the eighteenth century, Arthur had been little more than a laughable anachronism, a 'worthy' most amenable to parody, as in Henry Fielding's mock-heroic *Tom Thumb*. Still out of fashion in the early decades of the nineteenth century, Arthurania was widely seen as unfit material for serious artistic or intellectual consideration. As late as 1833 Samuel Taylor Coleridge stated his disdain for Arthur as a potential subject of epic poetry. With apparent reference to the legendary king's origins in Celtic history and Continental literature, he wrote: 'As to Arthur, you could not by any means make a poem on him national to Englishmen. What have we to do with him?'¹⁰

But even as Coleridge penned those words, a renewed appreciation of knightly chivalry, of which King Arthur was a prime representative, was already underway. Sir Walter Scott's phenomenally popular *Ivanhoe*, published initially in 1819, raised

---

2   *The Times*, 14 January 1895.

3   George Bernard Shaw, 'King Arthur', *Saturday Review*, **79**, 19 January 1895.

4   William Archer, *The Theatrical 'World' of 1895* (London, 1896), p. 20.

5   *Theatre*, 1 February 1895.

6   Bram Stoker, *Personal Reminiscences of Henry Irving* (London and New York, 1906), Vol. 1, p. 255.

7   From the inscription on Arthur's tomb, '*Rex quondam, Rexque futurus*', as recorded in Sir Thomas Malory's *Le Morte Darthur*, Book XXI, ch. 7.

8   J. Comyns Carr, *King Arthur; A Drama in a Prologue and Four Acts* (New York and London, 1895).

9   Alan Lupack, 'A Checklist of Printed Arthurian Drama in English', in Alan Lupack, ed., *Arthurian Drama: An Anthology* (New York, 1991), pp. 331–2.

10   S.T. Coleridge, *The Table Talk of Samuel Taylor Coleridge*, in T.M. Raysor, ed., *Miscellaneous Criticism of Samuel Taylor Coleridge* (London, 1936), p. 29.

interest in chivalric heroism at a time when, after the much-commemorated sacrifice of Nelson at Trafalgar and the final defeat of Napoleon, it seemed that the last of the great heroes had fallen. Sparked by Scott's novel, the ensuing Victorian obsession with all things medieval (including chivalry, heraldry, gothic and Romanesque architecture, banqueting, hunting and even jousting)[11] would enable the rehabilitation of Arthur as a central figure in this rediscovered heritage. In 1833–35, the future poet laureate, Alfred Tennyson, put Arthur at the core of the poem that would eventually anchor *The Idylls of the King*, the blank-verse narrative cycle that would prove Coleridge wrong by achieving the status of a national epic. By the mid-century, subjects drawn from the *Idylls* and other chivalric texts, including new editions of Sir Thomas Malory's *Le Morte Darthur*, had become staples in the art of Pre-Raphaelites and Royal Academicians alike. Medieval knights and ladies appeared in easel paintings, prints, stained-glass windows and other visual media produced by William Morris, Burne-Jones, John William Waterhouse, and founding Pre-Raphaelite brothers Dante Gabriel Rossetti and William Holman Hunt, among many others. Through the work of these artists, Arthur came to signify the social, political and moral ideals of England itself. By the time of the Irving–Carr production, he would be hailed once again as a British Aeneas – a symbolic point of origin and personification of national pride – as he had been in the Dryden–Purcell opera.

The elevation of King Arthur to a place of honour in the Victorian national consciousness coincided with the emergence of Great Britain as the world's pre-eminent power. In this age of colonial expansion, global commerce and rapid technological advancement, Britons turned, with increasing nostalgia, to thoughts of simpler times – to an idea of their nation as a small principality, founded upon the personal virtues of an ideal monarch. By reference to this largely invented history, citizens of the British Empire could see their country as originating in the just moral code of chivalry, as they read and dreamed of it in the legends of Arthur and his elite circle of hero-knights. For the leaders of a far-flung empire that thrived on bureaucratic efficiency, rather than the heroic acts of noble men, chivalry provided a means of defining their nation and themselves according to straightforward principles of honourable behaviour. It was in this context that chivalry, the honour code of the medieval knight, was redefined and re-tasked as the core ideology of the Victorian gentleman.

Nowhere was the political invocation of chivalry more apparent than in the Arthurian frescoes at the neo-gothic Palace of Westminster, where they were installed to inspire the powerful to noble deeds. Commissioned at the behest of Prince Albert (to whom Tennyson dedicated the *Idylls* in 1862), the scenes painted by William Dyce between 1847 and 1864 reflect the taste and values of the monarchy.[12] They illustrate the knightly virtues of mercy, generosity, hospitality, courtesy and piety, all of which were considered antidotes to the corruptions and complexities of nineteenth-century

---

11 Marc Girouard, *The Return to Camelot: Chivalry and the English Gentleman* (New Haven, 1981), p. 34ff, p. 90ff.

12 On the enthusiasm for chivalry of Queen Victoria and the Prince Consort, including the commissioning of the Dyce frescoes and other art, see Girouard, *The Return to Camelot*, p. 112ff.

life. For example, as Marc Girouard explains, the scenes of *Mercy* and *Courtesy* 'stress the obligation on gentlemen to be courteous to women and come to their protection', while in *Generosity*, 'Sir Lancelot spares his opponent King Arthur when he is unhorsed and at his mercy; all Victorian gentlemen knew that one did not hit a man when he was down'.[13] A key strategy of the Lyceum *King Arthur* would be to incorporate these values into the redemptive ideology of 'the once and future king'. As played by Irving, Arthur would embody all of the virtues depicted in the Westminster frescoes – most dramatically in sparing a prostrate Lancelot (Illustration 8) in a neat reversal of their roles in Dyce's *Generosity*.

In domestic settings, where Victorian chivalry dovetailed easily with the familiar patriarchal structure of the bourgeois family, Arthurian themes were introduced largely through the poetry of Tennyson and illustrated books. Along with public art along the lines of the Westminster frescoes and Pre-Raphaelite paintings, book illustration provided Irving and his collaborators with a rich repository of images that could be referenced in theatrical design. Chivalric texts were routinely produced in lavish volumes such as Moxon's 1868 edition of *The Idylls of the King* with engravings by Gustave Doré, and the famous Dent edition of *Le Morte Darthur* illustrated by Aubrey Beardsley, which appeared in 1893–94 just as Irving's stage production was entering its later phases of development. Sidney Lanier's *The Boy's King Arthur*, a sanitised abridgement of Malory published in 1880 with drawings by Alfred Kappes, is a notable example of an Arthurian volume created especially for children. Chivalry was deeply ingrained in the minds of young Victorians. In his boyhood, William Morris was given 'a little suit of armour to ride through the forest'[14]; as a teenager, Ellen Terry played 'Knights of the Round Table with Tennyson's sons Hallam and Lionel, and the young Camerons'.[15] Adults, too, were inspired to re-enact Arthurian fantasies. Extended sections of *The Idylls of the King* (such as the central colloquy of 'Merlin and Vivien', the subject of Burne-Jones's famous painting of the wizard bewitched by a *femme fatale*) comprised dialogue that could be readily enacted in dramatic readings. At Tennyson's request, his neighbour Julia Margaret Cameron extended the visual components of home theatres into a permanent artistic form with a suite of dramatic photographs that illustrated the *Idylls*, with friends and relatives as actor/models. Published in 1875, these carefully staged, eerily lit scenes at once evoke a mystical otherworldliness and the amateur staginess of *tableaux vivants*.

These textual, visual and increasingly and theatrical manifestations of Arthurania suggest a deep-seated longing for a King Arthur who could be seen, heard and all but touched – as if to bodily confirm the moral and spiritual renaissance that his 'return' symbolised. A major production in a top-tier London theatre seemed the next logical step in the Victorian quest for an apotheosis of the king, yet the highly charged and ambiguous nature of this national symbol meant that a satisfying drama would yet be difficult to achieve. By the time of Irving's production, more versions of King Arthur

---

13 Ibid., p. 181.

14 Ibid., p. 185, citing J.W. Mackail, *Life of William Morris* (London, 1899), Vol. 1, p. 9.

15 Ellen Terry, *The Story of My Life* (London, 1908), p. 56.

were available than ever before, but the character still lacked a definitive origin, and in the absence of universally accepted attributes he could inspire diverse or even contradictory expectations. Some of these were almost impossibly elevated. A commentator in the *London Quarterly Review* characterised Arthur as 'a secondary saviour, spotless like the Christ, his predecessor', who 'makes war on the powers of darkness'.[16] Clement Scott added: 'He is a warrior, but still he is a demi-god. A halo of light should be about his head. His face should be one of transcendent majesty.'[17] Although by the 1890s the mode of Victorian theatre that Irving epitomised had progressed greatly in terms of stature and stagecraft, whether it could sustain this level of transcendence was an open question.

At the same time, Irving had to contend with humorous and contemptuous attitudes towards Arthur that had survived since the days of Fielding and Coleridge and were far from extinct in the 1890s. The core analogies of Victorian Arthurania – which equated medieval knights and the chivalry of Camelot with nineteenth-century gentlemen and the *Realpolitik* of the British Empire – were easily satirised. While Arthur had not been the focus of a serious Victorian drama prior to Irving's, the king and his court did appear in a succession of farcical burlesques and Christmas extravaganzas dating back to a memorable equestrian spectacular by Isaac Pocock, staged at Drury Lane in December 1834. This parallel tradition of King Arthur as a figure of fun and light entertainment may explain why the Tennysonian character that Irving hoped to dramatise took so long to reach the stage. A lavishly appointed, high-minded Arthurian drama would court financial disaster if it reminded audiences of a lowbrow class of stage show.[18] To prevent this association, Irving relied upon his well-established ability to identify and assimilate the work of talented collaborators and adapt high-culture aesthetics such as the Pre-Raphaelites' to the tastes of a general audience.[19] *King Arthur* would ultimately draw upon six decades of precedents in poetry, painting, and illustration. Before all, however, Irving needed the right text – one that would infuse gravitas into material that might otherwise provoke laughter and derision.

The playwright most suited to Irving's purpose would have been Tennyson himself, but the poet laureate, now at an advanced age, was ambivalent on the

---

16 'The Literature of King Arthur', *The London Quarterly Review*, **CLXVII**, New Series 47, April, 1895, p. 108. The same article credits Arthur with god-like powers of resurrection: 'Arthur was a kind of British "Mercury" ... Every winter he withdraws from the struggle wounded and faint, and returns again with every spring, glorious in strength. That is the original meaning of the cry, "Arthur is come again – come again and thrice as fair!"'.

17 Clement Scott, *From 'The Bells' to 'King Arthur'* (London, 1896), p. 375.

18 On Pocock's extravaganza see Martin Meisel, *Realizations: Narrative, Pictorial and Theatrical Arts in Nineteenth-Century England* (Princeton, 1983), p. 43. Examples of Arthurian burlesque and extravaganza that survive in the archives of Harvard University include: W.M. Akhurst, *Arthur the king, or, The knights of the Round Table and other funny-ture: a burlesque extravaganza* (London: [1871?]); Akhurst, *King Arthur, or, Launcelot the Loose, Gin-Ever the Square, and the knights of the Round Table and other furniture: a burlesque extravaganza* (Melbourne, [1868?]); William Brough, *King Arthur, or, The days and knights of the round table, a new and original Christmas extravaganza in one act* (London, [1863?]). Further examples can be found in the British Library.

19 Meisel, *Realizations*, pp. 402ff.

prospect of seeing his vision of Arthur realised on a professional stage. In his youth, around the time of the Pocock extravaganza, Tennyson had sketched a scenario for a five-act 'musical masque' based on Arthurian romance,[20] but the time was not yet ripe for such a venture[21] and he settled instead on the poetic form of the *Idylls*. Sixty years later, in spite of his past support for domestic theatricals, he was yet unsure that the moment for a full-fledged drama had finally come. When a group of producers asked his permission to mount a dramatisation of his idyll 'Lancelot and Elaine' in London, Hallam Tennyson replied on his father's behalf: 'The *Idylls* seem to be so ideal that King Arthur and Lancelot live in a realm apart from common earth. Surely Arthur and Guinevere are more suitable for musical treatment after Wagner's fashion (but not Wagnerian fashion).'[22] When Irving approached Tennyson to write an Arthurian script of his own for the Lyceum, the poet demurred, even though the two had collaborated successfully in the past.[23] Although Irving did not propose an opera, he would incorporate music, and he would surely deliver a high level of stagecraft. Yet the laureate declined to participate and thus lend his imprimatur to the project, which would have gone a long way towards ensuring its commercial success. According to Stoker, he 'could not see his way to it. He had dealt with the subject in one way and did not wish to try it in another'.[24] The truth is that Tennyson did not see Irving as an actor capable of playing the prince of Camelot. 'Do what you think best', he added 'privately' at the end of Hallam's letter on the 'Elaine' project, '– only Irving will not do for King Arthur.'[25]

Rebuffed by Tennyson, Irving commissioned a script from the painter and playwright W.G. Wills, which he subsequently bought although, in Stoker's words, 'he did not think it would act well'.[26] Since Irving's next move was not to another poet or established playwright, this is probably less a critique of Wills's writing per se than of a failure to invoke a certain ambiance – that is, the context in which an

---

20 Alfred Tennyson, *The Poems of Tennyson*, ed. Christopher Ricks (London, 1969), p. 1461, quoting Hallam Tennyson. On pp. 1461–2 Ricks reprints a 'rough draft of a scenario' that Hallam found in one of his father's notebook's from 1833–40.

21 Kathleen Tillotson wrote, 'There is no clearer instance of a poet creating the taste by which he was enjoyed'. See 'Tennyson's Serial Poem', in Geoffrey Tillotson and Kathleen Tillotson, *Mid-Victorian Studies* (London, 1965), p. 82.

22 Hallam Tennyson, letter to Sir Baldwyn Leighton, 10 September 1891, in, Alfred Tennyson, *The Letters of Alfred Lord Tennyson*, ed. Cecil Y. Lang and Edgar F. Shannon (New York, 1981–90), pp. 428–9. As far as I can determine, the play under discussion, *Elaine* by George Lathrop, which had been produced successfully in New York, did not appear on the London stage in the 1890s; however, a French opera of the same name by Hermann Bemberg with libretto by Paul Ferrier did run for five performances at Covent Garden in July 1892. See *The Times*, 6 July 1892; and J.P. Wearing, *The London Stage, 1890–1899: A Calendar of Plays and Players* (Metuchen, 1976).

23 Irving produced Tennyson's plays *The Cup* in 1881 and *Becket* in 1893, the latter shortly after the laureate's death.

24 Stoker, *Personal Reminiscences*, Vol. 1, p. 253.

25 In a private addendum added to the letter from Hallam Tennyson to Leighton, cited above at footnote 22.

26 Stoker, *Personal Reminiscences*, Vol. 1, p. 253.

audience could accept Irving's embodiment of the king.[27] In turning to his friend Comyns Carr, initially to revise Wills's script, Irving sought an element he might have expected to get from Wills – an intense understanding of visual precedent. Carr had some – mostly amateur – theatrical experience (including a translation of French love poetry for a private recital by Sarah Bernhardt)[28] and some backstage knowledge of the Lyceum (his wife designed costumes for Ellen Terry),[29] but his main profession had been that of an art critic and curator. Most notably, he had been co-director of the Grosvenor Gallery in London, which exhibited both old masters and contemporary artists, including the most prominent Pre-Raphaelites.[30] Although he wrote serviceable blank verse and was conversant with key Arthurian texts, including those of Malory, Dryden and Tennyson, his crucial contribution was to recognise which images *had* to be presented on stage and find efficient ways to include them.

Discarding Wills, Carr wrote an entirely new play, organising each of his five acts (including a crucial establishing prologue) around an indispensable visual element: Arthur obtaining the sword Excalibur, the departure of his knights in Quest of the Holy Grail, the woodland scene of the Queen's Maying, the corpse of the broken-hearted maiden Elaine, and the fallen king's journey to Avalon. As conceived by the theatrical novice Burne-Jones, who had been recruited by Carr,[31] and executed by scenic painters Hawes Craven and Joseph Harker, these stage pictures were universally hailed as marvellous and were greeted (according to Stoker) by applause each time the curtain went up.[32] It was principally through the language of imagery that *King Arthur* tapped into the collective unconscious of Victorian Arthurania. With sardonic wonder, Shaw marvelled at the production's ability to match images that 'would be recognised with delight' with the 'stories [and characters] we long to have as the subject of these deeply desired pictures ... What Mr. Comyns Carr has done', he continued, 'is to contrive a play in which we have our heart's wish, and see these figures come to life.' To Shaw, this strategy of referencing and recreating familiar iconography was a lamentable abandonment of artistic originality – but it was one that even he acknowledged as highly effective.[33]

---

27 After Wills's death in 1890, his brother Freeman published a detailed synopsis and excerpts from the unproduced script, insisting that it could have been workable if Irving had allowed W.G. to revise it. See Freeman Wills, *W.G. Wills, Dramatist and Painter* (London, 1898), pp. 233–62.

28 Armand Silvestre, *Poèmes d'amour; tableaux vivants* designed by Cyprien Godebski, with music by Isaac Albeniz; rendered into English verse by Justin Huntly McCarthy, J. Comyns Carr, Alfred Berlyn, André Raffalovitch, H. Savile Clarke, Joseph Knight, Cotsford Dick and Clement Scott (London, [1892]).

29 Terry, *The Story of My Life*, p. 160.

30 Colleen Denny, *At the Temple of Art: The Grosvenor Gallery, 1877–1890* (Madison, 1996), p. 27. On Carr's varied career and theatrical ambitions, which included taking over the lease of the Comedy Theatre as a producer, see Alice Carr, *Mrs. J. Comyns Carr's Reminiscences*, ed. Eve Adam, 2nd ed., (London, 1926).

31 J. Comyns Carr, *Some Eminent Victorians* (London, 1908), p. 83. Clearly Carr's working relationship with Burne-Jones was a major asset to the production.

32 Stoker, *Personal Reminiscences*, Vol. 1, p. 255.

33 Shaw, 'King Arthur'.

In concert with his ingenious deployment of key images, Carr devised a thematic framework that ensured *King Arthur* a warm reception from patriotic, socially conservative audiences. As played by Irving, Carr's version of the legendary king was a paragon of masculine morality and beneficent suzerainty – a carefully crafted combination that would flatter the personal self-image of the Victorian gentleman and the benevolent self-image of the Victorian empire. Conversely, Carr scripted Terry's Guinevere as an archetype of feminine beauty and moral weakness; she is the poison in the may that tragically undermines king and country. By framing Arthurian legend as part morality play, part foundation myth, and by insisting on the queen's corrosive sexuality as the proximate cause of her husband's downfall, Carr deftly reinforced the social–political–erotic nexus of Victorian gender ideology.

These intertwined sexual and political themes are established during Carr's Prologue, 'The Magic Mere', which opened the drama with one of its most breathtaking images. Clement Scott, in his review for the *Daily Telegraph*, describes the scene (Illustration 4):

> All is dreamy, fantastic, mysterious. The music, always suggestive, never pronounced, helps the imagination ... Water nymphs and lake spirits, half hidden, play and sing on the water's surface. This remote nook, hidden from all the world, is the casket that holds Excalibur, the enchanted sword.[34]

Illustration 4   *King Arthur*: The Prologue: Scene – 'The Magic Mere' by Hawes Craven, based on designs by Sir Edward Burne-Jones

This atmospheric opening – an element not present in Wills's script – immediately established the mystical ambiance that Carr and Irving deemed necessary for Arthur. A masterpiece of lighting and stagecraft, the scene dispelled any whiff of amateurism or parody, which might have quickly attached to Arthur in a more

---

34   Scott, *From 'The Bells' to 'King Arthur'*, pp. 374–5.

prosaic environment. Here and throughout, Burne-Jones's costumes defied historical accuracy, referring instead to the fantasy of the medieval that he and other artists had manufactured. Arthur and Merlin (Sydney Valentine) appeared on stage as they would have in a Burne-Jones painting.[35] Their encounter with Excalibur, the magic sword raised aloft from the lake by an arm clad in white samite, was a familiar icon for Victorians. In book illustrations, Arthur and Merlin would row out to retrieve it, but Irving and Carr dispensed with the mundane labour of such a voyage. Instead, they had the blade quietly withdraw from the centre of the lake and then reappear close to shore at the climactic moment, allowing Arthur to grasp and raise it high from where he stood, in firm acceptance of his mission (Illustration 5).

Illustration 5   *King Arthur*: The Prologue – 'Excalibur' (Henry Irving as King Arthur) by Bernard Partridge, based on designs by Sir Edward Burne-Jones

The Prologue strongly implies a connection between Arthur's sacred mission – to achieve peace through battle by uniting the warring tribes of his contentious island

---

35 Arthur's inauthentic black armour is reminiscent of that of the young knight in the artist's *Briar Rose* series, discussed below. Burne-Jones cheerfully told pedants that the armour was designed 'To puzzle the archæologists!' (Stoker, *Personal Reminiscences*, Vol. 1, p. 254). Clement Scott was among those who thought the colour inappropriate for the saintly Arthur (Scott, *From 'The Bells' to 'King Arthur'*, pp. 375–6).

– and the present-day British Empire. Like Dryden before him, Carr made Arthur the spiritual ancestor of the current regime by giving him premonitions of its future sea power. He also invoked oceanic origins for Excalibur, the sword Arthur receives from the freshwater Spirits of the Lake. The play's Merlin explains:

> Long time, ere Time began
> 'Twas forged beneath the sea; its glittering blade,
> Was tempered by the waves; sea-maidens wrought
> Its jewelled scabbard, and that warrior king,
> Whose arm is strong to wield it in a fight,
> Shall rule a kingdom that shall rule the sea.
> Now art thou called! Stand forth and take thy sword
> Whose might alone can stay these wasting wars,
> Whose might alone shall bring the realm of peace.[36]

The same sense of election that Carr and Irving ascribed to Arthur – the strength of a leader driven by a sense of moral superiority – was applicable to the Victorian empire and the men who ruled it. An ideology of power assigned by destiny and asserted nobly, not merely in pursuit of territorial hegemony and commercial advantage, was integral to the honourable self-perception of Victorian nationalism.

Reviewers welcomed the play's jingoistic connection of King Arthur 'to the naval supremacy of his country in after ages'.[37] When mortally wounded at the end of the play, Arthur would underscore his role as imperial forebear by ordering Excalibur to be cast into the ocean, rather than having it returned to the mystical lake (as in Malory and Tennyson):

> Then cast it in the sea, to wait that day
> When upward from the shrieking waves shall spring
> A vast sea-brood of mightier strain than ours,
> Bearing across the world from end to end
> One cry to all, 'Our sword is in the sea'.[38]

Reiterated by the chorus in the play's closing line, 'England's sword is in the sea',[39] this 'restoration of the conquering blade to its parent waters'[40] bracketed *King Arthur* as a patriotic foundation myth. One commentator, who counted 'not less than six hundred place names in Britain ... connected with the name of Arthur', insisted that '[i]f Tennyson had been content with such a use of symbolism – *natural and inherent* in the story itself – his *Idylls* would have had a deeper and more human interest'.[41] This nationalistic embrace of Arthurian legend, which Coleridge had judged antithetical to Englishness, is emblematic of the success of the Lyceum *King*

---

36 Carr, *King Arthur*, pp. 2–3.
37 R. Warwick Bond, '"King Arthur" on the Stage', *The Fortnightly Review*, **CCCXLI**, New Series, 1 May 1895, p. 720.
38 Carr, *King Arthur*, p. 65.
39 Ibid., p. 67.
40 Bond, '"King Arthur" on the Stage', p. 720.
41 *London Quarterly Review*, **108**, p. 124, emphasis added.

Arthur. It attests to the canniness with which Irving and his collaborators understood and manipulated the role of Arthurania in the Victorian psyche.

In several instances, stage pictures necessary to meet audience expectations were extraneous to the play's principal themes of adultery and political treachery; fortunately, Carr was a master at working them in. The most clearly tangential of these essential images was the knights' departure for the Grail Quest at the end of Act I (Illustration 6). The Grail story was a popular element that audiences would expect to see, even if it traditionally had little to do with Guinevere and Lancelot's affair or the subsequent downfall of Arthur's realm. *The Times* rightly called it 'a pretext for filling the stage with a brave array of armed men in glittering mail and for an impressive passage in Sir Arthur Sullivan's score'[42] – after which the subject would never be mentioned again.

Illustration 6 *King Arthur*: Act I: The Great Hall at Camelot, by Hawes Craven, based on designs by Sir Edward Burne-Jones

During the build-up to this climax, Carr's script efficiently employs the Christology of the Grail in framing Arthur as an emblem of saintly purity, in direct contrast to the queen's decadent depravity. First, the Grail appears in a vision, witnessed by Lancelot and other knights, of a veiled cup borne by a mysterious maiden, 'crossing at the back of the stage in a beam of limelight, to the accompaniment of a peal of thunder'.[43] Then, in a speech declaring her love to Lancelot, who has just pledged to answer the holy call, Guinevere cites an image of the crucified Christ that she explicitly associates with Arthur:

---

42 *The Times*, 14 January 1895.
43 Ibid.

> ... oft when we kneel and pray,
> Before God's image bleeding on the Cross,
> We cheat our souls, for our vain hearts still seek
> The manhood not the God: 'twas so with me.
> That hour when Arthur came, it seemed as though
> Christ's hand had beckoned, and I knelt to him,
> And, in the midst of worship, thought I saw,
> The wingèd heart of love. But when you came,
> His great ambassador from Camelot,
> I saw Love's heart indeed, and knew I loved –
> But not the king.[44]

By announcing her adulterous affection in this context, when the Vessel of God's Blood has just been invoked, Carr's Guinevere begins to establish herself as the Judas whose unfaithfulness will lead to the death of her lord and master. The play connects the love of Christ with the love of Arthur, its standard of moral goodness, while presenting Guinevere's lust for Lancelot as the ultimate moral turpitude.

The cuckolding of Arthur, in other words, is tantamount to the betrayal of Christ – a point that Carr underscored by connecting Arthur to the image of the Saviour in Hunt's well-known painting *The Light of the World* (1851–53). This pensive, mystical figure, wearing a jewelled robe over a simple white shift and a diadem beneath a crown of thorns, was an apt model for the 'spotless' warrior-king that Carr and Irving strove to present. Hunt's Christ holds a lantern with star-shaped apertures that pierce the darkness of a woodland setting. In Act I of Carr's script, Guinevere refers to Arthur as 'a star ... that lamp / Which shines o'er half the world'.[45] After she has betrayed and been forgiven by Arthur, her repentance will redouble her reverence for the saviour-king. Upon his death at the end of the play, she will call her martyred husband 'the light of all the world'.[46]

From the beginning, Carr's Guinevere draws a distinction between the guilty love of adulterers and 'The love of Heaven, of honour, and of – him' – the love of Christ, chivalry and Arthur. She succumbs to a feminine moral weakness that she readily acknowledges, declaring that 'a woman is too weak / To guard what's best in what she loves the best'.[47] By leading Lancelot towards transgression and away from the holy purity of the Grail, she betrays her lover no less than her king: she deflects the finest knight in the realm from the sacred worship of Christ toward the erotic service of herself. In this transposition of Victorian misogyny onto an ostensibly medieval scene, Carr offers a warning to his contemporaries: it is the duty of men as morally superior beings to resist female sexuality and guard women from temptation. The failure of Lancelot to do so implicates him – and Arthur, too – in the tragedy that is to come. Guinevere herself is not evil; she is the instrument of an eminently foreseeable danger, and a victim herself of female drives that she is 'too weak' to resist without help.

---

44 Carr, *King Arthur*, p. 24.
45 Ibid., p. 18.
46 Ibid., p. 66.
47 Ibid., p. 25.

This impending threat is prophesied during the Prologue, in which the future king is shown his future queen in a vision accompanied by a cautionary fairy chorus:

> Love and beauty, hope and fear,
> Wait for thee in Guinevere.
> Love and Hate are born in May;
> Love, the bird upon the wing,
> Hate, the worm devouring.

Arthur equates Guinevere's beauty with all that is good and noble in himself, believing her to be as integral to his mission as Excalibur. To him, she symbolises the regenerative power of peace and the domestic tranquillity of the Round Table – the goal and reward of his uniting war. Confident that such a visage could not also represent danger, he scoffs at the supernatural warning:

> These fairy tongues are false, for, see, she bears
> The emblems of the spring: all the new world
> Leaps into flower about her; and the may
> Trails its white blossom round those stainless brows.

Arthur would not be Arthur without his idealism; he is inclined to believe that all that is beautiful must be good. Sensing naught but purity and renewal, he disregards Merlin's caution that 'full many a poisonous weed / Grows rank amid the blossoms of the may'.[48]

In Act II, this erotic 'weed' would come to fruition in a luscious Burne-Jonesian landscape identified in the programme as 'The Whitethorn Wood', the scene for the iconic pastoral of 'The Queen's Maying' (see Illustration 11, p. 105).[49] Guinevere and Lancelot meet in this prickly paradise to consummate their sin – a catastrophic fall in a setting that Stoker would recall as a 'fairyland' of 'transcendent beauty':

> The scene was all green and white – the side of a hill thick with blossoming thorn through which, down a winding path, came a bevy of maidens in flowing garments of tissue which seemed to sway and undulated with every motion and every breath of air. There was a daintiness and a sense of purity about the whole scene which was very remarkable.[50]

The 'sense of purity' here, like the backdrop of the Grail Quest earlier, is despoiled by aggressive female sexuality. Guinevere snares Lancelot in the Whitethorn Wood much as Vivien traps Merlin in Burne-Jones's famous painting, which provides a visual precedent with its encroaching vegetation. The reference to *Merlin and Vivien* is apparent in a drawing reproduced in the *Souvenir of King Arthur* sold at the theatre (Illustration 7): as she lurks in the may waiting for her lover to arrive, Terry's Guinevere strikes a *contrappotso* similar to Vivien's. But Arthur's queen is

---

48 Ibid., p.5.
49 This is another scene included primarily for visual effect. The Maying is shorn of its associated plotline in *Le Morte Darthur*, Book XIX, ch. 1, which involves the kidnapping of Guinevere by a renegade knight.
50 Stoker, *Personal Reminiscences*, Vol. 1, p. 254.

no sorceress; unlike Vivien, her act of seduction will cause herself no less suffering than her lover or her husband. Burne-Jones's design of the 'Whitethorn Wood' is also reminiscent of the overgrown vegetation in his *Briar Rose* series at Buscot Park in Oxfordshire, an illustration of Tennyson's poem 'The Day-Dream' in which a fairytale knight, clad in black armour similar to the artist's design for *King Arthur*, enters to wake a Sleeping Beauty and her entire kingdom from a supernatural thrall. This youthful rescuer redeems feminine innocence in a converse scene to the play's tragic fall of Camelot in the thicket of the Whitethorn Wood.

Illustration 7   *King Arthur*: Act II: The Queen's Maying (Ellen Terry as Queen Guinevere), by Hawes Craven, based on designs by Sir Edward Burne-Jones

Even as the stainless knight that Irving and Carr conceive him to be, King Arthur makes a crucial error that would have been instructive to Victorian gentlemen: he entrusts his wife with too much power, to the point that she is allowed and encouraged to interfere in matters of state. In political terms, Guinevere is a foil to Victoria herself – the queen who functions as a symbol of national morality but leaves day-to-day governance to men. As the invasive embodiment of female sexuality, Guinevere deprives her husband of political virility. The valiant bachelor prince who lofts his sword heroically at the end of the Prologue, with bloody work still to come (Illustration 5), is succeeded by the complacent married monarch of Act I who has completed his uniting wars and left Excalibur hanging placidly in its sheath. (In a use of symbolism that would be hilarious to a post-Freudian audience, Carr repeatedly equates the king with his adamantine blade and the queen with its still-more-powerful scabbard.) Believing that his beautiful queen personifies the peaceful realm he has achieved, Arthur sees Guinevere as a feminine check on his masculine belligerence, much as a good Victorian wife would be expected to temper her husband's aggressiveness.

The tragedy, at once personal and political, is that the king fails to restrict his wife's influence to its proper domestic sphere, and the emboldened queen's venturesome sexuality overcomes the masculine resolve of his ideal state. Following Guinevere's soft-hearted advice, Arthur weakens his realm by releasing captured spies. Then he insists that *she* determine whether a suddenly indecisive Lancelot should join the Grail knights or remain behind as the kingdom's principal defender. By retaining and then distracting her lover from his duties, Guinevere provides an opportunity for one of the play's traitorous schemers, Morgan le Fay (Genevieve Ward), to steal the king's magic scabbard. When he discovers its absence and Guinevere's concurrent adultery in Act III, Arthur refers to both in one anguished, accusatory statement: 'Lancelot, the scabbard of Excalibur / Is stolen'.[51] The double theft finally restores the king to his formerly active stance: unsheathed at last, his sword will be once more raised in battle in the final act – but too late to repair the essential link between gender regulation and imperial strength. The damage done by rampant femininity makes the fall of Camelot inevitable.

To emphasise Guinevere's pivotal position in the play as feminine destroyer, Carr invoked a cherished icon of girlhood innocence to represent the opposite extreme of femininity. The inclusion of Elaine, the Lily Maid of Astolat, fulfilled another obligatory image in *King Arthur*. An iteration of Tennyson's Lady of Shalott, Elaine was an even more popular figure in Victorian iconography.[52] She was known from *The Idylls of the King* and countless illustrations as the trusting, romantic naïf who dies of unrequited love for Lancelot when she learns of his affair with the queen. An Ophelia-like daughter and younger sister, with no mother to shield her from guile, she is tragically misunderstood by her father and brothers, who fail in their duty to protect her. This archetype of innocence appealed to Victorians of both sexes: 'Men wanted to rescue her, while woman wanted to mother her.'[53] She was commonly depicted in the throes of her obsession with Lancelot, gazing out of her tower window, examining the shield he left in her care, or sewing a sheath to protect

---

51 Carr, *King Arthur*, p. 51.

52 Christine Poulson has counted no fewer than 25 *Elaines* exhibited at the Royal Academy, Royal Scottish Academy and Royal Society of British Artists between 1860 and 1871. After a slight fall-off in the 1870s, artistic interest in *Elaine* revived after 1880 and continued well into the 1900s. See Christine Poulson, '"The True and the False": Tennyson's *Idylls of the King* and the Visual Arts', in Debra N. Mancoff, ed., *The Arthurian Revival* (New York, 1992), p. 101.

53 Debra N. Mancoff, *The Return of King Arthur* (New York, 1995), p. 80.

it from stain. Most typically, she was pictured as a recumbent corpse, struck down in the flower of her youth, being rowed to Camelot by a silent, Charon-like figure. Floating on her funeral barge, in a posture reminiscent of Sir John Everett Millais' *Ophelia* (1851–52), Elaine is a trenchant exemplar of the 'beautiful corpse' motif in Victorian poetry: the utterly helpless, utterly displayed, permanent virgin.[54]

For Irving and Carr, this exemplar of feminine purity and passivity was an irresistible foil to Guinevere. As for the Pre-Raphaelites before them, Elaine presented an opportunity to present the other pole of Victorian femininity – the helpless innocent, as opposed to the dangerous emasculator.[55] As usual, however, the Lyceum version of this character (played by Lena Ashwell) was no slavish imitation of a familiar model, but a canny adaptation, adjusted to fit the imperatives of the play's central themes. Although 'The Black Barge' is listed in the programme as the title of Act III, Elaine's funeral vessel was so well known that there was no need to depict it on stage.[56] The corpse itself was the essential image; brought in from the river by knightly bearers, it was placed upstage to lie in state for most of Act III. The staging made the martyred girl a silent witness to the king's confrontation with the adulterers, which ensues from her posthumous epistle naming Lancelot as her unrequited love and exposing him as the queen's lover. In the melodramatic climax of the love triangle, with a frantic Guinevere trying to intervene, Arthur cannot bear to strike down his apologetic friend, who offers no defence before his brandished sword (Illustration 8). The blocking poignantly aligned Arthur with Elaine as kindred spirits whose faith in the beauty of love is destroyed by the same sex-crime. For Victorian audiences, this betrayal of romantic idealism was the play's most tragic element.[57]

---

54 For an analysis of this motif in feminist criticism, considering both Elaine of Astolat and the Lady of Shalott, see Constance W. Hassett and James Richardson, 'Looking at Elaine: Keats, Tennyson and the Directions of the Poetic Gaze', in Thelma S. Fenster, ed., *Arthurian Women: A Casebook* (New York, 1996), pp. 287–91. See also Sandra M. Gilbert and Susan Gubar, *The Madwoman in the Attic: The Woman Writer and the Nineteenth-Century Literary Imagination* (New Haven, 1979, 2000), p. 43; and Barbara Johnson, '*Les Fleurs du mal armé*: Some Reflections on Intertextuality', in Chaviva Hosek and Patricia Parker, eds, *Lyric Poetry: Beyond New Criticism* (Ithaca, 1985), p. 273.

55 One of the reasons why the story of Arthur was so appealing to these painters was because it allowed them to construct femininity in this bipolar way.

56 As in the prologue, Irving avoided a boat scene that could have detracted from Arthur's similar funeral voyage, which he was saving for the final moment of the production.

57 The Elaine who appears in the play should not be confused with Malory's other major character of the same name, although at least one observer, on the barest of evidence, argued that Carr combined the two. In *Le Morte Darthur* and *The Idylls of the King*, Elaine of Astolat makes her first and only journey to court after her death, whereas in the play the lovesick maid first follows Lancelot to Camelot before discovering the truth and returning as an accusatory corpse. While this is a significant difference between Carr and his sources, in every other respect his Elaine is the much more widely known Lily Maid. Only the most pedantic of Arthurians could have read the naïve Elaine of the play as also alluding to the much more worldly daughter of King Pellas who bears Lancelot a son, Galahad, in *Le Morte Darthur*. See Bond, '"King Arthur" on the Stage', p. 718.

Illustration 8   *King Arthur*: Act III: The Tower Above the River at Camelot (Lena Ashwell as Elaine, Johnston Forbes-Robertson as Lancelot, Ellen Terry as Guinevere and Henry Irving as Arthur), by Hawes Craven, based on designs by Sir Edward Burne-Jones

Clearly, even to some observers at the time, Carr's treatment of adultery transposed nineteenth-century psychology onto ostensibly medieval characters.[58] Within the literary conventions of medieval romance, extramarital sex is not the ultimate sin; it can even be celebrated, as in the stories of La Beale Isoud and Sir Tristram, whose long-standing affair parallels that of the queen and her knight in *Le Morte Darthur*. For Malory's version of the king, the catastrophe is less his wife's infidelity per se than the rupture of the Brotherhood of the Round Table. When forced to acknowledge what has been an open secret, this Arthur is more inclined to mourn the loss of Lancelot than Guinevere, as others use the affair to drive a wedge between him and his erstwhile First Knight. Carr put the adultery at the centre of the tragedy, radically telescoping the onset of the affair with its discovery. This contraction – which permitted the guilty lovers no interstice of happiness – proved highly effective, even for those who perceived the play's anachronisms. *The Times* commented: 'Despite the several points at which it touches on the modern French drama of conjugal infidelity, the story is told with a rare elevation and a beautiful nobility of sentiment.'[59] Another critic, writing in the *London Quarterly Review*, explicitly approved the play's melding of a medieval tale with contemporary values,

---

58 Ibid., p. 717.
59 *The Times*, 14 January 1895.

declaring, after a survey of literary precedents, that Carr's version of the legend 'is as true to the spirit of our own times as to that of the far-back days of chivalry'.[60]

If Carr oversimplified in ascribing the fall of Camelot almost solely to the queen's adultery – veering decisively from medieval toward Victorian norms of sexual propriety – he nonetheless provided his leading lady with a far more interesting part to play than he did Irving or Forbes-Robertson. Irving's role was so passive, unconflicted and two-dimensional that only 'an actor of his commanding personality'[61] could have sustained it until the closing scenes, when he finally springs into action. This King Arthur is certainly guilty of no sexual transgressions himself, such as the intemperate instances of lust and incest ascribed to him in Malory. Following the Victorian standard set by Tennyson, Carr excises any hint that Arthur contributes to his own destruction by begetting Mordred on his own half-sister Margawse, as the king does in *Le Morte Darthur*. Also unlike Malory's version, the Arthur of the play does not attempt to murder his prophesied destroyer in infancy, perpetrating a desperate slaughter of the innocents. As to Johnston Forbes-Robertson, the second male lead was 'something of a carpet knight',[62] largely deprived of sexual initiative and manly heroism. This Lancelot waits for Guinevere to initiate their affair and is deprived of his customary heroic deeds in her defence. There is no room for him on stage in the final act when she is captured and about to be burnt at the stake; instead, it is Arthur who rescues her and fights for her honour (a deed Malory attributes to Lancelot). As presented to the Lyceum audience, Sir Lancelot was more or less merely the man who sleeps with his best friend's wife.

In contrast to these relatively inert men, Carr's Guinevere is a complex, multi-faceted character whose initiative (along with that of the villains, Mordred and Morgan le Fay) drives the central plot. An intelligent and passionate woman, she fights her own inclinations and submits to them, experiencing all the sensations of love, conflict and remorse. Perhaps the only downside of the role for Ellen Terry was that it required her to perform the queen's humbling penance in the final scene, first kneeling at Arthur's feet and then falling prostrate before his fallen body. Although not recorded in the souvenir programme (where such obeisant postures might have been shocking), these searing images of contrition and reconciliation were nonetheless essential for Irving's audience, for they reinstated the normative gender hierarchy that Guinevere had disrupted. They invoked the monarchs' final dialogue in *The Idylls of the King*, in which the wronged husband similarly forgives his prostrate and apologetic wife. To most in the Lyceum audience, this abject repentance seemed just – although, as *The Times* opined, there were undoubtedly 'some' who 'would have her meet the fate of the fair Elaine'.[63]

For the fallen Arthur in his final moments, the image of the repentant queen reprises the blissful feminine vision that first enraptured him – and prefigures, once again, the age of Victoria:

---

60 *London Quarterly Review*, p. 124.
61 *The Times*, 14 January 1985.
62 Bond, '"King Arthur" on the Stage', p. 717.
63 *The Times*, 14 January 1895.

> See, 'tis the spring!
> Down in the vale the blossoms of the May
> Are swinging in the sun! and there she stands
> That shall be England's queen![64]

By laying down the adulterer and looking forward to a succession worthy of his own moral goodness, Arthur signals the final confirmation of the play's national and gender politics. The image of Guinevere at his feet would give way to the last obligatory vision of the evening – the voyage of the king in the company of three mystical queens to the Isles of Avalon. This 'Passing of Arthur', commemorated in the frontispiece of the souvenir programme, signified not only his leave-taking, but also his deification and survival in the hearts of Victorian audiences, who were invited to count themselves among his spiritual descendants. With its closing image, *King Arthur* completed the conveyance of Arthurian chivalry to Victorian London.

As the production's only unequivocal detractor among the critics, Shaw took particular offence at the mortification of Terry as Guinevere, protesting that her prostrate obeisance to Irving's Arthur was needlessly demeaning.[65] Implicit in this complaint was the accusation that male resentment influenced the way in which the queen was written and staged – resentment, if not of Terry personally, then of actresses in general as women who enjoyed unusual levels of self-sufficiency and freedom in the 1890s. The erotic licence taken by the queen had to be repudiated not only by the character but also by the woman who portrayed her. As performed by a leading Victorian actress, the humbling of Guinevere could be taken as doubly appropriate by those who classified actresses as inevitably promiscuous. In an interview published in 1897, Clement Scott would articulate this attitude with unusual frankness:

> It is nearly impossible for a woman to remain pure who adopts the stage as her profession. Everything is against her. The freedom of life, of speech, of gesture, which is the rule behind the curtain, renders it almost impossible for a woman to preserve that simplicity of manner which is after all her greatest charm ... Temptation surrounds her in every shape and on every side; her prospects frequently depend on the nature and extent of her compliance, and, after all, human nature is very weak.[66]

This statement is strikingly close to the doctrine of feminine weakness by which Carr's Guinevere explains her own susceptibility to temptation – namely that unaided women cannot help themselves, a dogma that invited male theatregoers to self-congratulation by ratifying their sense of moral superiority.

Only Shaw took Carr and Irving to task for pampering the egos of Englishmen at the expense of Englishwomen. Condemning 'costume plays' such as *King Arthur* as nothing more than 'foolish flatteries written by gentlemen for gentlemen', he

---

64 Carr, *King Arthur*, p. 66.
65 Shaw, 'King Arthur'.
66 See Tracy C. Davis, *Actresses as Working Women: Their Social Identity in Victorian Culture* (London, 1991), p. 94. Davis quotes the Scott interview, first published in the magazine *Great Thoughts*, from the penny reprint: Reymond Blathwayt, '"Does the Theatre Make for Good?" An Interview with Mr. Clement Scott' (London, 1898), pp. 3–4.

announced in *The Saturday Review* that the Lyceum production was clinging to the outmoded attitudes of a bygone era.

> That vision of a fine figure of a woman, torn with sobs and remorse, stretched at the feet of a nobly superior and deeply wounded lord of creation, is no doubt still as popular with the men whose sentimental vanity it flatters as it was in the days of "The Idylls of the King." But we are learning that a woman is something more than a sweetstuff to fatten a man's emotions.[67]

These words recall Shaw's advocacy, six years earlier, of a production of Henrik Ibsen's *A Doll's House* that had shocked London audiences and critics. Shaw applauded Ibsen's portrayal of a pampered wife and mother who abandons her home and condescending husband as a worthy indictment of 'middleclass chivalry'.[68] Insisting now that 'Mr. Comyns Carr miscalculated the spirit of the age', he renewed his battle against the reactionary gender politics of Victorian chivalry, and called upon his contemporaries to level 'a stinging dose of wholesome ridicule' upon the 'amateur King Arthurs' who still propagated it.[69] But Shaw's was a voice in the wilderness; the commercial success of the Lyceum production demonstrates that it was his own evaluation of female subjectivity – not Irving's and Carr's – that was out of step with prevailing social attitudes.

In fact, Irving and Carr were expertly attuned to the cultural logic of their age. In *King Arthur* they created the 1890s equivalent of a Hollywood blockbuster – one with fine-art pretensions that deftly balanced spectacle and star power with high-culture cachet – within the physical immediacy of the theatre. Irving's offstage role in conceiving, commissioning and staging *King Arthur*, with Carr jobbed in like a screenwriter, invites comparison with film directors and producers who would bring explicit claims of authorship to their work. As a performer embodying the quintessence of chivalry, in his last new role prior to his unprecedented knighthood, Irving deployed his own personal fame in a manner that would become commonplace in the age of movie stars. As film actors would soon do on screen, Irving and his co-stars brought their own glamorous auras to the characters they portrayed. But with the intimacy that can be achieved only by physical proximity, Irving's art surpassed the capacities of film. No one in a Lyceum audience who knew Henry Irving could forget that the most celebrated actor of his time was present on the stage, whether he was playing King Arthur or anyone else. Irving's celebrity enabled him to render Arthur actual while sustaining the prevailing Victorian fantasy of a chivalric heritage. In an uncanny yet familiar alchemy, the larger-than-life presences of Irving, Terry and Forbes-Robertson at the Lyceum made it possible for Arthur, Guinevere and Lancelot to be there too.

But the price of theatrical immediacy is its fleetingness. The play that Irving commissioned from Carr is inextricably bound to its moment in time. However

---

67 Shaw, 'King Arthur'.
68 'Asides', *Penny Illustrated Newspaper* (1 June 1889), in George Bernard Shaw, *Bernard Shaw: The Drama Observed*, ed. Bernard F. Dukore (University Park, 1993), Vol. 1, p. 119.
69 Shaw, 'King Arthur'.

satisfying it was in 1895, *King Arthur* does not endure as literature, but merely as an exquisite artefact of the cultural dynamics that created it. As a conventional and reactionary playwright, history would soon consign Carr's name to obscurity. Yet, as thoroughly as the play and its writer have been forgotten, Irving's *King Arthur* has nonetheless exerted far-reaching, if largely unrecognised, influence as the performative culmination of Victorian Arthurania. The gender positions attached to King Arthur and Queen Guinevere at the Lyceum have adhered long after they should have fallen off, and have made the medieval charms of these figures all the more difficult to perceive. In this respect, Irving and Carr have still to answer charges levelled long ago – if not for *presenting* these archetypes of chivalry in what Shaw considered an outmoded theatrical form, then for *burying* them within the conventions of Victorian ideology.

Chapter 6

Sins of the Fathers: Dostoevsky and the Murders of Henry and Laurence Irving

Laurence Senelick

All the great novelists of the world are Russian, and foremost among them is Dostoevsky. So Arnold Bennett declared, speaking for a generation that was bowled over by the publication in 1912 of Constance Garnett's translation of *The Brothers Karamazov*.[1] The Dostoevsky craze spread so rapidly that, the following year, the inimitable Max Beerbohm felt called upon to issue what purports to be a biographical sketch of another esteemed Russian novelist. This prodigy is said to have, at the age of 18, murdered his grandmother as a sign of his precocious genius. Such a conflation of Dostoevsky with his characters is named Luntic Kolniyatsch. Give the name a Cockney inflection and it sounds like Colney Hatch, the lunatic asylum.[2]

Beerbohm's bemusement at Dostoevsky's seemingly overwrought situations reflected the attitude of the English common reader. In Victorian Britain, many of Dostoevsky's novels, apart from *Karamazov*, first became available in poorly received English translations by Frederick Whishaw, published by Henry Vizetelly between 1886 and 1888.[3] In a review of a French translation of *Crime and Punishment* which appeared in the same year as Whishaw's version (1886), the *Spectator* called Dostoevsky the 'most highly gifted' of the Russians, but doubted that he would ever achieve popularity with the English public. He did, however, have an appeal for the professional literati. In a letter, George Gissing wrote that Bill Sikes and Jonas Chuzzlewit 'show but feebly after we have watched that lank student with the hatchet under his coat, stealing up the stairs; when we have seen him do his deed of blood, and heard the sound of that awful bell tinkling in the still chamber'.[4] Another letter, this one to J.A. Symonds from Robert Louis Stevenson in 1886, after

---

1 'It would be hard to exaggerate the impression made upon young readers in 1912 by the appearance of "The Brothers Karamazov"': Frank Swinnerton, *The Georgian Literary Scene. A Panorama* (London, 1935), pp. 146, 295. See also Carolyn G. Heilbrun, *The Garnett Family* (New York, 1961), p. 181. Incidentally, Swinnerton also regarded the increased popularity of detective fiction and mysteries as symptomatic of the post-war mentality.

2 'Kolniyatsch' (1913), repr. in Max Beerbohm, *And Even Now* (New York, 1921), pp. 47–54.

3 W.J. Leatherbarrow, 'Introduction: Dostoevskii and Britain', in W.J. Leatherbarrow, ed., *Dostoevskii and Britain*. (Oxford/Providence, 1995), pp. 24–5.

4 Quoted in Gilbert Phelps, *The Russian Novel in English Fiction* (London, 1956), p. 164.

he had written *Jekyll and Hyde* and *Markheim*, declared 'Raskolnikoff[5] is easily the greatest book I have read in ten years ... Many find it dull: Henry James could not finish it: all I can say is, it nearly finished me. It was like having an illness.' Coming from a consumptive, this is high praise indeed. For the common reader, however, Dostoevsky remained outlandish and unsavoury – in George Moore's words, 'Gaboriau with psychological sauce'.[6]

Therefore, when Laurence Irving, Sir Henry's younger son, adapted *Crime and Punishment* for the stage in 1908, four years before Garnett's *Karamazov* appeared, he was taking a considerable risk. However, he was eminently qualified for the task. After education at Marlborough College and the Collège Rollin in Paris, he was brought to St Petersburg in September 1888 at the age of 16 by his mother, who was said to have a library of 50 Russian books. On the shores of the Neva, he learned to speak Russian fluently, acted in amateur English circles and adopted Tolstoyan principles of pacifism and sobriety.[7] He entered the acting profession shortly after his return to England, working for Frank Benson, J.L. Toole and Beerbohm Tree. His first play, *Time, Hunger, and the Law*, was a one-act Gorkian study of the lower depths of Russian life, produced at a benefit at the Criterion Theatre in 1894 (he also was to translate Gorky's *Lower Depths*). Thereafter, Irving concentrated on playwriting, with occasional forays into acting on his father's tours between 1899 and 1904.

Dramatizations of *Crime and Punishment* had already had some success on the Russian and German stages, and even in Paris. The popular Russian tragedian Pavel Orlenev had toured one to New York in 1905. In England little attention had been bestowed on Robert Buchanan's *The Sixth Commandment*, published in 1890. Five years later, a very literal version by Charles Henry Meltzer entitled *Rodion the Student* had been staged in the United States by Richard Mansfield and was deemed by some to be 'the most imaginative and powerful expression of his genius'.[8] Nevertheless, Mansfield soon dropped it from his repertory.

Laurence Irving's five-act play, bearing the unwieldy title *The Fool Hath Said in His Heart 'There Is No God'*,[9] opened, after a trial run in Boston, at the Lyric Theatre, New York, on 8 May 1908. E.H. Sothern, the Shakespearian actor who had already appeared in Irving's *Richard Lovelace*, played the central role of Rodion Raskolnikoff. Irving compressed the action into 26 hours, and updated it from 1866 to 1905, so that he could make references to the Duma and put his onstage crowd in danger of being arrested as revolutionaries. Similarly, Irving's Raskolnikoff was not a penniless philosophy student drunk on German metaphysics, but a political radical, a type made familiar to audiences by the popular press. References to recent events in the Russian Empire helped to conjure up a contemporary St Petersburg in their mind.

---

5   When quoting or citing Irving's play or reviews thereof, I reproduce the spelling Raskolnikoff; when referring to Dostoevsky's novel, I transliterate the name Raskolnikov.

6   Quoted in Phelps, *The Russian Novel in English Fiction*, pp. 156–65.

7   Austin Brereton, 'Laurence Irving. Life in Russia', *The Times*, 31 August 1921; Laurence Irving, *The Successors* (London, 1967), pp. 137–8, 148–53.

8   Philip Hall, 'The Theatre', *Boston Herald*, 20 December 1931.

9   Over the course of the run, the title was progressively shortened to *The Fool Hath Said There Is No God*, *The Fool Hath Said in His Heart* and *The Fool Hath Said*. Oliver M. Sayler, *The Russian Theatre* (New York, 1922), p. 300.

As the critics were quick to point out, Irving has emasculated Dostoevsky's novel, perhaps to please the American public, perhaps to satisfy his own dramatic requirements. Sonia, the prostitute who sells her body but preserves the purity of her soul, was far too extreme a type for the Edwardian stage; so Irving converted her into 'a thin, frail vessel of religious hysteria',[10] a poor seamstress supporting a younger sister. The distinguished critic Walter Pritchard Eaton complained that, as represented in the play, Sonia's religion, 'trivial superstitions and a pack of stale conventions ... could not impress such a mind as *Rodion*'s except with pity'; 'Mr. Irving is in the ridiculous position of the man who used to answer the arguments of an evolutionist by quoting the Book of Genesis.'[11]

Consonant with this diminution of the novel's spiritual content, Raskolnikov's crime and its rationale were transformed from the economic and philosophic to the melodramatic: he is trying to save his beloved Sonia from sexual harassment by a brutal, bewhiskered landlord. The love motivation is left rather vague, – part theory, part pity, part admiration – and the murder is committed offstage. Irving's handling reveals none of the careful unfolding of character, the growing awareness of guilt present in Dostoevsky, even though the action is regularly retarded by verbose discussions of religion and social conditions. Most reviewers felt that the drama was sluggish, disjointed and devoid of atmosphere, until Raskolnikoff's encounter with the examining magistrate who applies 'the third degree'. The fourth-act cross-examination was judged the most stirring scene in the play and regularly greeted with applause. (Later, Irving admitted that the scene had been foreshadowed by one in Brieux's *La Robe Rouge*, which Arthur Bourchier had staged in London as *The Arm of the Law*.[12]) The magistrate's cat-and-mouse game is about to culminate in a confession when a man already arrested pre-empts it with his own admission of guilt. Ultimately, Irving's Raskolnikoff makes his confession not out of belief in Nietzsche or God, but out of his half-hearted love for Sonia, and is sentenced to three years in Siberia.

The New York critics were harsh: they rebuked the playwright for 'obliquity, cowardice, or commercialism', in omitting the scenes in which Sonia's mother kisses her feet and in which the whore and the student read the Bible together, and producing a 'sneaking, weak-kneed steal, a melodramatic gold brick'.[13] A few put the blame on Dostoevsky, whose story was judged too 'somber, too heavily overshadowed by that feeling of the futility of human endeavor against existing conditions – with the conditions distinctly foreign – to make a vital appeal to an American audience'.[14] The star system meant that Sothern was supported by a mediocre company, but he himself was exculpated from general blame, praised as a romantic actor who could mould 'gold bricks' from very little straw. Even so, one observer felt that his

---

10 'New plays at the theatres', New York *Globe and Commercial Advertiser*, 10 March 1908.

11 Walter Pritchard Eaton, 'Of Justifiable Homicide', *Sunday New York Sun*, 15 March 1908.

12 'Mr Laurence Irving. His Garrick and other "futures"', 13 November 1910, unidentified clipping, Harvard Theatre Collection. The role of Bezak may also have owed something to Beerbohm Tree's cunning Russian police spy in *The Red Lamp* (1887).

13 'New Plays at the Theatres', unidentified clipping, Harvard Theatre Collection.

14 *Theatre Magazine*, April 1908.

sepulchral voice, hollow-eyed make-up and obvious guilt would pin the blame on him so that 'even the house policeman might have recognized' it.[15]

For all the complaints of its tedious length and the illogicality of Raskolnikoff's conversion, Sothern's popularity and the audience's approval of poetic justice won the play a decent run. Its stay in New York was extended through April, and then it toured to Chicago. Eaton pointed out that audiences, as a whole, approve of justifiable homicide, especially when it is depicted as a 'thing of moral beauty, of ethical satisfaction'; the play thus wound up as a successful plea for the morality of murder. He facetiously suggested that the police be called in for it was more corrupting than the banned *Mrs Warren's Profession*.[16]

Irving then attempted to give the play a hearing in England, but no popular actor-manager was willing to take on such a lugubrious role. The piece was now called *The Unwritten Law*, a title unavailable in the United States where a play of that name by Edwin Milton Royle had already been produced. After a trial run in Croydon, Irving reduced it to five scenes in three acts, with minimal intervals for the scene-changes, and plunged into West End management, casting himself in the leading role, although protesting that it required a stronger actor.[17] When *The Unwritten Law* opened at the Garrick Theatre on 14 November 1910, the London critics were far more laudatory than their brethren across the pond. They appreciated its attempt to treat a serious subject seriously, and frequently alluded to *Macbeth*. While deploring the younger Irving's occasional indulgence in violent hysteria, described by the *Pall Mall Gazette* as 'quite remote from anything in the natural order of human conduct',[18] they praised his acting overall as 'deliberate and sure, elaborate yet seeming inevitable', conferring a sense of tragedy on what would otherwise be a 'crude tale of murder and remorse'.[19]

Describing Raskolnikoff as a 'Russian Hamlet', Irving defended the play from charges of gloom by pointing out that its 'terrible and intense' tragic issues end in 'what Americans call "an ultimate uplift"'.[20] He toured it through England in autumn 1911, in tandem with his earlier murder drama *Margaret Catchpole*, but provincial audiences were put off by the play's sombre theme and open religious discussions. Irving's wife, Mabel Hackney (Illustration 9), who played Sonia, explained to a reporter that the public outside London were 'hurt by the repetition of the Lord's Prayer by me, and made uncomfortable by the fact that I speak some of Christ's well-known words as if they had some real meaning, and not in the usual holy

---

15 Charles Darnton, 'The New Play', *Evening* –, 10 March 1908. Harvard Theatre Collection.

16 Eaton, 'Of Justifiable Homicide'.

17 These sentiments were conveyed in the opening-night curtain speech. *Morning* – 1910, unidentified clipping, Harvard Theatre Collection.

18 Quoted in unidentified clipping, 18 December 1918, Harvard Theatre Collection; see also Mordred, 'Drama à la russe', unidentified clipping, Harvard Theatre Collection.

19 John Palmer, 'Laurence Irving', *Saturday Review*, 6 June 1914. Austin Brereton refers to this production as Laurence Irving's 'first sterling and ending success in London'. See Austin Brereton, '*H. B.' and Laurence Irving* (London, 1922), p. 186.

20 'Mr Laurence Irving. His Garrick and other "futures"', unidentified clipping, Harvard Theatre Collection.

drawl'.[21] When the season ended, Irving dropped the play.[22] However, in establishing his reputation as a playwright and an actor, it served much the same function as *The Bells* had for his father and for much the same reason. Henceforth, Laurence Irving would be in demand for parts 'requiring a subtle intelligence, a sensitive spirit' and 'a refined humour'.[23]

Illustration 9   Laurence Irving as Raskolnikoff with Mabel Hackney in *The Unwritten Law*

---

21 She continues, 'It is sad in England how they like to shut up all references to the Bible and religion, as they shut up the churches, only to be thought of once a week with a large Sunday dinner.' Unidentified clipping, Harvard Theatre Collection.

22 After Irving's death in the sinking of the *Empress of Ireland* in 1914, the play enjoyed a brief after-life. With a reduced cast, the three-act version, now retitled *The Humble*, was revived at the Greenwich Village Theatre in New York on 13 October 1926, with Basil Sydney as Raskolnikoff and Sydney Greenstreet as Bezak. The Broadway critics in that more cynical age were merciless, finding it antiquated and artificial: they scoffed at a murder committed to preserve 'the respectability of a maiden music teacher upstairs' and sneered that the 'great Russian equivalent of "An American Tragedy"' should be rendered in 'small, glum London terms'. See Gilbert W. Gabriel, 'Dostoievsky to the Contrary', *New York Sun*, 14 October 1926; also Alexander Woollcott, '"Crime and Punishment" Again', *New York World*, 14 October 1926; J. Brooks Atkinson, 'Literary melodrama', New York *Times*, 15 October 1926; Percy Hammond, 'The Theaters', *New York Tribune*, 15 October 1926. (Woollcott presciently saw Greenstreet's feline detective as a rehearsal for Count Fosco in *The Woman in White*, a role he was later to play in the movies.)

23 *The Times*, obituary, 1 June 1914.

One of Walter Pritchard Eaton's disappointments had been had that Irving's Raskolnikoff was the victim less of conscience than of his nervous system. In his performance, a salient moment had shown the student haunted by 'the dead man's face with its bared teeth'.[24] Earlier, E.H. Sothern's interpretation had been praised for depicting how the 'gnawings of conscience' created a 'gradual collapse of sick nerves'.[25] Indeed, one American critic noted that this dramatization of *Crime and Punishment* is 'primarily a study in abnormal psychology; its chief interest is neither narrative nor philosophical, nor religious, but neurotic'. It presented 'the sufferings and the mental conditions of a high strung, intensely nervous young man who had done a physically horrible thing which has shattered all the lower senses of his being, while the higher centers – his will and his moral sense – remain untouched'.[26]

Irving was, perhaps unwittingly, copying the most successful aspects of his father's performances. Austin Brereton astutely noted in 1922 that Laurence Irving's Raskolnikoff 'goes through a world of torture, somewhat similar to that inflicted upon the happy burgomaster in *The Bells*'.[27]

Over the course of his long career, Henry Irving had been extolled for his expertise at portraying what Ruth Rendell has called 'murderous minds', leading some commentators to suggest that his true mission was to dramatize the *Newgate Calendar*. Homicidal motives and their detection fascinated him. There is the story of his visiting the Paris morgue in 1888, the same year Laurence went to Russia, and becoming convinced that a man who had stopped twice to view a corpse was its murderer. He then 'rehearsed the motive and methods of the crime which his imagination reconstructed'. As well as Robert Macaire and Dubosc in *The Lyons Mail*, he played a physically unlikely Bill Sikes and long considered commissioning a play about Thomas Griffiths Wainewright, the Regency dilettante, forger and poisoner.[28]

The seal on Irving's fame had been set by his performance in 1871 of Mathias (Illustration 10) in *The Bells*, the signature role favoured by Irving impersonators, and which he revived for over 30 years. A good-hearted family man and neighbour who, overcome by a sudden wave of cupidity, commits a murder on impulse and then falls prey to fear of discovery – this constituted the originality of Irving's concept. As in Dostoevsky, the murder is committed with an axe and the victim is a contemptible figure of commerce – here, a Jewish grain merchant; and, again, as in Dostoevsky, the murderer is subjected to a reasoned reconstruction of the murder, without revealing his guilt. But there is no intellectual or spiritual underpinning in Leopold Lewis's clumsy play carpentry. 'Remorse', neither in word or concept,

---

24 'London Theatres', unidentified London clipping, 1910, Harvard Theatre Collection.

25 S.C. Williams, 'Sothern's Rodion Clear and Adroit', Boston –, 16 January 1908, Harvard Theatre Collection.

26 'The Morality of Murder', unidentified New York clipping, 10 March 1908, Harvard Theatre Collection.

27 Brereton, *'H. B.' and Laurence Irving*, p. 187.

28 Laurence Irving, *Henry Irving. The Actor and His World* (London, 1951), p. 498; H. Chance Newton, *Crime in the Drama* (London, 1927), p. 27. A collateral Brodribb relation of Henry Irving had been transported to Australia on the same convict ship as Wainewright had.

appears in the play: Mathias is more exercised at the idea of being found out than at the heinousness of his deed.²⁹

Illustration 10 An artist's impression of Henry Irving in *The Bells*. The background figures are not allegories of conscience, but the hypnotist, the Polish Jew and other characters in Mathias's dream

Benoît Constant Coquelin, who had created the role of Mathias, pointed out that Henry Irving made no effort to reproduce the behaviour of a French provincial malefactor, but concentrated instead on the peculiarities of a generic psychology.³⁰ Such a psychological element could be better elaborated in an intellectual than in an innkeeper – hence Irving's enduring interest in Eugene Aram. Aram, a Yorkshire schoolmaster devoted to philological studies, had, with an accomplice, brained a shoemaker named Daniel Clark and buried him beneath a rock in Knaresborough on 7 February 1745. The motive, like that of Aram's petty thefts, was purely mercenary, and the crime lay undetected for 13 years, until Clark's remains were accidentally dug up. Continuing to deny his guilt, despite the fact that his accomplice, Houseman,

---

29 For the text, see David Mayer *et al.*, eds, *Henry Irving and 'The Bells': Irving's Personal Script of the Play* (Manchester, 1987); and Leopold Lewis, *The Bells*, in George Rowell, ed., *Nineteenth Century Plays* (London, 1953), pp. 467–502.

30 Newton, *Crime in the Drama*, p. 264.

turned Crown's evidence, and insisting that the bones were those of a medieval hermit, Aram was found guilty and, after a failed suicide attempt, was hanged in 1759.

The interest of posterity lay not in the crass crime itself, but in Aram's character; that there should be, in H.B. Irving's words, 'in the one man the attributes of the thoughtful and gifted scholar and those of the sordid and deliberate murderer'.[31] This theme of the divided soul appealed to the romantic imagination. The first influential literary treatment was Thomas Hood's poem 'The Dream of Eugene Aram' of 1831, infused with macabre hysteria and introducing an element of remorse absent in the actual perpetrator. Bulwer Lytton intended a tragedy on the subject, but instead produced a novel (1832, revised 1840), which laid its emphasis on Aram's schizophrenic enigma.[32]

Irving had first recited Hood's poem in 1869, when 'the agony of the murderer as he unburdened his soul, was acted with a power which was new and strange, and thrilling in its intensity'.[33] Having brooded on the poem for many years, and seeing its histrionic potential, Irving commissioned W.G. Wills to turn the *cause célèbre* into a play. Once again, the murder would not be portrayed on stage, for Wills conceived the central situation as 'a young fresh girl find[ing] that the lover of her bosom is a murderer'.[34] This discovery, of course, was not to rise to the religious epiphany of Sonia in *Crime and Punishment*, but would remain on the level of a pastoral love story. The mercenary motives of the historic Aram were changed to avenging the dishonour of his beloved, just as Laurence was to change Raskolnikov's motive to expunge an assault on Sonia. As in *The Bells*, the protagonist would undergo agonies of remorse, but because Aram is a more cerebral type, the membranes of a guilty conscience would be peeled back without an elaborate dream sequence. The first act established the idyllic romance, the second brought in the conflict with Aram's blackmailing accomplice, and the third was an extended soliloquy culminating in a public admission of guilt and death in the arms of his beloved.

Played in 1873 and revived in 1879, *Eugene Aram* was more a *succès d'estime* than the runaway hit *The Bells* had been, possibly because, as Frederic Daly put it, '[t]he British public prefers, in the main, being amused to being terrified'.[35] Nevertheless, Irving's Aram was, in some respects, a more virtuoso performance than Mathias. This was a 'refined and sensitive nature' surrounded by love and respect, capable of overcoming accusations by 'sheer superiority of mind' until evidence of his crime is uncovered. Then his resolution falters before his conscience:

---

31 H.B. Irving, 'The True Story of Eugene Aram', *Occasional Papers, Dramatic and Historical* (Boston, 1907), p. 141.

32 For a full discussion of the historical Aram and his treatment by Hood and Bulwer, see Laurence Senelick, *The Prestige of Evil. The Murderer as Romantic Hero from Sade to Lacenaire* (New York, 1987), pp. 174–200.

33 Frederic Daly, *Henry Irving in England and America 1838–44* (London, 1884), pp. 23–4; Austin Brereton, *The Life of Henry Irving* (London, 1908), Vol. 1, p. 107. Irving regularly repeated this recital as his party piece at benefits and evening parties, at least as late as 1898.

34 Irving, *Henry Irving*, p. 227.

35 Daly, *Henry Irving in England and America*, p. 28.

In this transition from courage to despair, Mr Irving presented a picture of mental agony which was almost unendurable ... The whole of the last act was occupied by Aram's dying confession. For half-an-hour the actor sustained a monologue in which frenzy at the thought of the injuries which had provoked the crime, and the remorse of the departing soul, were painted with singular skill.[36]

In Clement Scott's words:

In Act II, when denounced by his accomplice, the whole tone of Aram's demeanour changes, and from being a white-hot, passionate man, he is a hang-dog, beaten, defeated fellow. This is a splendid change on the part of the actor, and, if we mistake not, will be accepted as a triumph of Mr. Irving's acting in this most difficult scene. It was so sudden and complete, it electrified the audience, and the play was deservedly stopped for the applause. Left alone with his conscience, once more he gives himself up to a soliloquy, with which Mr. Irving brings down the curtain ... It made, deservedly, a deep impression on the audience.[37]

The *Spectator* was even more graphic in its description:

Then comes the terror, abject, indeed for a while, with desperate, breathless rally, thick incoherent speech, failing limbs, ghastly face, dry lips and choking throat, as dreadful as only fear can be, and horribly true ... [In Act III, which is almost all soliloquy] In accents of heartrending grief and contrition, he implores Heaven for a sign of pardon, and flings himself down by a cross, the white, mute, impersonation of mental despair and physical exhaustion.[38]

Significantly, when Irving came to create Macbeth in 1875, finding himself out of sympathy with the protagonist's warrior aspect, he turned the Thane of Cawdor into a similar figure of abject terror and contrition, leading Henry Labouchère to call the revival of 1888 '[a] Macbeth based on recollections of *Eugene Aram*'.[39]

Irving's performance as Aram seems to have made a profound impression on Laurence's elder brother H.B. (who, incidentally, had been at Oxford with the facetious Max Beerbohm).[40] An amateur criminologist, H.B. believed that everyone contains seeds of crime, whose cultivation or suppression is mysteriously determined, forcing us to fight our criminal natures at all times. Influenced no doubt by his theatrical background, he spends a good deal of the introduction to his *Book*

---

36 Ibid., p. 33. For a description of Irving's rapid shifts in temperament in Act II, see Bram Stoker, *Personal Reminiscences of Henry Irving* (London and New York, 1906), Vol. 1, p. 128.

37 Clement Scott, 'Irving as Eugene Aram', in H.A. Saintsbury and Cecil Palmer, eds, *We Saw Him Act. A Symposium on the Art of Sir Henry Irving* (New York 1939, repr. 1969), p. 68.

38 *Spectator*, 19 April 1873.

39 In *Truth*, quoted in Irving, *Henry Irving*, p. 889. Dostoevsky was equally familiar with the Scottish play. See Iurii D. Levin, 'Dostoevskii and Shakespeare', in Leatherbarrow, ed., *Dostoevskii and Britain*, pp. 39–82.

40 The Aram story, as presented by Bulwer Lytton, had been perpetuated on stage in the meantime by John Martin Harvey in *After All* by Frederick Wills and F. Langridge (1901).

of *Remarkable Criminals* analysing not historical malefactors, but Iago, Claudius, Cassius and the Macbeths. His prime English example, however, is Eugene Aram, a man of culture and studious habits, whose succumbing to his homicidal instincts strikes H.B. as unfathomable. 'He would seem to have thought himself a superior person, above the laws that bind ordinary men ... Being something of a philosopher, he had no doubt constructed for himself a philosophy of life which served to justify his own actions ... He emphasised the fact that his life had been unpolluted and his morals irreproachable.'[41] This statement could come from a character sketch of Raskolnikov.

To bring the wheel full circle, let me point out that the murders in Dostoevsky's fiction have their correlatives in genuine cases, documented by contemporary newspapers. Like the Irvings, Dostoevsky was drawn to accounts of true crime and justified this addiction in a letter of 1869, saying that however fantastic the facts, they are truth.[42] As editor of the newspaper *Vremya*, he published serial versions of Armand Fouquier's *Causes célèbres de tous les peuples*, from February 1861 to April 1863. Bulwer's novel *Eugene Aram* was first published in Russian in the early 1860s, and Dostoevsky read it.[43] There the notion of the scholar ridding the world of a worthless parasite and thereby alleviating his own plight is chronicled in the most forthright manner. Aram's irritation and his fear of exposure are also present as elements in Raskolnikov. Although they may never have heard of one another, Henry Irving and Fyodor Dostoevsky shared, in this case, an identical source of inspiration.

A year after *The Unwritten Law* had closed, Laurence Irving was asked to write an introduction for the Everyman edition of an anonymous translation of *Crime and Punishment*.[44] In attempting to acclimatise the British reader to Dostoevsky in a few paragraphs, Irving makes some idiosyncratic emphases. He refers to the characters and 'those weird dreams and trances into which they fall'. '[Dostoevsky] seems ever on the verge of making to his reader some great psychic revelation; yet in a wonderful way, in the way of the realist, he will reattach the wondrous ramifications of slumber to the material world.' Suppress the name of the novelist and this could as easily refer to Mathias's vision of his trial or Aram's narrative of his crime; the realist shaping dreams to material reality could as easily be Henry Irving. Irving's manner as the burgomaster had, in John Oxenford's words, 'a dreaminess in his

---

41 H.B. Irving, *A Book of Remarkable Criminals* (New York, 1918), pp. 14–18. See also Cary Mazer, 'The Criminal as Actor: H. B. Irving as Criminologist and Shakespearean', in Richard Foulkes, ed., *Shakespeare and the Victorian Stage* (Cambridge, 1986), pp. 106–20.

42 Quoted in George Steiner, *Tolstoy or Dostoevsky* (New York, 1959), pp. 142–3.

43 The first comparison of Bulwer's Eugene Aram and Raskolnikov seems to have been made by Kazimierz Waliszewski in his introduction to *Crime and Punishment* in the Harvard Classics Shelf of Fiction (1917). Waliszewski finds Aram to be 'of a superior species' to the Russian, but 'the subject and the story ... appear identical in their essential lines'.

44 The old translation had been out of print for five years, and Constance Garnett's new translation would not be published by Heinemann until 1914. See Phelps, *The Russian Novel in English Fiction,* pp. 161, 169.

manner, which bespoke his existence in two worlds, his inner world being a kind of purgatory'.⁴⁵ The similarity to Raskolnikov is striking.

Laurence Irving then defends Dostoevsky against charges of 'reverting to melodramatic expedients'. Citing Shakespeare as a model, he dismisses denigration of the melodramatic impulse. 'What does this matter where the insight is so deep, the evocative power so unfailing, the flux of the emotion so sure, the analysis so keen, the idea propounded so daring and so subtle? ... illumined ...by a gleam of something almost fantastic, almost grotesque, something wholly national.'⁴⁶ Despite that last reference, suggesting that the *outré* is a native Russian trait, this special pleading could serve as a defence of his father's predilection for melodrama. The adjectives – 'fantastic', 'grotesque' – are those which recur in critiques of Henry Irving's performances. Lady Marie Dickens, describing the actor reciting 'The Dream of Eugene Aram', uses the words 'weird and thrilling' and recalls 'the most terrifying manner [of] the schoolmaster's despair and remorse at the ghastly deed of which he had been guilty. He actually made you see the corpse of the murdered man – as though you were hypnotized.'⁴⁷ In other words, in a trance, the spectator is made to see the material manifestation of a psychic phenomenon. For Laurence Irving, Dostoevsky writes in the way in which Henry Irving acted.

In Henry Irving's interpretations of Mathias, Aram and Macbeth, as in Dostoevsky's major novels, a soul-shattering experience is precipitated by a murder. This is not only the direst act of violence, but also a moment of intense revelation and ordeal to both participant and observer alike. By reabsorbing the murderer into the Christian cycle of sin and redemption, and by subordinating the passions and the intellect to faith, Dostoevsky powerfully reversed the romantic tradition of the demiurgic criminal. With his keen attention to the convolutions of the guilty conscience and its pangs, Henry Irving was, in a more secular way, also refashioning – psychologising, as it were – the romantic outlaw. When Laurence Irving came to transfer Dostoevsky's complex and tormented student to the stage, he naturally cast him in the mould of his father's homicidal heroes. *Mutatis mutandis*, the Victorian melodrama and the Russian realistic novel touch through the agency of Laurence Irving's stagecraft.

---

45 John Oxenford's review in *The Times*, quoted in Brereton, *The Life of Henry Irving*, Vol. 1, pp. 117–18.

46 Quoted from the reprint in the Constance Garnett translation of *Crime and Punishment*, issued by Heritage Press in 1938, pp. viii–ix. For Dostoevsky's own relationship to stage melodrama, see A. Al'tshuller, 'Dostoevskii i russkiy teatr ego vremeni' and A. Gozenpud, 'O teatral'nykh vpechatleniyakh Dostoevskogo (Vodevil' i melodrama 40-kh i 60-kh godov XIX veka)', in A.A. Ninova, ed., *Dostoevskiy i teatr. Sbornik statey* (Leningrad, 1983), pp. 52–102.

47 Saintsbury and Palmer, eds, *We Saw Him Act*, p. 81.

Chapter 7

Irving and his Scenic Artists

Jeffrey Richards

It was in the 1880s that a fully pictorial stage was achieved in Victorian England, blending actor and crowds in the setting with a sustained atmospheric and compositional unity.[1] This necessitated ever more elaborate and three-dimensional sets and scenery. By the end of the nineteenth century it had become an article of faith for many that this was the only way to present drama, particularly Shakespeare's plays, to the public. Typically, the architect Alfred Darbyshire in his book *The Art of the Victorian Stage* (1907) asked:

> Can we be surprised that enthusiastic devotees exist who have taken advantage of the resources of the nineteenth century to worthily and adequately produce his works? Is it to be wondered at that the great actor-managers, Kean, Phelps, Calvert, Tree, Courtneidge, Benson and Irving, have spent the best years of their lives, and their treasure, in efforts to place Shakespeare upon our stage with all the accessories and surroundings calculated to secure an honourable setting for the jewels of his mind?[2]

Significant changes had occurred in stagecraft from the 1850s and 1860s. These were partly in response to the prevailing philosophy of the leading practitioners of the drama. Their watchwords became spectacle and verisimilitude. At the Princess's Theatre, Charles Kean, who had a passion for historical antiquarianism, sought accurately to re-create the past in his stagings of Shakespeare and Byron. He was recognised generally as 'the pioneer of this great movement'.[3] Madame Vestris at the Lyceum and Tom Robertson at the Prince of Wales's strove for realism of costumes, props, settings and manners, whether in historical or contemporary drama. Leading theorist E.W. Godwin wrote 33 articles prescribing the precise and accurate costumes and settings for all of Shakespeare's plays. Archaeology and authenticity became terms of praise when applied to such productions.

The search for both transformed staging, however. Until the mid-century, scenery consisted, as Russell Jackson describes it, of 'either cloths (painted canvas on rollers), suspended from the flies, or flats (painted canvas stretched on wooden frames), and originally supported in wooden grooves'.[4] But from the 1860s onwards the box set

---

1 On this development, see Martin Meisel, *Realizations: Narrative, Pictorial and Theatrical arts in Nineteenth-Century England* (Princeton, 1983).
2 Alfred Darbyshire, *The Art of the Victorian Stage* (New York, 1969), pp. 10–11.
3 Ibid., p. 11.
4 Russell Jackson, 'Victorian and Edwardian stagecraft: techniques and issues', in Kerry Powell, ed., *The Cambridge Companion to Victorian and Edwardian Theatre* (Cambridge,

became the norm, with side walls at an angle to the flats and, later, three-dimensional built-out scenery to enhance the flats and cloths. This necessitated the scrapping of the grooves and the propping up of flats on stage, fixed by braces and later screws.

The scenic artists working with the new system found themselves and their actor-manager employers now regularly accused of overloading and swamping the stage with unnecessary furniture and distorting and slowing down the plays – particularly Shakespeare's plays – with the long waits necessary to construct ever more lavish and elaborate three-dimensional sets. There were three main critical standpoints: the traditionalists who supported simple painted backcloths and flats and opposed built-out scenery, the atavists who sought to return to plain Elizabethan staging techniques and the modernists who advocated abstract scenery and lighting effects in place of realistic scene-painting and properties.[5]

The debate between these various groups raged in the pages of the theatrical journals throughout the last three decades of the nineteenth century, but the pictorial viewpoint remained the dominant one.[6] It is a view that is best described as holistic, and it was fully articulated by Henry Irving in 1885:

> Today we are employing all our resources to heighten the picturesque effects of the drama, and are told this is a gross error. It may be admitted that nothing is more objectionable than certain kinds of realism, which are simply vulgar; but harmony of colour and grace of outline have legitimate sphere in the theatre, and the method which uses them as adjuncts may claim to be 'as wholesome as sweet, and by very much more handsome than fine'. For the abuse of scenic decoration, the overloading of the stage with ornament, the subordination of the play to a pageant, I have nothing to say. That is all foreign to the artistic purpose which should dominate dramatic work ... You perceive that the nicest discretion is needed in the use of the materials which are nowadays at the disposal of the manager. Music, painting, architecture, the endless variations of costume, have all to be employed with strict regard to the production of an artistic whole, in which no element shall be unduly obtrusive.[7]

It was generally agreed during Irving's lifetime that the final responsibility for achieving the compositional harmony, artistic cohesion and dramatic flow of the Lyceum productions was Irving's. For not only was he the star, but he was also the director or, as he was then called, the stage manager. However divided they may have been about his acting, the critics were generally agreed about one thing – he was a great director.[8]

Tighe Hopkins, writing in the *Westminster Gazette* confirmed his concern with every aspect of the production:

2004), pp. 53–4.

5 On these developments see Sybil Rosenfeld, *A Short History of Scene Design in Great Britain* (Oxford, 1973), pp. 111–64.

6 On the debate in the pages of *Theatre* see James F. Stottlar, 'The Theatre Magazine under Clement Scott' (Chicago University, PhD dissertation, 1966), pp. 286–331.

7 Jeffrey Richards, ed., *Sir Henry Irving, Theatre, Culture and Society: Essays, Addresses and Lectures* (Keele, 1994), p. 46.

8 On Irving as director, see Jeffrey Richards, *Sir Henry Irving: A Victorian Actor and His World* (London, 2005), pp. 217–58.

He is a martinet on the boards, as every manager who understands his art should be, and his rule is autocratic. His success lies in his authority ... When Sir Henry has a new play in hand, the study of his own part is merely one item in the labour of preparation ... He considers the play as a whole, then in detail, and scene by scene, and in his mind he has beheld it all enacted before the first rehearsal is called ... Scenery, costumes, properties, music, are matters scarcely less important than the management of scenes.[9]

Reviewing Irving's 1882 production of *Romeo and Juliet* in the *Theatre*, Clement Scott praised:

... the innumerable beauties of a series of Shakespearean pictures, which show the stage in a new light, and put poetry into motion and action. Mr Irving told his audience that it had been a labour of love to all concerned to build up and arrange these lovely and elaborate tableaux, but a master-mind was indeed required to suggest and organise what was so splendidly carried out. That mastermind and guiding spirit was Henry Irving.[10]

In what remains the only full-length sustained analysis of the work of Irving's scenic artists at the Lyceum, Joseph T. Gardner Jr seeks to downplay Irving's influence over the scenic design of his productions. He claims that, at the Lyceum, 'there existed a constant tension between Irving's authority and the autonomy of his scene painters, a tension which was resolved differently in each play he produced' and 'the lack of a clearly defined philosophy, regarding the design concept and his critical inadequacy in visual areas flawed his creative leadership'.[11] He says that Irving was too busy perfecting his own acting and directing the other actors to pay too much close attention to the visuals. But the idea that Irving had no clearly defined philosophy, concentrated on the acting at the expense of the visuals and left his scenic artists to get on with it flies in the face of the evidence, some of it assembled by Gardner himself.

Irving was quite clear that there was an overall picture into which the actor must be incorporated:

It is most important that an actor should learn that he is a figure in a picture, and that the least exaggeration destroys the harmony of the composition. All the members of the company should work towards a common end, with the nicest subordination of their individuality to the general purpose. Without this method a play when acted is at best a disjointed and incoherent piece of work, instead of being a harmonious whole like the fine performance of an orchestral symphony.[12]

In an essay on stage production Irving outlined his approach to every play. He sets the work of the scene-painters in the context of the overall production:

This branch of stage-work has, in itself, three natural divisions – the preparation, the rehearsal and the working of the play. The first of these deals mainly with the *mise*

---

9   Charles Hiatt, *Henry Irving: A Record and Review* (London, 1899), pp. 262–3.
10 Clement Scott, Review of *Romeo and Juliet*, *Theatre*, **5**, (1882), pp. 230–3.
11 Joseph T. Gardner Jr, 'Hawes Craven, William Telbin and Joseph Harker: An Analysis of the Scenographic Practices of Henry Irving's Principal Scene Painters at the Lyceum' (Florida State University PhD dissertation, 1977), pp. 12, 69.
12 Richards, ed., *Sir Henry Irving: Theatre, Culture and Society*, pp. 44–5.

en-scène. It is necessary to select the scene-painters, as usually none of these are specialists in their craft. This choice having been made, and the 'interiors', the 'exteriors', the 'cloths' and 'sets' having been duly apportioned, it is imperative that models should be prepared, so that harmony of action may not be endangered, or labour wrong or useless, undertaken ... When I say that scenes have frequently to be worked in conjunction, like the several parts of a complicated machine, the difficulty of securing perfect cohesion will be understood. Moreover the tone of the scenery has to be determined in relation to the costumes, for it would be an obviously unhappy arrangement for a lady and gentleman to make love in yellow with a background of the same tint. Nor are the labours of this department yet exhausted, for as the rehearsals prosper, and new schemes of stage-management are developed, the scene-painter and machinist follow in miniature the various necessities of the action. Then comes the choice of appointments ... And be it never forgotten, that such accessories must be only helps to the acting, not on the one side too meagre to assist or stimulate imagination, nor on the other, so extravagant in detail as to smother it ... The dresses alone need elaborate care – for they must be picturesque – they must be suitable to the wearers – harmonies of colour must be maintained – combination and possible effects must be studied, and all the dresses must be made and fitted so that the actors and actresses ... are satisfied with their comfort, and above all, their appearance ... The lighting of the scenes is a special department, for on this depends, in a great measure, the picturesqueness of the play. The change from night to morning, or from daylight to darkness, is often an essential element of the illusion. The resources of various systems of lighting has to be in a measure experimental, so as to benefit by accidental combinations.[13]

Bram Stoker produces much evidence to show that Irving customarily had a fully formed visual picture in his mind of the stage scene. Stoker, watching as the rehearsals of *Faust* (1885) proceeded, and aware of the cost of the enterprise, became more and more concerned about its visual appeal. His misgivings culminated at a partial dress rehearsal of the Brocken scene: 'It was then, as ever afterwards, a wonderful scene of imagination, of grouping, of lighting, of action, and all the rush and whirl and triumphant cataclysm of unfettered demoniacal possession. But it all looked cold and unreal – that is, unreal to what it professed.' He communicated his feelings to Irving, who replied:

As far as tonight goes, you are quite right; but you have not seen my dress. I do not want to wear it till I get all the rest correct. Then you will see. I have studiously kept as yet all the colour to that grey-green. When my dress of flaming scarlet appears amongst it – and remember that the colour will be intensified by that very light – it will bring the whole picture together in a way you cannot dream of. Indeed I can hardly realise it myself yet, though I know it will be right. You shall see too how Ellen Terry's white dress and even that red scar across her throat will stand out in the midst of that turmoil of lightning!

Stoker concluded: 'He had seen in his own inner mind and with his vast effective imagination all these pictures and these happenings from the very first; all that had been already done was but leading up to the culmination.'[14]

---

13 Ibid., pp. 113–14.
14 Bram Stoker, *Personal Reminiscences of Henry Irving* (London, 1906), Vol. 1, pp. 146–7.

Irving had clear views on the role, nature and structure of scenery. Ellen Terry recalled, for instance, that Irving believed in 'front scenes', seeing how necessary they were to the swift progress of Shakespeare's plots: 'These cloths were sometimes so wonderfully painted and lighted that they constituted scenes of remarkable beauty.' The best, she thought, were the Apothecary scene in *Romeo and Juliet* and the exterior of Aufidius' house in *Coriolanus*.[15] It was Irving's perfectionism which gave the Lyceum productions their reputation for beauty.

Irving was ruthless in discarding scenery if it did not conform to his mental image of a scene or if it conflicted with the demands of stage-management. Ellen Terry recalled:

> There was enough scenery rejected in *Faust* to have furnished three productions and what was finally used for the famous Brocken scene cost next to nothing. Even the best scene-painters sometimes think more of their pictures than of scenic effects. Henry would never do anything that was not right *theatrically* as well as pictorially beautiful. His instinct in this was unerring and incomparable.[16]

Stoker gives a specific example from *Faust*. For Margaret's death scene with its flight of angels, William Telbin had devised a rainbow, 'suggestive of Hope and Heavenly Beauty'. Irving studied it, lit it and then ordered the whole thing to be struck, apart from the ladder of angels. He then ordered a dark blue backcloth to be placed behind it, sapphire mediums on the limelights on both sides and white limelights on the angels. Telbin was then to complete it by painting in some stars on the blue backcloth. Stoker recalled: 'Then we saw the nobly simple effect which the actor had had in his imagination. Never was seen so complete, so subtle, so divine a vision on the stage. It was simply perfect, and all who saw it at once began to applaud impulsively.'[17]

Irving did the same on his production of *Dante* in 1903. Lena Ashwell, who was acting in the production, recalled:

> The scenery, like the play, came from Paris, the Inferno painted as a cyclorama, a back-cloth continually revolving. It had cost a fortune. Irving sat an entire day in silence watching it ... and then with an indescribable scream of rage flung (his) hat into the pit and said; 'They can take it away and burn it. Do they think I'm a damned showman?.'[18]

Although archaeological accuracy was regularly stressed in accounts of Irving's work, and was part of his gospel of the stage as a vehicle for education, Irving was far from being a slave to accuracy. He wrote: 'Nor do I think that servility to archaeology is an unmixed good. Correctness of costume is admirable, and necessary up to a certain point, and when it ceases to be "as wholesome as sweet", it should, I think, be sacrificed.'[19] What mattered to Irving was what worked theatrically and pictorially.

---

15 Ellen Terry, *The Story of My Life* (London, 1908), p. 172.
16 Ibid.
17 Stoker, *Personal Reminiscences of Henry Irving*, Vol. 1, pp. 180–2.
18 Lena Ashwell, *Myself a Player* (London, 1936), p. 87.
19 Richards, ed., *Sir Henry Irving: Theatre, Culture and Society*, p. 46.

In an article on the stage as a school of art and archaeology, published in 1888, Henry Herman took Irving to task for the 'strange incongruities foisted upon an unsuspecting public' in his production of *Romeo and Juliet*, in which the actors wore a mixture of costumes ranging over a period of a hundred years. Stoker explained that Irving had engaged Alfred Thompson, a well-known costume designer, to design the costumes. But, in the event, he did not think they fitted his visual picture and used none of them. Instead, he selected costumes from old prints and books and arranged the colours and the stuffs to be used.[20] Irving's decision is vindicated by the reviews. Clement Scott, for example, writes:

> [Irving] was attired unlike all other Romeos that we had seen, but in a costume that was singularly becoming, however strange. The prevailing tone to doublet, hose and cloak was reseda or mignonette green, contrasted with a deep crimson cap ... Attired in pale primrose satin, with light brown hair falling unfettered over one shoulder, Miss Ellen Terry was surely a Juliet that enchanted every eye ... The contrast in colour between the gay Mercutio and the sober Romeo was cleverly devised ... The first dress of Juliet had now been abandoned for one equally becoming of blue and gold brocade.[21]

So when the critics praised, as they often did, the 'perfect accuracy' of Irving's stagings, they were in fact praising an illusion of accuracy – something that looked and felt right rather than something that was necessarily chronologically and stylistically correct.[22]

Irving's visual sense was influenced by pre-existing imagery. Edward Gordon Craig, who studied Irving's production methods closely, says that, in seeking to establish the atmosphere and style of a production, Irving would turn to illustrators: John Gilbert, Honoré Daumier and, in particular, Gustave Doré.[23] Doré (1832–83) had made celebrated illustrated editions of Cervantes' *Don Quixote*, Dante's *Divine Comedy*, Tennyson's *Idylls of the King* and Milton's *Paradise Lost*. These works undoubtedly provided Irving with inspiration for the visuals in his own productions of *Don Quixote*, *Dante*, *King Arthur* and *Faust*.

At the Lyceum Irving regularly employed the three men who were, by common consent, the greatest scenic artists of their day: Hawes Craven (1837–1910), William Telbin (1846–1931) and Joseph Harker (1855–1927). Hawes Craven was described by *The Compact Dictionary of National Biography* as 'probably the greatest scene painter of his century'.[24] The *Magazine of Art* declared: 'In the records of scenic art no name is held in higher repute than that of Telbin.'[25] Sir Johnston Forbes-Robertson

---

20 Stoker, *Personal Reminiscences of Henry Irving*, Vol. 1, p. 94.

21 Scott, Review of *Romeo and Juliet*, p. 235.

22 It was Wilde who praised the perfect accuracy of *Much Ado*. But, as Irving himself revealed, one of the scenes – Leonato's garden – contained cedars which, a writer pointed out, were unknown in Messina at the time of the play, and an eminent painter informed him that the sword worn by one of the characters belonged to the time of Charles I. See Richards, ed., *Irving, Theatre, Culture and Society*, pp. 113, 114.

23 Edward Gordon Craig, *Henry Irving* (London, 1930), pp. 127–34.

24 *Compact Edition of the Dictionary of National Biography* (Oxford, 1995), Vol. 2, p. 2585.

25 *Magazine of Art*, **25**, 1902, p. 371.

wrote that Harker 'stands bravely in the front rank [of scene painters], together with Stansfield, Roberts, Beverley, Telbin and Hawes Craven'.[26]

Irving, unlike the previous lessee of the Lyceum, Colonel Hezekiah Linthicum Bateman, did not have a resident scenic artist. This was probably due to the fact that the new system of long runs for plays, coupled with the demands placed on the painters by Irving's ever more elaborate productions, meant that it was more appropriate to contract painters for each individual production. However, Hawes Craven, who had been Bateman's resident scenic artist, leased the Lyceum painting rooms as his studio and worked almost exclusively for Irving from 1878 to 1898. This was a situation with which he was apparently well satisfied, telling an interviewer in 1893 that he had joined the Lyceum under Bateman and 'here I intend to remain as long as Mr Irving sees fit to retain my services'.[27]

Despite Craven's prominence, Irving employed several painters on each production, and no one painter had overall control. The overall control and ultimate vision was Irving's. Gardner has calculated that at least 69 per cent of the 200-plus scenes in the 25 productions he has studied were the work of Craven, Telbin and Harker. He has also significantly discovered that Craven (Illustration 11) was usually responsible for the exteriors, Harker (Illustration 12) for the interiors and Telbin (Illustration 13) for the three-dimensional built-out scenery and scenes that were dramatically pivotal, such as the Capulet tomb in *Romeo and Juliet*, the church in *Much Ado About Nothing* and the Brocken in *Faust*.[28] This very fact indicates that Irving recognised the strengths of the individual painters and deployed them for those strengths in complementary fashion.

Illustration 11 *King Arthur*: Act II: The Queen's Maying, by Hawes Craven, based on designs by Sir Edward Burne-Jones

---

26 Sir Johnston Forbes-Robertson, 'Introduction' to Joseph Harker, *Studio and Stage* (London, 1924), p. 4.

27 'Scene Painters and Scene Painting: A Talk with Mr. Hawes Craven', *Sala's Journal* (4 March 1893), pp. 208–9.

28 Gardner, 'Hawes Craven, William Telbin and Joseph Harker', pp. 71, 118–19, 128.

Illustration 12   *Ravenswood*: Act IV Scene 1: Ravenswood – A Room, by Joseph Harker

Illustration 13   *Faust*: Act IV: Summit of the Brocken, by William Telbin

But the painters were not left without guidance from the actor-manager. All three scene painters have testified to Irving's active involvement in the design process.

Hawes Craven acknowledged the relative lack of autonomy that the scene painter enjoyed:

> The life of a scene-painter is an exceedingly arduous one. Compare his position with that of the picture painter. The latter has entire control of his work. Not so the scene painter. He has to submit to changes, and to produce a scene which has no other purpose from a pictorial point of view except the use that is made of it.

He went on to outline the nature of his relationship with Irving:

> Mr Irving is always desirous that everything shall be as perfect as possible, and when a new play is decided upon and there is occasion to travel to the locality from which the scenes are taken, I invariably accompany him in order to make sketches. I was five or six weeks in Germany for 'Faust'; I visited Scotland for 'Macbeth'; I went to Venice prior to the production of 'The Merchant of Venice', and to Paris for 'The Bells'. It is only in this way that it is possible to attain to anything approaching reality. Mr Irving is also careful to supply such archaeological works as may assist with information, and models are prepared of each scene, and submitted before the actual work itself is commenced. Here, for instance ... is the woodman's hut in 'King Lear'. Here is another, only different, of the same scene. Oh! Yes we often make more than one model before a final decision is come to.[29]

In his autobiography Joseph Harker is intensely critical of some of the actor-managers he worked with, but of Irving he writes:

> Irving was one of the most painstaking producers I ever knew ... Irving's attention to detail extended, of course, to the scenic side. Absolute accuracy was an ideal from which he never knowingly swerved. One of the scenes in *Coriolanus* showed a fish-monger's shop in a Roman thoroughfare. Anxious to achieve the necessary degree of realism, I painted outside the shop a life-like representation of a turbot. The scene, it must be understood, had to be shown twice in the play – once in the opening stages, and again towards the final fall of the curtain. Irving was down on the turbot as soon as he set eyes on it. 'Take that fish out, my boy!' was his command, 'I'm going to the wars in the play, and it won't keep till I get back'.[30]

William Telbin noted that scene-setting was not complete until the set or backdrop had been lit. Lighting was an integral part of the creation of the stage picture:

> The best scene ever designed and painted can be ruined by injudicious lighting; for the illumination is the last and most important touch to the picture – its very life. Oh, for a hint from Henry Irving (the much-praised, and justly so, 'gas-man' of the Lyceum is no less a person than the manager himself); no one knows how well to light a scene as he does, veiling its defects and enhancing its merits.[31]

Irving was acknowledged as a master of stage lighting which, for him, meant gaslight and limelight. He developed increasingly sophisticated means of lighting

---

29 'Scene Painters and Scene Painting', p. 209.
30 Harker, *Studio and Stage*, pp. 124, 127–8.
31 William Telbin, 'Art in the Theatre', *Magazine of Art*, 12, 1889, p. 200.

scenes by applying coloured lacquers to the limelight mediums and dividing the footlights into independently controlled colour circuits. This meant, says Bram Stoker, that Irving could use 'the media of coloured lights as a painter uses his palette'.[32] Percy Nash, who stage-managed *Robespierre* in 1899, recalled: 'Scenes lit by Irving had always the effect of oil-paintings, the boundaries lost in shade, highlights focusing the points of greatest interest.'[33] Writing in 1939, H.A. Saintsbury remembered: 'He performed miracles with gas and calcium lights; the sunset on the quicksand in *Ravenswood*, the dawn in *Romeo and Juliet*, the mystic lake and apparition of Excalibur [in *King Arthur*]; they have never been rivalled ... We have seen nothing in design or lighting since his time that he did not anticipate.'[34] Irving also seems to have been the first actor-manager to reduce or extinguish the house lights during performance, thereby enhancing the impact of the stage pictures.

Despite the fact that Irving had at his disposal the most eminent scene-painters in the business, he turned at various points in his career to established painters and, in doing so, revealed his knowledge of nineteenth-century Romantic painting and indicated further influences on his artistic vision. He was also well aware of the publicity value to be gained from involving leading artistic figures in the activities of the Lyceum. So, just as he called on the services of Sir Arthur Sullivan, Sir Alexander Mackenzie, Sir Julius Benedict and Sir Charles Stanford to score his productions, he engaged Sir Lawrence Alma-Tadema (*Coriolanus*, *Cymbeline*), Ford Madox Brown (*King Lear*) and Sir Edward Burne-Jones (*King Arthur*).

Alma-Tadema, 'the best known and best paid of all Victorian classical painters',[35] was celebrated for the fidelity of his genre paintings of everyday life in the Ancient World. Alma-Tadema said: 'If I am to revive ancient life, if I am to make it relive on canvas, I can do so only by transporting my mind into the far off ages, which deeply interest me, but I must do it with the aid of archaeology. I must not only create a *mise-en-scène* that is possible but probable.'[36] It was his archaeological accuracy and sense of dramatic composition that was to lead to him becoming the established painter most often employed by the actor-managers. For he not only designed *Coriolanus* and *Cymbeline* for Irving, but also *Hypatia* and *Julius Caesar* for Beerbohm Tree.

Although Irving first contacted Alma-Tadema in 1879, it was not until 1901 that he staged *Coriolanus*, utilising Alma-Tadema's designs and Alexander Mackenzie's score. Stoker recalled: 'Irving felt that with such an artist to help – archaeologist, specialist and genius in one – he would be able to put before an audience such work as would not only charm them by its beauty and interest them in its novelty, but would convince by its suitability.'[37] Alma-Tadema's designs were faithfully executed by Hawes Craven, Joseph Harker and Walter Hann. The praise for the sets and the properties was lavish. The *Era* declared: 'A visit to *Coriolanus* ... is

---

32 Bram Stoker, 'Irving and Stage Lighting', *Nineteenth Century*, **69**, May 1911, p. 911.
33 H.A. Saintsbury and Cecil Palmer, eds, *We Saw Him Act* (London, 1939), pp. 262–3.
34 Ibid., p. 398. See Illustration 4, p. 72.
35 Christopher Wood, *Olympian Dreamers* (London, 1983), p. 28.
36 Vern Swanson, *Sir Lawrence Alma-Tadema* (London, 1977), p. 44.
37 Stoker, *Personal Reminiscences of Henry Irving*, Vol. 2, p. 68.

a liberal education in the attire, the furniture, the weapons and the architecture of Rome five hundred years before Christ.'[38] Richard Phené Spiers, calling the designs a 'revelation', devoted a lengthy article in the *Architectural Review* to an analysis of them – an article subsequently published as a free-standing pamphlet.[39] But the play, which had never been popular with audiences, flopped and was withdrawn after 36 performances.

Alma-Tadema also clearly admired the effects achieved by Irving in his stage productions. Alfred Darbyshire was sitting next to Alma-Tadema at Irving's production of *The Cup*, which received rapturous applause for its classical sets and backdrops. Darbyshire reported that: 'With a sigh and a shrug of his shoulders, he exclaimed: "Ah! How poor my art is after this". The great artist repeated this opinion to the great actor-manager. Irving, with that sad smile which sometimes passed across his features, said, "Ah! Tadema, when I am dead and gone my art is gone, while yours lives for ever".'[40]

When Irving decided to produce *King Lear* in 1892, there was only one artist he could turn to – Ford Madox Brown, who had had a career-long interest in the play. Irving had an engraving of Brown's painting *Cordelia's Portion* on his dressing-room wall and, according to the painter Graham Robertson, he 'admired it immensely'.[41] He also acquired 16 pen-and-ink drawings of scenes from *King Lear* that Brown had executed in the 1840s. These, together with the painting *Lear and Cordelia* (1848–54), would set the style of the production. In addition, Irving engaged Brown to design the Romano-British interiors of Lear's Palace and Albany's hall as well as the exterior of Gloucester's castle with a Roman temple in the background. The actual scene-painting was undertaken by Harker and Craven.[42]

Graham Robertson, who noted the inspiration provided by Brown, recorded:

The result was fine, sombre and austere throughout until the final heartrending scene of the old king's death beside the body of Cordelia, which was enacted amongst flowery down-lands where white chalk cliffs towered out of a sea of dazzling blue under skies full of pitiless sunshine; a daring and most poetical touch which seemed to isolate the two tragic figures and to intensify the darkness of their doom.[43]

For *King Arthur*, the obvious painter to turn to was the man who had made the Arthurian legends his own particular subject – Sir Edward Burne-Jones, Bart. Stoker recalled that Irving enormously enjoyed working with Burne-Jones:

This man had such mighty gifts that in his work there was no waste; all the creations of his teeming brain were so fine in themselves that they simply stood ready for artistic use.

---

38 *Era*, 20 April 1901.

39 Richard Phené-Spiers, 'The Architecture of *Coriolanus* at the Lyceum Theatre', *Architectural Review*, **10**, 1901, pp. 2–21.

40 Darbyshire, *Art of the Victorian Stage*, p. 105.

41 W. Graham Robertson, *Time Was* (London, 1931), pp. 168–9.

42 Helen Borowitz, '*King Lear* in the Art of Ford Madox Brown', *Victorian Studies*, **21**, 1978, pp. 309–34.

43 Robertson, *Time Was*, pp. 168–9.

His imagination working out through perfected art peopled a whole world of his own and filled that world around them with beautiful things.[44]

Yet, even such an eminent a figure as Burne-Jones was not immune from Irving's veto; the actor-manager completely changed his designs for Merlin's costume and Arthur's armour in order to fit his own preconceptions of the overall picture.[45] Irving was, however, vindicated by the rapturous reception *King Arthur* received. Each scene was applauded by the audience as the curtain rose, and Irving's work at the Lyceum was directly compared with Wagner's *Gesamtkunstwerk* at Bayreuth. One critic wrote:

> The glory of all the blended arts that he gives us – poetry, acting, music, painting, all – surely this is a new thing, a thing only now possible on the stage and realised as yet only by Irving at the Lyceum and Wagner at Bayreuth. Bayreuth I have not seen, but it is inconceivable that it should have anything to show more beautiful than the series of 'Burne Jones' pictures which go to make up 'King Arthur'. The mind is thronged with their memories – the dark blue of the Magic Mere, with that glowing vision of Guinevere, gold against silver, in its midst: the sober brown and gray of the heavy masonry, rough hewn with earliest Norman ornament: the knights with glaive and burnie – 'clad in complete steel' as they clashed round the usurper king – or in their robes of solemn hues, purple and russet and sombre red; white maidens singing through the wood of ash and blossoming may, cool with the green of leaves and grey tree-trunks, and the clouded sky beyond: the orange sunset, dying behind deep blue hills, and sky of pale green, barred with grey clouds and edged with smouldering red. Throughout these pictures held and charmed one.[46]

However, the bringing in of professional painters provided the potential for conflict with the established scene painters, who were extremely sensitive on the subject of their status. Typical of their reactions is that of Joseph Harker who, in his autobiography, is quick to record slights to his profession by artistic grandees such as Sir John Millais and Sir Aston Webb.[47] He declared roundly:

> My heart and soul are filled with scorn for the type of artist or critic who seeks to differentiate scene-painting from any other branch of the whole art of painting. Paint is paint the world over, whether it is applied to a large canvas or a small canvas. The man who knows how to apply paint is a painter. The man who does not understand the finer uses of paint may live to be a useful plumber or decorator, but he will most certainly never become a capable scene-painter.[48]

But he points out that some of the greatest contemporary artists (Alma-Tadema, Poynter, Burne-Jones, Edwin Abbey and Seymour Lucas), all of whom he had worked with, 'seemed genuinely anxious to create designs worthy of our art, [and]

---

44 Stoker, *Personal Reminiscences of Henry Irving*, Vol. 2, p. 73.
45 Christine Poulson, 'Costume Designs by Burne-Jones for Irving's production of *King Arthur*', *The Burlington Magazine*, **128**, 1986, pp. 18–24.
46 Unattributed review, *Percy Fitzgerald Collection*, Garrick Club, Vol. 14, p. 61.
47 Harker, *Studio and Stage*, pp. 51, 96.
48 Ibid., p. 170.

... what impressed me still more was the fact that none of these great artists desired to teach me my job'.[49]

Harker was not alone in his sentiments. In his interview with *Sala's Weekly*, Hawes Craven lamented: 'the scene painter's work is not always sufficiently recognised. We sometimes feel that we are in the position of the unfortunate individual who receives more kicks than ha'pence.'[50]

Burne-Jones's ignorance of the theatre initially led to some difficulties with Irving's regular scene painters, Hawes Craven and Joseph Harker, who were responsible for executing his designs. Stoker recalled: 'When it was objected that the suggested scenes were impossible to work in accordance with stage limitations, Irving pointed out that there was in itself opportunity for the ability of the scene-painters' skill and invention. Burne-Jones suggested the effect aimed at; with them rested the carrying it out.'[51] The problems were overcome. Burne-Jones went to see Hawes Craven painting the backdrops, but his daughter recalled: 'Father seemed to have nothing to suggest or criticize, only to wish to be shewn things, and they talked like brother artists.'[52]

There was something of a contretemps when Ford Madox Brown was advising on design for *King Lear*. Joseph Harker recorded that he was caused 'some heartburnings on account of the scarcity of architectural records on which to base my design for the Palace scene'. Irving was pleased with the model he designed and insisted on them taking it over to show Brown, who was ill in bed at home. Brown took one look at it and declared: 'Good gracious! It looks like the palace of an Ojjibway Indian.'[53]

Many of the greatest artists of the nineteenth century lent their support to the scenic artists as they fought to be recognised as artists in their own right rather than mere craftsmen. In a lecture in 1892, Sir Hubert von Herkomer said:

> Scenic art should in no way be held an inferior art ... the greatest artists of the day should find some pleasure in such work, if only out of pure revenge for the inadequacy of our paints and canvases to reach some of rare effects in nature. All art is a struggle with the inadequacy of our materials for expression. But in stage work the artist has more materials at his command than in any other form of artistic expression.[54]

The campaign for recognition reached a climax in 1904. A complimentary dinner for the principal scenic artists of the day was given on 31 January 1904 by a committee of artists, authors and composers convened by the painter Sir Philip Burne-Jones. Among the leading painters present were Alma-Tadema, Sir Edward Poynter, Marcus Stone, John Singer Sargent and Hubert von Herkomer. In a generous and good-hearted tribute, Alma-Tadema declared that 'the scenic painter had long since deserved some recognition beyond the occasional off-hand mention of his

---

49 Ibid., p. 97.
50 'Scene Painters and Scene Painting', p. 209.
51 Stoker, *Personal Reminiscences of Henry Irving*, Vol. 1, pp. 254–5.
52 Georgiana Burne-Jones, *Memorials of Edward Burne-Jones* (London, 1912), Vol. 2, p. 247.
53 Harker, *Studio and Stage*, p. 127.
54 *Magazine of Art*, **15**, 1892, p. 318.

endeavours in the papers'. A telegram was received from Irving, on tour in America, regretting his inability to be present 'to do honour to an art and its artists to which and to whom I am in so many ways indebted'.[55] Three months later the Scenic Artists Association was established with Hawes Craven as president and Joseph Harker as vice-president; within a year it had 80 members.

Irving's production of *Romeo and Juliet* in 1882 was, by common consent, the first of the grand Lyceum spectacles. Clement Scott called it 'probably the grandest production of a play by Shakespeare the stage has ever seen', and *The Times* said that, with regard to staging and production, '*Romeo and Juliet* reaches a height of perfection that has seldom been approached and that certainly has never been surpassed'.[56] Austin Brereton, in *Dramatic Notes*, said: 'Never before had such a glorious setting been given to one of Shakespeare's plays.'[57] Irving spent nearly £10,000 on staging it and engaged Sir Julius Benedict to provide the romantic score.

Ellen Terry, who thought that *Romeo and Juliet* did not surpass *The Cup* in beauty, nevertheless pronounced it 'the first of Henry Irving's great Shakespearean productions ... it was very sumptuous, impressive and Italian. It was the most elaborate of all the Lyceum productions.'[58]

In the programme Irving wrote: 'In producing this tragedy, I have availed myself of every resource at my command to illustrate without intrusion the Italian warmth, life and radiance of this enthralling love story.' Irving explained his concept of the play to Ellen Terry: '"Hamlet" could be played anywhere on its acting merits. It marches from situation to situation. But "Romeo and Juliet" proceeds from picture to picture. Every line suggests a picture. It is a dramatic poem rather than a drama and I mean to treat it from that point of view.'[59]

The critics recognised and acknowledged this approach. *Punch* said:

> Magnificent it is. As a series of stage pictures it is unprecedented and can scarcely be surpassed. Some of the scenes – notably *Capulet's* garden and *Juliet's* chamber – might be transferred to canvas with but little alteration, and accepted as striking and satisfactory works of Art, having a grace of composition worthy of DICKSEE or of FREDERICK WALKER, and a charm of colour suggestive of BURNE-JONES or HOLMAN HUNT.[60]

There were 17 separate scenes in *Romeo and Juliet*: Craven did 11, Telbin four and William Cuthbert two. As always, Irving had firm ideas about what he wanted. One of them provided for the dramatic climax of the play. Ellen Terry recalled:

> It is usual for Romeo to go in to the dead body of Juliet lying in Capulet's monument through a gate on the <u>level</u>, as if the Capulets were buried but a few feet from the road. At rehearsals Irving kept on saying: 'I must go <u>down</u> to the vault.' After a great deal of consideration he had an inspiration. He had the exterior of the vault in one scene, the

---

55 *Era*, 6 February 1904.
56 *The Times*, 9 March 1882.
57 Austin Brereton, ed., *Dramatic Notes*, 4, 1882–83, p. 11.
58 Terry, *The Story of My Life*, p. 208.
59 Ibid.
60 *Punch*, 18 March 1882.

entrance to it down a flight of steps. Then the scene changed to the interior of the vault, and the steps now led from a height above the stage. At the close of the scene, when the Friar and the crowd came rushing down into the tomb, these steps were thronged with people, each holding a torch, and the effect was magnificent.[61]

What the critics noted about the production was the overall coherence of the vision presented. One critic wrote:

> The life in southern cities, roused only from stagnation by the fierce excitement of civil broil, is presented with unsurpassable fidelity; and Verona, as Ruskin has seen it, with 'the crescent of her eastern cliffs, whence the full moon used to rise through the bars of the cypresses in her burning summer twilights, touching with soft increase of silver light the rosy marbles of her balconies' stands revealed. That variety of architecture which except in Rome is elsewhere unexampled is exhibited, and the very beauty of the ironwork, which is a feature of the city is preserved.[62]

The Times also, noting the 'perfection of the production', said:

> There is a prodigal wealth about the whole arrangements, a multiplicity of scenes, a crowding of the stage with life, a richness, a beauty, and a degree of artistic arrangement in the costumes and grouping of the players that fairly distances all that has been done before ... From the time when the curtain ... rises on Mr. Hawes Craven's market scene down to the end there is no cessation of the beautiful effects that are presented to the eye.[63]

The scene-painting undoubtedly contributed to this in a major way. *The Times* thought 'the scenery was as good as it could be'. One critic was moved to comment on how much improved the scene-painting now was:

> Time was, and that not far remote, when a mediaeval street scene or two, a conventionally gloomy Friar's cell, a Juliet's chamber which might have been ordered at will from the nearest upholsterer's, and a tomb of the Capulets which suggested nothing more noble than can be found at a venture in the side walks of Kensal Green were deemed amply sufficient for a representation of Shakespeare's immortal love story. Now we have the play illustrated with what seems to the spectator an inexhaustible series of really fine pictures of old Verona and Mantua, including both interior and exterior scenes in their most picturesque aspects ... The eyes of spectators at the play can rarely have rested upon anything more picturesquely noble than Mr. Craven's scene at the opening of Act III, with the trellised walk between the walls of some fair garden, its ancient arches, and the cool stone recesses, and sculptured alcoves. The fine gloom of the scene of the interior of the tomb, or rather deep vault of the Capulets ... is again very striking to the imagination.[64]

Several of the reviews paid tribute to the individual scenic artists. The *Era*, for instance, noted that after the Chorus spoke the prologue:

---

61 Terry, *The Story of My Life*, p. 215.
62 Unattributed review, *Fitzgerald Collection*, **5**, p. 44.
63 *The Times*, 9 March 1882.
64 Unattributed review, *Fitzgerald Collection* Vol. 5, p. 48.

Then speedily our attention is arrested by Mr. Hawes Craven's beautiful stage picture representative of the market-place in Verona, with its strongly built-up bridge in the rear, with its effective groupings, and all the bustle and animation of busy every-day life ... The next scene to take admiration by storm is that of the festival in Capulet's house. The eye is fairly baffled in the attempt to take in all the blaze of light and evidence of luxury that here abound; the maskers with their rich dresses, the dancers in white and gold, the gay gossiping crowds, and the well-grouped minstrels who supply the music ... This scene ... is the handiwork of Mr. W. Cuthbert. Mr Hawes Craven is responsible for all six scenes of the second act, the most noticeable being the Garden lying low beneath the terrace, where stands Capulet's house, with its massive pillar-supported balcony ... The 'set' is a splendid one and called forth a general buzz of admiration. Another fine stage picture, reflecting the highest credit on Mr. Craven, is the Public Place at the beginning of the third act, where Mercutio and Tybalt meet their deaths. Juliet's chamber displays once more the artistic skill of Mr. Cuthbert; while later on, the services of Mr. W. Telbin have been brought into play with the most satisfactory results. The street in Mantua, where Romeo seeks out the apothecary ... takes us in imagination to the squalid 'quarter' of an Italian city. But the 'last scene of all that ends this strange eventful history', if not the most picturesque, is the most impressive, and will linger longest in the memory. This is 'the tomb of all the Capulets'.[65]

What is striking about the reviews is how often they couple a discussion of sets and scenery with a discussion of the management of the crowd. Looking back from 1908, Ellen Terry recalled of *Romeo and Juliet*:

In it Henry first displayed his mastery of crowds. The brawling of the rival houses in the streets, the procession of girls to wake Juliet on her wedding morning, the musicians, the magnificent reconciliation of the two houses which closed the play, every one on the stage holding a torch, were all treated with a marvellous sense of pictorial effect.[66]

It seems that Irving had learned lessons from the celebrated visit to London in 1881 of the Saxe-Meiningen company which performed, in German, a series of Shakespeare plays, beginning with *Julius Caesar*. The Saxe-Meiningen company were renowned for 'the extraordinary accuracy and picturesqueness of stage-management, especially in the handling of mobs or other great masses of humanity'. George Odell concluded that their visit had a lasting effect on the English stage and, in particular, on Irving.[67] Several contemporary critics identified the influence of the Saxe-Meiningen company.[68]

Clement Scott thought Irving's crowd-handling in its 'variety, suddenness, and effect' superior to that of the Saxe-Meiningen company ('not nearly so mechanical').[69] *The Times* noted approvingly:

---

65 *Era*, 11 March 1882.
66 Terry, *The Story of My Life*, p. 208.
67 George C. Odell, *Shakespeare from Betterton to Irving* (New York, 1920), Vol. 2, pp. 377–8.
68 *Era*, 11 March 1882; unattributed review, *Fitzgerald Collection*, 5, p. 48.
69 *Theatre*, 5, 1882, p. 234.

The most brilliant of the spectacular effects were the frequent seemingly spontaneous groupings which marked the most striking situations. Such, for example, were the ball scene, culminating in the lovely 'torch dance', in which all the dancers appeared clothed in white and gold; the grouping of Romeo and the Nurse, in the fourth scene of Act 2; the sudden gathering over the dead Tybalt; and the extremely subtle arrangement of colours in the scene round the fancied death-bed of Juliet. Each of these is a picture of great beauty, studied with immense care.[70]

Another critic commented on the reality of the crowd scenes: 'Through the streets meanwhile ... circulates a crowd of real men and women, dressed in appropriate and artistic costumes and occupied with their own affairs, but not so occupied but that the slightest incident in the life around them sets them astir.'[71] What completed the widely recognised perfection of the staging and complemented the scene-painting and the management of the crowds was the lighting. In his essay on the play Edward R. Russell pointed out:

> Throughout the play the management of the lighting is a thing wholly new in its perfect and accurate graduation, and here in the first scene we have the first example of it in the creation of what the *Spectator* well described as 'an atmosphere'. Pictorially it is a very striking 'set' of the market-place of Verona, carefully and agreeably softened by shade and by a central fountain, giving a delightful feeling of repose while beyond over a bridge is seen the glaring brilliancy of the unshaded sunny atmosphere.[72]

Many critics commented on the 'baking sun' effect on the early scenes – an effect enhanced by a brilliant new pigment developed by Craven to create a clear bright blue Italian sky. Juliet's chamber was bathed in a sunrise, which showed pink, orange and purple tints, culminating in golden sunlight. The Capulet tomb was partially lit by a shaft of moonlight and, later, by the torches carried by the mourners down the steps.

There was criticism of both Irving's Romeo and Ellen Terry's Juliet – some of it very harsh – but there was almost no criticism of the production itself. It ran for a triumphant 160 performances and set the standard for all future productions of the play. It also demonstrated perfectly the application of Irving's holistic approach – an approach that was to characterise all the future productions in his career.

All the evidence suggests that the whole conception of every production staged at the Lyceum was Irving's. He prepared the text, selected and rehearsed the cast, devised the lighting, selected the scene painters, assigned them their scenes and supervised their activities. The painter Sir Hubert von Herkomer, who staged amateur productions of music dramas with his own scenery at his house at Bushey, and lectured on stage lighting and stage scenery, was certainly in no doubt about whose vision was being realised on the Lyceum stage in every aspect:

---

70 *The Times*, 9. March 1882.
71 Unattributed review, *Fitzgerald Collection*, Vol. 5, p. 44.
72 Edward R. Russell, '*Romeo and Juliet* at the Lyceum', *Macmillans Magazine*, **46**, 1882, p. 326.

Now I rejoice whenever I see a noble effort to bring about 'an artistic whole' on the stage notably from the hands of that great artist, Henry Irving, who, with a giant's strength, carries through schemes that would crush any other actor or manager. I suspect there is but one mastermind behind the Lyceum proscenium, and that is the secret of all success. If a thousand people are needed to carry out an art scheme, it must be planned and directed by <u>one man</u> who stamps it as his work.[73]

---

73 *Magazine of Art,* **15**, 1892, p. 261.

Chapter 8

'Henry and 250 Supers': Irving, *Robespierre* and the Staging of the Revolutionary Crowd

Jean Chothia

Peter Brook, in *The Empty Space,* famously described his 'acid test' of memorable theatre:

> When a performance is over, what remains? ... The event scorches on the memory an outline, a taste, a trace, a smell – a picture. It is the play's central image that remains, its silhouette ... When years later I think of a striking theatrical experience I find a kernel engraved on my memory.[1]

The metaphors might be mixed, but Brook's insistence on the essential mark left by the 'striking theatrical experience' goes to the heart of why theatre might matter. Contemporary accounts suggest that Henry Irving's 1899 production of *Robespierre,* commissioned from Victorien Sardou and translated by Irving's son, Laurence, offered such an experience to many in his audience. Personal factors made audiences more than usually responsive to the actor, as well as his role in what turned out to be Irving's last successful production. Central to what remained was the encounter between his Robespierre and the revolutionary crowd in a period in which effective crowd work had become the signature feature of illusionist staging and the new field of 'crowd psychology' had emerged as an area of concern, feeding the contemporary middle-class fear of the increasing confidence of the underclass. My chapter explores this in the light of other significant Anglo-French encounters evident in the ever-complex interaction of play, production and cultural moment.

Robespierre was the culminating production of a vogue for French Revolution melodramas, launched on the London stage in 1889.[2] These embodied an English revolutionary imaginary which, derived largely from Carlyle's *French Revolution* and Dickens's *Tale of Two Cities,* centred on displaced aristocrats, the dark thrill of the guillotine and the savagery of French mobs. Further stimulus had been provided by lurid reporting of the fight for the 1871 Paris Commune; by vivid scenes of rioting

---

1 Peter Brook, *The Empty Space* (Harmondsworth, 1990), pp. 152–3.
2 Kristan Tetens lists five in the 1889–90 London season. See her 'Commemorating the French Revolution on the Victorian Stage: Henry Irving's *The Dead Heart*', *Nineteenth Century Theatre and Film,* **32**, 2005, pp. 36–69. I am grateful to Ms Tetens for a preview of her article.

workers evoked in Emile Zola's *Germinal* (1885); and by the sudden rise and equally sudden evaporation of mass support for General Boulanger and his Parti National, between 1886 and 1889. All of this reinforced the belief, held by much of the English press, that the French populace and system of government were much more unstable than the English, even while it simultaneously generated a fascination with that more dangerous or – depending on perspective – freer society across the Channel.

More immediately, interest in 1789 was fired by the centenary of the first Revolution, which was celebrated in Paris, despite protests from the European monarchies, with fireworks and gun salutes, the staging of the Exposition Universelle, and the opening of the newly constructed Eiffel Tower. Progressively since 1870, revolutionary emblems – the *tricoleur*, Bastille Day and the *Marseillaise* – had been adopted into the national self-identification of the Third Republic and a 'Museum of the Revolution' inaugurated. Now, heroes of the Year II were reinterred in the Panthéon and, even as Hippolyte Taine was identifying a pathology of 'the crowd mind' as he traced the upheavals of the present back to the disasters of 1789, a National Edition of Jules Michelet's earlier, more celebratory, history was commissioned.[3]

The London melodramas shared, to a notable extent, the typological characteristics identified in *The Times*:

> ... persecuted aristocrats are in imminent danger of death, but are saved by the self-sacrificing heroism of a leader of the people; a noisy rabble of *sans culottes* invades the stage from time to time, or shouts hoarsely in the wings; the guillotine throws its shadow athwart the scene.[4]

So, intriguingly, did the two most notable contemporary Parisian stage versions of the Revolution, although with very different effect, given the sharper French fault lines. The *Théâtre Libre*'s 1889 staging of *La Patrie en Danger* so extended the role of the *sans culottes* that the Goncourts' romance of a revolutionary leader risking all to aid his former master was transformed into a celebration of the popular voice of the Revolution was transformed. Sardou's own *Thermidor*, which featured similar efforts by Labussière, a leader of the people who had lost faith during the last days of the Terror, stimulated the anger of the contemporary popular voice when students, deeming the play hostile to the Revolution and therefore the Republic, rioted at its second performance at the *Théâtre Français* in 1891. Clemenceau then famously declaring '*La Révolution est un bloc*' – in other words, it was to be accepted whole or not at all – gained a ban on performance of the play in any subsidised French theatre by a vote of 315 to 122.[5]

The impetus for *Robespierre* was Irving's. The press had decried his revival of Watts Phillips' 30-year-old *The Dead Heart,* as his centenary offering in 1889. *Time*, 'long[ing] for something better', had compared it unfavourably with historical

---

3   Hippolyte Taine, *Origines de la France contemporaine*, 6 vols (Paris, 1876–94); Jules Michelet, *Histoire de la révolution française* (Paris, 1847–52).

4   *The Times*, 13 May 1890.

5   F.W.J. Hemmings, *The Theatre Industry in Nineteenth Century France* (Cambridge, 1993), p. 86.

romances on the French stage.⁶ Sardou recalled that, after acting Napoleon in *Madame Sans-Gêne* 'with great success' in 1897 and 'feeling that he would be still more successful in a part better suited to his physique', Irving asked for a play 'on the Revolution, with Robespierre as the chief character'.⁷ George Bernard Shaw might deride 'Sardoodledom'⁸ and Europe's new, independent theatres might engage with avant-garde writing but, as Irving and his potential audiences well knew, Sardou was still pre-eminent in the French theatre. Although his plays are now so completely eclipsed that none is currently in print except as an opera libretto, *Fédora*, *La Tosca* and *Madame Sans-Gêne* were classics in their own day, triumphantly toured by such luminaries as Sarah Bernhardt, Eleonora Duse and Benoît Constant Coquelin. The success in 1895 of Beerbohm Tree, pretender to Irving's crown, in an English version of *Fédora*, Sardou's representation of emigré Russian revolutionaries, was a further spur. Moreover, while in no way tempted by Shaw's Napoleon in *The Man of Destiny*, Irving commented that Sardou's was a man who 'even in his domesticity learned always to be an actor and to act his acting while at all times maintaining the imperial illusion'.⁹ In Sardou he had found another dramatist able to supply the kind of duplicitous historical *monstre sacré* he had relished when playing Wolsey (1895) and Richard III (1896).

Sardou for his part, although he spoke no English and never braved the Channel, was aware of Irving's ascendancy on the London stage and of his reputation for creating unsurpassable stage pictures and filling his stage with people. As passionately interested in the Revolution as he was appalled by what he saw as its excesses, Sardou had good reason to revisit it. After the ban on *Thermidor*, he had published a series of pamphlets taking issue with Ernest Hamel's hagiographic history of Robespierre. Subsequently, he used various invited prefaces to attack radicals such as Michelet or Louis Blanc who, he claimed seemingly without irony, wrote 'not the history but the romance of the Revolution'.¹⁰ When *Thermidor* was revived, without incident, in 1896, he interpolated a scene of Robespierre's downfall before a hostile National Convention. This scene he would substantially reuse as the climax to Irving's play.¹¹

Both parties in this curious Anglo-French collaboration were concerned with historical accuracy. Sardou, famous since the late 1860s for the historical research that informed the settings of his plays, drew on contemporary documents for his detailed recreation of the pageantry of the *Fête* of the Supreme Being (Act II) and for the Convention scene (Act V). While trusting the more fully fictional sequences to

---

6   *Time*, January–June 1890.
7   16 October 1905, Memorial tributes, Laurence Irving Collection, Theatre Museum, THM/37/8, (hereafter THM).
8   George Bernard Shaw, *Our Theatres in the Nineties* (London, 1932), Vol. 1, p. 133.
9   27 April 1897, THM/39/3.
10 Jean Sardou, *La Maison de Robespierre, réponse à M.E. Hamel* (Paris, 1895); 'Preface', Frantz Funck-Brentano, *Legends of the Bastille*, trans. George Maidment (London, 1899), 6; 'Preface', Paul Stefane-Pol, *Autour de Robespierre* (Paris, 1901). Translations are mine unless otherwise stated.
11 Jean Sardou, ed., *Théâtre Complet*, Vol. VI: *Thermidor, Odette, Robespierre*, (Paris, 1935), p. 603.

Irving's chosen designers – Harker, Harford and Hawes Craven – he insisted that the sets for these two scenes be built, overseen by him, by the Parisian company, Amable, and then shipped over. Irving reported first receiving for approval Sardou's scenario 'with every essential of the story elaborately mapped out. With this he supplied drawings, which he had made himself, and copious documents.' Accepting the dramatist at his own estimation, Irving added: 'Sardou is not only an accomplished draughtsman, but also probably the greatest living authority on the Revolutionary period.'[12]

Although Irving immediately posted Laurence to France to negotiate a good hour's worth of cuts, including the lengthy exposition, and later insisted that Laurence 'condense' Robespierre's monologues,[13] he followed scrupulously Sardou's drawings and detailed stage directions for costume, set and ritual. The Lyceum programme registered the authenticity of the music 'specially composed' by George Jacobi which, like the score Jacobi had previously provided for *The Dead Heart*, incorporated celebrated period works: Méhul's *Chant du Depart*, the *Marseillaise* and Gossec's *Cantata* (1794). It announced, too, that *Robespierre, the Sea-Green Incorruptible*, 'profusely illustrated', and *The Life of Maximilien Robespierre*, by G. H. Lewes, could be bought from theatre attendants for 1s and 3s 6d respectively and, under the heading 'Argument', provided a résumé not of the fictional plot, but of the factual events of 1794.

Despite the claims to historical accuracy, Sardou's play is not unfairly dismissed as 'hardly ... a serious contribution to Robespierre historiography'.[14] To the 'escaping aristocrat' formula is added the complication that now the 'leader of the people' is Robespierre himself and the royalist in danger his putative adult son, Olivier, from what must have been a remarkably youthful liaison. Robespierre endures a *Richard III*-like haunting by past victims and, in the core sentimental scene, looks anxiously with his former lover, Clarisse, from a window on to the passing tumbrels for Olivier – a trope regularly recycled since a particularly affecting version in Tom Taylor's 1860 *Tale of Two Cities*. In a final travesty of history, Robespierre eludes the guillotine through a successful suicide in the Convention. His dying plea is for forgiveness from Clarisse.

Although a few contemporaries praised Sardou's ingenuity, most were disappointed by the anomalous conjunction of history and romance. Finding the plot commonplace, *Today* sniffed that it 'might serve for any age in any grade of society. A father in ignorance places his mistress and son in peril of their lives and, on discovering their identity, endeavours to regain their freedom.'[15] The *Illustrated London News* described it as a 'silly and historically unsatisfactory story';[16] the American ambassador to Germany, catching it in London, labelled it 'grotesquely

---

12 Unidentified clipping, 5 November 1899, Locke-Robinson Collection, New York Public Library (hereafter NYPL).

13 18 January 1899 (THM/37/7).

14 William Howarth, 'The Representation of Robespierre in European Drama', in Colin Haydon and William Doyle, eds, *Robespierre* (Cambridge, 1999), pp. 237–51, 243.

15 *Today*, 27 April 1899.

16 *Illustrated London News*, 6 May 1899.

unhistorical', its mystifications 'suited only to the lowest boulevard melodrama'[17] and even the admiring Clement Scott thought it demonstrated the 'arbitrariness of the playwright's licence'.[18] But, for all that, the production was an immense success – Irving's last. As Ellen Terry wrote to Shaw from America, 'this beastly *Robespierre* is what they call a boom over here, and we can carry it on for a long time.' Indeed, it was such a boom that it more than recouped Sardou's huge fee of £1,000 for the script, £1,000 more, if toured to America, and 5 per cent of the takings.[19]

The necessary question is less 'Why Sardou?' than 'Why the success?' Factors extraneous to the play contributed. As Irving's first new production since the devastating fire which destroyed the Lyceum stores in their Southwark warehouse on 18 February 1898, it floated on a surge of sympathy. In that disaster 260 scenes from 44 plays – costumes, properties and sets – had all been lost. Bram Stoker, Irving's business manager, lamented 'the deprivation of all he had built up'. Then, later the same year, a long illness from which, Terry recorded, 'he nearly died' put Irving out of action for months and contributed to the financial crisis that led to his handing control of his theatre to a limited liability company.[20] American headlines, announcing 'Career of England's Greatest Actor Closing' and 'America has certainly seen the last of Sir Henry Irving', reflected the sense of finality.[21] The new production, anticipated in accounts of lavish preparations and multitudes of historically accurate costumes, promised a resurgence.

Queues famously formed early for Lyceum premieres, but those forming before breakfast for the opening of *Robespierre* were phenomenal and, while it was customary for audiences to applaud the first entrance of favoured actors, the collective 'tumult of acclaim' was 'exceptionally warm, even for him'.[22] From all parts of the house, 'the pent up warmth of welcome continued for some minutes. The gallery shouting, the pit cheering, and the dress circle, startled from its propriety, waving handkerchiefs'.[23] The numerous illustrations and cartoons that appeared of Irving in costume, including several 'sketched from life' by Harry Furniss in the *Telegraph*, a widely syndicated portrait by Bernard Partridge and two in Charles Hiatt's biography

---

17 Andrew D. White, *Autobiography* (London, 1905), Vol. 2, p. 276.

18 *Telegraph*, 17 April 1899.

19 Terry, THM/37/8. The play had 105 performances in London, 43 in the provinces and 109 in America, visiting some 30 cities between October 1899 and May 1900. American receipts were £111,000 of which Irving's profit was £24,000. See Charles Hiatt, *Henry Irving: A Record and Review* (London, 1899), p. 264; and Bram Stoker, *Personal Reminiscences of Henry Irving* (London, 1906), Vol. 2, p. 330.

20 Stoker, *Personal Reminiscences*, Vol. 2, p. 302; Ellen Terry, *The Story of My Life* (London, 1908), p. 325. By agreement with the Lyceum Company, chaired by J. Comyns Carr, Irving was to bear 60 per cent of the cost of new productions and spend at least four months annually touring. The company collapsed in 1902.

21 13 January 1899, NYPL.

22 Hiatt, *Henry Irving*, p. 258; Stoker, *Personal Reminiscences of Henry Irving*, Vol. 1, p. 268.

23 *Telegraph*, 17 April 1899.

published later the same year[24] suggest a quickened consciousness of the transience of even such a dominant fixture as Irving. His departure from Tilbury, with a touring company of 87 and 300 tons of scenery, was sufficiently newsworthy to be recorded by the new-fangled cinematograph and, once in America, headlines declared 'Irving Here Once More', 'Henry Irving Is Himself Again' and interviews reported him 'now in splendid health' and 'sound as a bell' with 'no trace of the serious illness'.[25] Terry, who hated her underwritten, maternal role, wrote succinctly: 'He is afloat again. It is a bad play but a wonderfully showy one. Much variety in scene, no development of character. A one-man piece. Henry and 250 supers.'[26]

Reviews make clear that more than sympathy powered the success. Those '250 supers', or supernumerary performers, their 'lifelike deportment'[27] and the 'absolutely perfect' management of them,[28] were germane. The magnificent Act II pageant of the *Fête* of the Supreme Being, complete with huge Statue of Liberty and golden incense-burning tripod, was much praised, but it was the final scene, V. ii, adapted from the 1896 *Thermidor,* in which Robespierre faced a riotously hostile Convention, which made the real impact. As Stoker noted, 'everywhere the piece was played the scene in the Convention went with uncontrollable effect'.[29] Stages teeming with supers were familiar to late nineteenth-century audiences. The tour of the Saxe-Meiningen company to Drury Lane in 1881 famously reawakened London theatre to the possibilities of aesthetically ordered stage crowds and sharpened the discrimination of critics and audiences. As Terry later noted, 'very little was attempted with crowds on the English stage after Charles Kean, who had admirable stage crowds, until the Saxe-Meiningen Company visited London. From that moment there was reform amounting to revolution.'[30] The impact was evident across a range of theatrical events, from popular – and populated – spectacles at Drury Lane to attentively grouped pictures in Shakespearean production, one of the first manifestations of which was Irving's own disposition of Capulets and Montagues in his 1882 *Romeo and Juliet.*

Beyond the aesthetic appeal of the populated stage, fictions of riot and revolution shadowed contemporary concerns about socialism and the rise of militant trade unionism that had seen waves of strikes across the industrial world in the late 1880s and early 1890s in what has been fairly described as a period of 'extraordinary coincidence of intellectual and public concern about crowds'.[31] The year 1889 had

---

24 Portraits by Scotson Clark and Oliver Bath, Hiatt, *Henry Irving*, pp. 259, 265. The Theatre Museum has a fine wood engraving by Gordon Craig and the Bram Stoker Collection has an unsigned watercolour.

25 *Daily Graphic*, 16 October 1899; *New York Herald* and *Evening Journal*, 17 October 1899; clippings, NYPL.

26 Quoted, A.E. Wilson, *The Lyceum* (London, 1952), p. 145.

27 Max Beerbohm, *More Theatres 1898–1903* (London, 1969), p. 136.

28 *Pall Mall Gazette*, 25 April 1899.

29 Stoker, *Personal Reminiscences of Henry Irving*, Vol. 2, p. 269.

30 Terry, 'Stage Decoration', *Windsor Magazine,* n.d., but recalling the 'late Henry Irving', THM/37/8/8.

31 J. McClelland, *The Crowd and the Mob, from Plato to Canetti* (London, 1989), p. 198.

seen the declaration of the Second Socialist International as well as the centenary of the French Revolution and, the following year, the newly legal German Social Democratic Party had won 20 per cent of the popular vote. Among the most prominent English strikes the Bryant and May match girls' strike of 1888 had aroused public sympathy, while the great London Dock Strike of 1889 had publicised itself with brass bands, banners and the singing of the *Marseillaise*, the anthem of international socialism as well as of the French Republic[32] – the festivity and popular sympathy proving at least as worrying to the authorities as the economic consequences.

In 1889, when preparing his script of *The Dead Heart*, Irving had written to Terry of the need for 'a starving crowd – hungry, eager, cadaverous' in the opening Bastille scene and of the 'very terrible' effect if that could be achieved.[33] In the event, while most commentators found the staging better than the play and several praised the crowd activity, the revolutionary mob disappointed the expectations of others. Burne-Jones 'wanted rather more shouting and distant roar in the Bastille scene ... A good dreadful growl always going on would have helped.'[34] J.A. Froude, who had anticipated 'a fiercer intonation of the *Marseillaise*', missed the 'fury of enthusiasm' with which, he claimed, it was sung historically[35] and *Theatre* wanted 'more abandon' in the dancing of the *Carmagnole* and 'more ruffianism' in the singing of the *Ça Ira* and the *Marseillaise*.[36]

In Paris, André Antoine's near-simultaneous presentation of the revolutionary mob in *La Patrie en Danger* was, in contrast, all too real. In February 1889 he had seized the opportunity of a *Théâtre Libre* tour to London to see *Macbeth* at the Lyceum. Irving's staging of the discovery of Duncan's murder (Illustration 14) seemed derisively unnatural to William Archer:

> The only visible source of illumination is a small hanging lamp but miraculous shafts of moonlight break in on every hand and flashes of lightning make themselves visible (so far as one can understand) through walls of solid whinstone.[37]

To Antoine, already planning the Goncourt production, the *mise en scène* in this and the banquet scene was revelatory. The arrangement of the supers in seemingly haphazard clusters and the wonderful lighting effects seemed unlike anything yet imagined in France.[38] Some 30 years later, he still recalled that, 'in Irving's productions a shaft of moonlight or sun would always appear on the face of the leading character, one hardly knew how or why, but it was very fine, all the same'.[39]

---

32 See H. Llewellyn Smith and Vaughan Nash, *The Story of the Dockers' Strike, Told by Two East Enders* (London, 1890).
33 Quoted in Laurence Irving, *Henry Irving, the Actor and His World* (London, 1951), p. 516.
34 Letter 1889, quoted in Terry, *The Story of my Life*, p. 310.
35 Tetens, 'Commemorating the French Revolution'.
36 *Theatre*, 1 November 1889.
37 *New Review*, September 1889.
38 André Antoine, *Mes Souvenirs sur le Théâtre-Libre* (Paris, 1921), p. 136.
39 *Conferencia*, 1 March 1923.

Illustration 14   *Macbeth*: Act II: Court of Macbeth's Castle, with Irving (left) as Macbeth and Ellen Terry (right) as Lady Macbeth

Impressed as he was by the Meininger productions he had seen the previous year and intent on pursuing their methods, Antoine perceived the need to go beyond the 'incomplete realism' of their fixed postures and the silences that fell whenever a lead actor spoke, wanting a more ragged and chaotic impression.[40] His disposition of the revolutionary crowd to clustering effect and his atmospheric lighting he learned from Irving, with the difference that, whereas in Irving's virtuoso theatre the leading actor was always prominently lit, Antoine's streaks of light, falling seemingly randomly on faces and figures in the 200-strong crowd, focused attention on individuals within the swarming mass.[41] The diversion to crowd activity from the somewhat tedious speeches of the principals, however, created a disjunction between play and production. Moreover, where some commentators were disappointed by the lack of tumult in Irving's revolutionary mob, the clamour of Antoine's resulted in his leading actor, Mévisto, straining so realistically against it that he lost his voice, the actor's vital tool.[42] Antoine, the prototype modern director, and Irving, the doyen of actor-managers, each learned by trial and error that the more convincingly wild a stage crowd was to seem, the more carefully orchestrated it had to be.

---

40 *Le Temps*, 23 July 1888.
41 Antoine, *Mes Souvenirs*, p. 139.
42 Jean Chothia, *André Antoine* (Cambridge, 1992), pp. 70–2.

Interest in insurgent crowds and the ease with which crowd could be transformed into mob had intensified with the appearance in English in 1896 of Gustave Le Bon's *The Crowd: A Study of the Popular Mind*, his apocalyptic, popularising version of some 20 years of socio-psychology. Surveying the masses with deep pessimism, Le Bon identified reversion to savage, instinctual action as characteristic of the behaviour of people in crowds where individuals inevitably lost control to the collective through a process of contagion so that, in a moment, the public could become the mob. Weaker minds were affected by stronger minds, but regressive behaviour affected anyone caught up in mob activity.[43]

Audiences of European Naturalism had, meanwhile, been moved and thrilled by images of collective misery and riot among the underclass in Gerhart Hauptmann's famously heroless play, *The Weavers*. Staged at the *Freie Bühne* and the *Théâtre Libre* in 1893 and then, wherever it escaped censorship, at independent theatres across Europe, it had supplied Antoine with a more appropriate vehicle for his experiments in staging insurgency. His revival, when French public performance was finally licensed in 1898, was widely acclaimed. How aware of this activity Irving was is not recorded, although Elizabeth Marbury, who as Sardou's foreign rights agent, sat in for him at rehearsals of *Robespierre* and *Dante*, cryptically noted that Irving 'had at this period of his career, become infected with the New Art, and feared above all to be considered a victim of the old regime and its influences'.[44]

Also in 1898, revolution and its crowds were again in vogue on the London stage. Kyrle Bellew's *Charlotte Corday* ran at the Adelphi and Beerbohm Tree raised the stakes with a *Julius Caesar* that shifted attention definitively to the forum scene and the mob's role in it. Then, in February 1899, *The Only Way*, produced by John Martin Harvey, a former member of Irving's company, reputedly came alive with the Act III entrance of the *sans culottes*.[45] It is as if Irving not only returned from near–death, but did so determined to reclaim his crown. Interestingly, his cast for *Robespierre* included Bellew in the role of Olivier and, as Billaud-Varennes, Louis Calvert who had rehearsed the supers as well as playing Casca in Beerbohm Tree's *Julius Caesar*.[46]

Whether or not Irving was aware of Antoine's work, Sardou clearly was. Ubiquitous press commentary on the upstart *Théâtre Libre* included even his own most loyal advocate, Francisque Sarcey, in *Le Temps*. More directly, in 1888, immediately after

---

43 Gustave Le Bon, *Psychologie des foules* (Paris 1895). Among the most widely cited works of crowd psychology are Gabriel Tarde, *Les lois d'imitation* (Paris, 1890); Henri Fournial, *Essai sur la psychologie des foules* (Paris 1892), and Scipio Sighele, *La folla deliquente* (Turin, 1891). For detailed discussion of the arguments of the crowd psychologists, see, McClelland, *The Crowd and the Mob*; Jaap van Ginneken, *Crowds, Psychology and Politics, 1871–1899* (Cambridge, 1992) and Susan Barrows, *Distorting Mirrors* (New Haven, 1981), ch. 6.

44 Elizabeth Marbury, *My Crystal Ball: Reminiscences* (London, 1924), p. 101.

45 Max Beerbohm, *Around Theatres* (London, 1953), p. 119. See also Jim Davis, 'The Only Way and the Other Ways: A Dickens Adaptation for the 1890s', in Richard Foulkes, ed., *British Theatre in the 1890s* (Cambridge, 1992), pp. 59–70.

46 Richard Foulkes, 'Louis Calvert: a Shakespearean in the Nineties', in Foulkes, ed., *British Theatre in the 1890s*, p. 176.

Sardou had publicly dismissed Tolstoy's *Power of Darkness* as 'to be read not seen', it was staged triumphantly by the *Théâtre Libre* and, in 1891, Antoine's open letter offering his stage for the banned *Thermidor* had been gleefully reprinted throughout the French press.[47] It may well be that Sardou's stage direction in the Convention scene, '*salvoes of applause and shouts. Robespierre ... shouts, gets hoarse, but his voice is lost in the uproar. All are gesticulating, talking at once*',[48] derives from the reports of Mévisto losing his voice to Antoine's overenthusiastic supers. Certainly, a new interest in staging Revolutionary crowds had emerged in *Thermidor*. Although the supers are largely kept offstage, their cries of 'Vive la République!', 'A bas le tyran! A bas Robespierre!' recur and, in Act IV, they are directed to gather gradually onto the walls surrounding the Conciergerie yard, '*all joking, eating, drinking*'. They remain onlookers, but a self-conscious theatricality is introduced when Labussière denounces them: 'See the crowd ... the claque of the guillotine! ... They applaud the executioner!'[49] This perception of the crowd as carnivalesque would be developed in *Robespierre*'s Act II *Fête* scene, which opens with convivial exchanges of gossip, jokes and banter among the waiting crowd, including urchins perched in the Tuileries' trees or clambering on statues, but suddenly flared into brief but bloodthirsty hostility to Olivier and his protests before ending with a wildly danced carmagnole. The plot of *Robespierre* might be second-hand and the intrigues formulaic, but Sardou gave Irving rather more of a base than commentators have allowed.

As all this suggests, it was not just numbers that created the effect in *Robespierre*, although, with a speaking cast of 69 and up to 235 supers, these were huge.[50] Irving's stage had been crowded before: *Faust* used more than 200 supers in 1885, *The Dead Heart* some 300. In a period in which comparative citation was common, reviewers took pains to distinguish this achievement from celebrated earlier instances. Scott, in a cable to the *New York Herald*, listed famous crowd scenes from Charles Kean's *Richard II*, through the Meininger *Julius Caesar*, to Beerbohm Tree's 'infinitely better' one, before concluding that 'all sink into insignificance' beside Irving's 'wild tumult ... the most impressive accomplishment we have yet beheld', since 'never has a more exactly animated and spontaneous rendering of a wild mob's irresponsible fury been seen'.[51] The *Sketch* claimed that even the Meininger crowds were not as 'intensely individualised'[52] and, in New York, the *Dramatic Mirror* insisted that 'no such superb management of the stage mob [has] ever been seen here'.[53]

The paradox of realist theatre – that the more wild and spontaneous the action is to seem, the more thoroughly rehearsed it must be – was acknowledged, if unconsciously, in accounts which, even while attesting to the 'completeness' of

---

47 Antoine, *Mes Souvenirs*, pp. 224, 227.
48 Prompt copy, trans. Laurence Irving, THM, p. 118.
49 Sardou, *Théâtre Complet*, Vol. VI, pp. 155, 176.
50 Figure from Alan Hughes, *Henry Irving, Shakespearean* (Cambridge, 1981), p. 16. It probably fluctuated: Stoker, *Personal Reminiscences of Henry Irving*, Vol. 2, p. 269, recorded 'more than a hundred' supers.
51 *New York Herald*, 22 April 1899.
52 *Sketch*, 19 April 1899.
53 *Dramatic Mirror*, 4 November 1899.

the illusion, praised the control, 'the perfect stage management'[54] that underlay it. Although finding Irving's crowd so real it seemed that 'the intensity almost destroyed the natural partition between stage and audience', Scott nevertheless recognised 'the master-hand of the Lyceum director in every department and detail'.[55] The arrival in New York of H.J. Loveday, Irving's stage manager, well in advance of the company, to train the supers, was much noticed. The *New Penny Magazine* took its readers 'Behind the Scenes with Sir Henry Irving', to describe his 'wonderful way of handling a crowd' and the intensive drilling of 'every individual composing it'.[56] It also noted that eager students flocked to join the trainee crowd. In London, the drilling was assisted by the sergeant from the local barracks, whose men were encouraged to 'keep out of mischief' and augment their beer money as supers.[57]

The close attention Irving paid to gesture, positioning, crowd vocalising and the assigning of specific phrases to named actors is evident from the annotation in his prompt copy. He developed his own version of the Meininger practice of dividing the supers into groups, each led by an actor and, like Antoine and Beerbohm Tree, used a mixture of strategic blocking and operant conditioning – including a foreman's whistle – to train the supers to quick response. Marbury recalled that, initially, while the stage manager rehearsed the scene, Irving sat in the auditorium watching attentively and calling out suggestions for recording in the prompt book. Only when the new production was nearing completion would he be on stage himself and then 'rehearsals were incessant and exhausting'.[58] Choreographed movement of the crowd was crucial. As Terry wrote, 'every moment you must be considering its colour, its form, its movement, its human significance', and Stoker recalled that, in the Convention scene, much of the effect depended on 'the rush of deputies across the floor of the house, and the series of fights for the tribune'.[59]

The detail and exuberance of the festive Act II crowd, and their brief, but startling, ferocity, were an important preparation for the final scene. So, at a more technical level, was V.i, the scene immediately preceding the V.ii Convention scene. A 'carpenter's scene' of a kind familiar to Irving's audience, this was set up just inside the proscenium as if in an anteroom. Here, Robespierre's enemies conspired while noises of angry debate and the ringing of the President's bell emanated from the deep stage behind a drop curtain, where the Convention Hall was already set. The stage then remained in darkness for some three minutes during which, as the stage directions, heavily underlined in Irving's prompt copy, read: '*the tumult of the Convention and the ringing of the President's bell are heard – increasing in volume. The lights are suddenly turned up and the Convention is disclosed, uproarious.*'

The Convention scene itself was effectively shaped: 'howling', 'frantic' and 'frenzied' are the recurrent adjectives in reviews recording the savagery of the

---

54 *Sketch*, 13 May 1899.
55 *Daily Telegraph*, 17 April 1899.
56 'Behind the Scenes with Henry Irving', *New Penny Magazine*, **24**(II), 1899, pp. 601–7.
57 Stoker, *Reminiscences of Henry Irving*, Vol. 1, p. 157.
58 Marbury, *My Crystal Ball*, pp. 100–1.
59 Terry, THM/37/8/8; Stoker, *Personal Reminiscences of Henry Irving*, Vol. 2, p. 269.

crowd, and one declared that 'there is no resting place in it. Plot and tumult prevail throughout'.[60] Yet, more attentive observers registered significant shifts in tempo. It was 'the pauses, the silences' more than the noise of the mob that impressed an American reviewer, especially 'the most moving and tense moment':

> ... the moment when the brother of Robespierre, and Saint Just, and Couthon, and Lebas stepped forward to take their places by the side of the doomed 'incorruptible' and a great hush fell on the assembly as, in a flash, the creatures who had been clamouring for their tyrant's blood seemed to perceive for the first time the full audacity and the historical significance of their acts.[61]

In another potent use of silence, after Thuriot has called for a vote on Robespierre's arrest, the stage direction reads '*The whole of the Mountain rise, as one man, in dead silence*'. It is only after the 'Plain', rejecting an appeal from Robespierre, has risen in turn and Thuriot has declared the vote unanimous that an immense clamour breaks out in a frenzy of shouting and waving of caps. Indeed, although Olivier, clutching his assassin's weapon, is on stage throughout and Clarisse, having watched from the visitors' gallery, will rush forward in the final moments, Sardou's structuring of the scene drew on real events. Robespierre's struggles with Tallien for possession of the Tribune, his five attempts to answer the charges of different accusers and 'the moving and tense moment' of solidarity initiated by Robespierre's brother all echo eyewitness accounts in the *Moniteur Universel*, no. 311, of July 1794. Sardou's concentrated version of actual historical process in this scene provided the basis Irving needed for his representation of the fatedness of Robespierre's fall and his capacity to compel audience attention.

The posed production photograph of the Convention reproduced here (Illustration 15) is a composite image incorporating several disparate sequences – Robespierre's defiant challenges, the opposed parties combining against him and Clarisse already on the Convention floor, weeping. Despite this, and the indeterminate focus of the gaze of some of the less disciplined supers, the photograph gives a good idea of Irving's organisation of the scene. His renowned sense of the visual image is apparent in the height variations, the packed stage – although here with just 90 supers – and the potential for sound to ricochet between 'Mountain' dominating at stage left and 'Plain' at stage right. Irving occupies his characteristically strong position, as he would for Robespierre's initial defiance. Although the photographic lighting means the stage lighting is not registered, it is clear that Irving, who changed his wig, make-up and costume for this final scene, would stand out, pale against the assembled crowd, even when collapsed on the Tribune steps. His isolation, pallor and stillness were much noticed. As the *New York Dramatic Mirror* reported, 'in the midst of the clamour Robespierre stands like a gaunt rock'.[62] Even if silenced by 250 supers, there is no danger whatever of this Robespierre being lost in the turmoil.

---

60 NYPL.
61 4 November 1899, NYPL.
62 *New York Dramatic Mirror*, 4 November 1899.

Illustration 15   *Robespierre*: Act V Scene 2: The Convention Scene, with Irving as Robespierre in the foreground (in light-coloured costume), Ellen Terry as Clarisse (immediately behind and to Irving's right, weeping), Kyrle Bellew as Olivier (clutching his assassin's gun) and Laurence Irving as Tallien (at the lectern)

Although reviewers complained of the absurdity of Sardou ending the play with Robespierre's suicide, this may well have been one of Irving's interventions. It was dropped from the much reworked French version published in Sardou's *Théâtre Complet*, which ends with a guilt-wracked Robespierre risking all to free Olivier. A Convention scene, identical to that interpolated into the 1896 *Thermidor*, is then recycled as an epilogue. A novelisation of Sardou's play, published in 1899 and warmly endorsed by the dramatist, similarly had Robespierre walk proudly from the Convention and, after further excitements, including a touching parting from Clarisse and a change of heart by Olivier, go to his death at the guillotine.[63] The curtailed action in Irving's version was, perhaps, theatrically fortuitous. Just two months earlier, a succession of affecting scaffold scenes had found definitive form on the Lyceum stage itself. After Sidney Carton's self-sacrificing 'far, far better thing' spoken to a hushed crowd on the steps of the guillotine in *The Only Way*,[64] even Irving's Robespierre on the scaffold would have been anti-climactic. By eschewing the romanticism of the Anglophone stage guillotine and emphasising the ferocious

---

63 Ange Galdemar, *Robespierre* (London, 1899).
64 For a pedigree of descent of scaffold scenes through the Jacobite melodrama, *All for Her* (1875) and *The Dead Heart* (1889), to Martin-Harvey, see Davis, '*The Only Way*', in Foulkes, ed., *British Theatre*, p. 61.

and fickle nature of the crowd, Irving's distortion of history probably contributed to his scene's impact.

Attention to the real event is a logical result of ever more realistic use of historical detail in staging romantic melodrama. Despite objections to the ahistorical suicide and formulaic plot, and some carping about the precise ordering of events on 9/10 Thermidor, the Convention scene did register with audiences and reviewers as a notable re-enacting of history and its terrible ironies. One critic who claimed to 'lack words' to describe 'the portentous turmoil of the scene in the Convention, where "Plain" and "Mountain" meet to destroy the distracted Robespierre', nevertheless gave an eloquent account of the historical situation.[65] Another relished the image of Irving's Robespierre attempting 'in vain to speak against the clamour of a wolfish crowd ... reviled, insulted, despised ... swept away by the irresistible force and fury of those over whom he had until then held potent sway'.[66] Such recognition of the irony of the 'seething, gesticulating crowd of men and women ... dooming to the scaffold the men who had incarnadined it with human blood', informed Scott's account, too.[67] Press and audience were responding not to the turns of the melodramatic plot, but to the drama of a terrifying crowd turning on the creator of the Terror; of a demagogue silenced by the popular voice. Perhaps it was also responding to a dominant actor momentarily overwhelmed by his supers. This crowd, the simulacrum of a ferocious mob, could thrill but, in the final analysis, as an achieved example of finely balanced stage control, it was to be enjoyed rather than feared.

The execution of the Convention scene eclipsed the supposed high-points and emotional climaxes of lost and found love and newly aroused paternal feeling, creating a disjunction between plot and *mise en scène* even greater than in *La Patrie en Danger*. Olivier, at left front of the stage, clutching his assassin's weapon, seethes with hatred. Clarisse cries in horror as Robespierre shoots himself. The memoirs and press accounts were not concerned with them. It was not the fictional son, but the historical Tallien and his struggle with Robespierre for possession of the podium that electrified. The thrill was doubtless reinforced by another of those strange, but theatrically powerful, shadowings effected by the personal presence of the actors, since Tallien was played by Irving's actual son. Laurence's delivery of Tallien's wild denunciation of Robespierre was labelled 'brilliant' by *Today*[68] and was described by Max Beerbohm as marking him 'as a young actor with genius'.[69]

The impression, peculiar to staged history, of something which has already taken its course being shown again is made more complex by Irving's sleight of hand in drawing into service one of the iconic representations of the Revolution, Jacques-Louis David's *Serment du Jeu de Paume,* known as *The Tennis Court*

---

65 4 November 1899, NYPL.
66 THM/PN2598-I8.
67 *New York Herald*, 22 April 1899.
68 27 April 1899.
69 Beerbohm, *More Theatres*, p 135. Shaw commented of Laurence's performance in *Captain Brassbound's Conversion*, on 26 December 1900: 'I rather think that Tallien may have got you into the habit of shouting.' See Bernard Shaw, *Collected Letters*, ed. Dan H. Laurence (London, 1972), Vol. 2, p. 211.

Oath (Illustration 16). Disseminated in numerous engravings, and prominently displayed in the fine art section of the 1889 *Exposition*, this familiar image had become accessible as a signifier of Revolutionary fervour and at least momentary unanimity. It figures the launching event when, on 20 June 1789, the members of the Third Estate, defying the king's order in one of the Revolution's notably theatrical demonstrations, resolved to continue to meet until their constitutional demands were achieved. Viewed as if on a stage, the deputies, arms simultaneously outstretched, swear their collective oath. Just present at the upper windows, a theatrical curtain is blown by the wind of change and, beyond it, is glimpsed the street crowd who, on 14 July, would become the heroes of the conquest of the Bastille and the savage mob of late nineteenth-century imaginings.

Illustration 16   Jacques-Louis David, *Le Serment du Jeu de Paume (The Tennis Court Oath)*. Sylvain Bailly (elevated centre) leads the oath

That Irving frequently drew on the visual arts in organising his scenes is well documented. Edward Gordon Craig identified Honoré Daumier, John Gilbert and Gustave Doré as strong influences and, more recently, Alan Hughes noticed the importance to Irving's *Richard III* of Edwin Abbey's 1896 painting of Richard courting Lady Anne,[70] but the effect in *Robespierre* is particularly interesting. Since Irving's is the Revolution in the grip of the Terror, the blissful dawn long gone, he traduces the mood and historical moment of David's picture. This is Hippolyte Taine's or Gustave Le Bon's ferocious crowd, not David's optimistic one. Robespierre, hands ardently clutched to breast in David's picture, is now the one at odds with the dominant mood. But this very traducing contributes to the impact. Just as David had been forced to

---

70   Edward Gordon Craig, *Henry Irving* (London, 1930), pp. 127–134; Hughes, *Henry Irving*, pp. 158–9.

abandon the painting as his figures, carefully drawn from life, were successively eliminated, so Irving's superimposition of the Terror's culminating moment on to this iconic image of revolutionary optimism, supplied a terrible historic irony, whether or not individual audience members so rationalised it.

That sense of intensified experience in an audience brought to witness the ironies of history was further complicated by the contemporary historical moment. Max Beerbohm might jeer that 'that orgy of prigs and cutthroats' had 'now no significance except as providing background for melodramas in London',[71] but some, at least, of Irving's audience found contemporary resonances. The stage image of a pack of French deputies turning on and silencing an individual to his destruction shadowed current events in France at the moment when certainty about the rights of such destruction were evaporating. Zola's publication of 'J'accuse'[72] and his subsequent prosecution for libel, had stimulated increasingly fierce and partisan debate over the conviction and deportation in 1894 of Captain Dreyfus, which would culminate in June 1899, during the run of *Robespierre*, in the announcement of a retrial. The *Westminster Budget* thought that the scene presented 'a vivid idea' of the current French convulsions,[73] while *Today* judged that 'the wild frenzy of the National Convention upon the 9th of Thermidor has only been equalled in the French Chamber during a Dreyfus interpellation'.[74]

The kind of transformation imposed, wittingly or not, on the play is a marker of the eclipse of romanticised history, at least in the theatre.[75] When Revolutionary leaders again made an impact on European stages it was in the intense drama-documentary format of *Danton's Death*, a play directly concerned with the crushing of individuals by the movement of history. Büchner's play, unperformed and probably unperformable when written in 1835, was first produced in Germany in 1902 and claimed its place in the international repertoire with its 1916 production by Max Reinhardt, the new master of stage crowds, who again 'filled the theatre with the fickle, lurid, terrifying cyclone of the French Revolution'[76] and prepared the way for the twentieth century's succession of 'plotless' history plays, from Shaw's *Saint Joan* (1924) through Stanislawa Przybyszewska's *The Danton Case* (1927), to Brecht's *Galileo* (1943) and Andrez Wajda's film based on Przybyszewska, *Danton* (1982).

How long do Brookian traces survive before they are lost, or absorbed into the collective memory? In 1907 journalists, attempting to convey the power of Granville Barker's staging of the Trafalgar Square suffrage meeting in Elizabeth Robins' *Votes for Women*, again engaged in comparative citation. The *Sunday Times* declared

---

71 Beerbohm, *More Theatres*, p. 136.
72 Published on the front page of *L'Aurore*, 13 January 1898.
73 *Westminster Budget*, 21 April 1899.
74 *Today*, 27 April 1899.
75 *The Only Way* toured into the twentieth century, and 'escaping aristocrat' intrigue figured in Baroness Orczy's *Scarlet Pimpernel* (produced by Fred Terry, 1903). Romain Rolland's *Danton* (1900) launched his 40-year attempt to present the revolution as epic theatre. Revolutionary romance flourished in cinema in, for example, Vitagraph's three-reel *A Tale of Two Cities* (1911) and Fox's seven-reel version, directed by Frank Lloyd (1917).
76 *New York Post*, 12 December 1929.

'Mr Tree's *Julius Caesar* crowd is quite eclipsed and M. Antoine at his best could not have done better',[77] while the *Sketch* found it 'the finest stage crowd that has been seen for years, not excepting the particularly good ones in Mr Tree's production of *Julius Caesar* and in *Robespierre*'.[78] Whereas the *Julius Caesar*s of Antoine and Beerbohm Tree were in current production, the mere name of *Robespierre,* six years since its last outing, could evidently provide a touchstone. But the cost of huge casts was already becoming prohibitive.

Barker's astonishing crowd, on a cusp between realist and representative staging, numbered only some 20 supers. Lady Benson was not alone in attributing Irving's ruin to the 'enormous sums lavished on the dressing and mounting of his tremendous productions' where 'each super was as correctly and properly dressed as the principals'.[79] Consciousness of this and of a wages bill that, for *Robespierre*, ran to £1,000 a week[80] no doubt informed Irving's curiously predictive suggestion:

> Why wouldn't it be a good idea to furnish biograph supernumeraries? You could by means of that wonderful invention, have a procession of four or five hundred on the stage at once, and think of the enormous expense spared. Why, in *Dante* I have four or five hundred people employed. Now with a biograph attachment – .[81]

Production costs contributed to Antoine's bankruptcy at the *Théâtre Libre* in 1894 and again at the *Odéon* in 1914. Beerbohm Tree stayed in profit but, in Hollywood in 1916, recorded his amazement at the 'veritable Babylon ... peopled by thousands of actors' he saw on the set of D.W. Griffith's *Intolerance*.[82] The first full-length feature film, Enrico Guzzoni's *Quo Vadis?* in 1912, featured a crowd of 3,000, and Antoine's first engagement in the silent film industry, an adaptation of Victor Hugo's *Quatre-Vingt-Treize* (1874, film released 1921), included resources for crowd scenes undreamt in his theatre. The contrast between theatre's constantly recurring wages bills and the capacity to recoup cinema's initial costs through multiply reproduced prints was stark. The camera's capacity for long-shot, close-up, and sharp or soft focus, and the ability to edit, also enabled a new kind of directorial control.

A century later, while cinema rejoices in its digitally enhanced crowd scenes, the theatre is mainly given over to small-cast plays, and crowd scenes present a recurrent staging problem. One of Deborah Warner's conditions for directing *Julius Caesar* at the Barbican in 2005 was that she be allowed a 100-strong crowd. The *Observer* quoted her as saying: '100 singing [in the opera chorus] is exciting, we have heard it before. A hundred actors shouting – rough, rude and anarchic – is utterly unknown.'[83] Disappointingly, Warner relied on voice, rather than movement, to suggest insurgency. Her crowd, updated to the present, was largely held at the sides of the stage, behind crowd control barriers. Sheer numbers did allow a glimpse

---

77 *Sunday Times*, 14 April 1907.
78 *Sketch*, 15 May 1907.
79 'I Knew Henry Irving', 2 February 1938, THM.
80 Irving, *Henry Irving*, p. 628.
81 *New York Sun*, 8 November 1903.
82 *The Times*, 8 September 1916.
83 *Observer*, 10 April 2005.

of the impact that anarchic crowds must have made on *fin de siècle* stages, but these registered more like an English holiday crowd than a mob precipitating the end of an Eastern bloc regime or protesting against Western infidels; it was difficult to believe such a crowd could change the course of history.

This was hardly the case a century earlier, when stages teemed with life. Irving's crowd management, like that of Antoine and Beerbohm Tree, was honed through trial and error and intensive rehearsal. The practice of colleagues and rivals, as well as the discriminating expectations of audiences and critics primed with sensitivity to crowd psychology and stage practice, supplied both challenge and spur.

Chapter 9

Serenade in a Gondola: Music and Interpolated Action in Irving's Production of *The Merchant of Venice*

Stephen Cockett

Irving made numerous cuts to *The Merchant of Venice*, first performed on 1 November 1879. He dispensed with the Prince of Arragon, eliminated deprecatory comments about Shylock by the Christians along with lines by Portia that might offend her audience's sensibilities, and abbreviated lyrically ornate passages in Bassanio's casket scene. At the end of the Act II, however, he added a carefully wrought after-piece that was entirely of his own creation. In this interpolation, Lorenzo steals Jessica away with his comrades over the canal bridge while a gondola carrying serenaders crosses the stage and disappears into the distance. Then a group of revelling masquers run on to the stage, pass Shylock's house and cross over the canal in the direction of the eloping lovers. The curtain falls and then rises after a few moments on the scene later in the evening: Shylock returns alone from dinner with the Christians back across the bridge to his empty house. As he approaches the door the curtain falls.

From our perspective, the interpolation seems not especially remarkable as an example of the director's art, but it took Irving's contemporaries by surprise. The *Saturday Review* described it as 'a singularly fine touch of invention'.[1] Ellen Terry, reflecting in her memoirs on the features of Irving's Shylock that touched people to their hearts, said that 'for absolute pathos, achieved by absolute simplicity of means, I never saw anything in the theatre to compare with Shylock's return home over the bridge to his deserted house after Jessica's flight'.[2] Even William Archer, in his withering study of Irving, actor and manager, cited the interpolation as an instance of Irving's genius as a 'regisseur'.[3]

Orchestral accompaniment was integral to Irving's concept of the elopement scene and its after-piece, the dynamic shape of which might be compared to a musical score. Indeed, Irving committed more orchestral support to the episode than to any other part of the play, and had entrusted the task of writing the score to Hamilton Clarke, his newly appointed musical director at the Lyceum and an established composer in his own right. While descriptions of the setting for *The*

---

[1] *Saturday Review*, 8 November 1879.
[2] Ellen Terry, *Ellen Terry's Memoirs*, ed. Edith Craig and Christopher St John (London, 1933), p. 146.
[3] William Archer, *Henry Irving Actor and Manager: A Critical Study* (London, 1883), p. 99.

Merchant of Venice with its exquisite detail and mellow tones figure prominently in critical reviews,[4] the musical score attracts no more than a passing mention. But this was so with most theatre music to spoken plays in the period and is not perhaps surprising given that orchestral accompaniment for the actor, to be effective, had to keep a low profile. This principle has changed little over time: film music today shares with the nineteenth-century theatre orchestra a similar purpose to heighten dramatic intensity, yet rarely does it receive the degree of critical acclaim afforded to acting and cinematography. Music should underscore the moving image without drawing attention to itself. Norman O'Neill, an experienced composer of music for stage plays, writing in 1911, said that 'it is not always so much the intrinsic value of the music as its appropriateness and aptness which make it successful from a theatrical point of view'.[5] Music should serve the drama, never the reverse.

The life span of a musical score in the nineteenth century was generally limited to the length of the production run. Excepting instances where incidental music by more celebrated composers such as Mendelssohn and Sullivan made it to the concert platform and eventually to the recording studio, music to spoken plays remained in the orchestra pit, only rarely to be archived. This lack of access to music to the spoken play in the nineteenth century hinders a retrospective view of how scenes worked in performance and of the specific contribution of orchestral accompaniment to the overall effect. Irving's *The Merchant of Venice* is a fortunate exception. Though the orchestral parts to Clarke's music no longer exist, a copy of a piano transcription of the score, published at the time of the opening performance in 1879, is held at the British Library. The transcription was a commercial enterprise (price £2s 6d) and gave members of the audience an opportunity to enjoy the music on the piano at home, rather like the CD of a popular show today, while earning extra revenue for the Lyceum. It includes all the main music cues as indicated in the production prompt book in the Theatre Museum, and provides a basis for exploring the function and effect of music in the production and, in particular, the interpolated episode.

Irving's instinct for the use of music within the performance event has been overshadowed by critical interest in his skills as actor and manager. Yet, more than any other theatrical figure of his time, he advanced the interrelationship between music from the pit and action on stage. In the first place, he eschewed the standard practice of underscoring every character entry and sensational stage business with 'hurries', 'melos' and sentimental hymn-like tunes, and he employed some of the finest composers of his day who could write without resort to musical cliché. But, more importantly, he applied an unerring sense of how music could make a distinctive contribution to the effect he was trying to create for his audience, and evidence suggests that he achieved this without the aid of a musical ear. He knew when the music was inappropriate, and would say so, and would pass deserved compliments when the music was 'right', but communicating exactly what he wanted the music to *do* was more of a problem. Musical ideas resist expression by words and gesture,

---

4 For a full description of set and costumes see Percy Fitzgerald, *Henry Irving: Twenty Years at the Lyceum,* (London, 1893), pp. 129–31.

5 Norman O'Neill, 'Music to Stage Plays', a paper given to the Musical Association on 21 March 1911, in Derek Hudson, *Norman O'Neill: A Life of Music* (London, 1945), p. 128.

and pressures of the production process made communication between Irving and his musical director all the more strained. In the case of *The Merchant of Venice*, the patience of both parties was yet more severely tried by a rehearsal schedule compressed into just three weeks between proposal and opening night.

Hamilton Clarke, no less than other musical directors, felt the force of Irving's demands. Ellen Terry remembered how

> Hamilton Clarke often grew angry and flung out of the theatre, saying that it was quite impossible to do what Mr Irving required.
>
> 'Patch it together, indeed!' he used to say to me indignantly, when I was told off to smooth him down. 'Mr Irving knows nothing about music, or he wouldn't ask me to do such a thing.'
>
> But the next day he would return with the score altered on the lines suggested by Henry, and would confess that the music had been improved.
>
> 'Upon my soul, it's better! The Guv'nor was perfectly right.'
>
> His Danish march in 'Hamlet', his Brocken scene in 'Faust' and his music for 'The Merchant of Venice' were all, to my mind, exactly *right*.[6]

The piano transcription of the music to *The Merchant of Venice* includes the overture, entr'acte pieces between all the acts (Irving restored Act V, traditionally omitted from productions of *The Merchant of Venice*), music in the two casket scenes with Morocco and Bassanio, including the song in Shakespeare's text 'Tell Me Where Is Fancy Bred?', a song in the final Belmont scene, and three pieces that make up the incidental accompaniment to the interpolated scene: music as a gondola crosses the stage, a serenade in a gondola, and the music of the carnival masquers. Clarke linked most of the pieces thematically: music for the masquers, the Prince of Morocco and the serenade in the gondola are 'announced' in the overture to facilitate recognition when heard again within the play. Music played as the Prince of Morocco chooses the casket repeats the preceding entr'acte music, but the song 'Tell Me Where...' is heard for the first time during Bassanio's casket scene. Clarke employs two contrasting rhythms throughout: the barcarolle, originally a folk song sung by Venetian gondoliers in 6/8 time with a strumming rhythm reflecting the stroke of the oar; and a faster 2/4 polka-like dance of the masquers.

Given the nineteenth-century practice of associating musical themes with particular characters and also Irving's determination to foreground Shylock and the bond plot at the expense of the romance scenes, it is surprising that not a single note in the score for *The Merchant of Venice* is associated directly with the Jew. Apart from musical 'flourishes' accompanying the entries and exits of the Prince of Morocco and the Doge, all the music belongs to Belmont and Venice carnival. In addition, each piece of music heard during the performance of a scene has a *diagetic* function – that is, it forms part of the narrative world of the play: the songs at Belmont are sung by musicians in Portia's employ, serenaders sing from the gondola, cavorting masquers play their own pipes and tabors, though all of them with off-stage orchestral support. The overture and entr'actes serve to reinforce the melodies and rhythms of the Christian world through anticipation and repetition.

---

6 Terry, *Ellen Terry's Memoirs*, pp. 121–2.

The world of Belmont is characterised in part by its music. Here, the notion that music is made up of the tones, intervals and rhythms emitted by movements of the spheres, popular in the sixteenth and seventeenth centuries, finds its fullest expression in Shakespeare. In the final scene, on a bank where 'sweet the moonlight sleeps', Lorenzo tutors the melancholy Jessica:

> There's not the smallest orb which thou behold'st
> But in his motion like an angel sings,
> Still quiring to the young-ey'd cherubins;
> Such harmony is in immortal souls,
> But whilst this muddy vesture of decay
> Doth grossly close it in, we cannot hear it.

He instructs musicians 'to wake Diana with a hymn, and with sweetest touches pierce their mistress' ear, and draw her home with music'. The world of Belmont induces surrender to the power of music. By contrast, Shylock's world allows no such possibility: here, music is 'the vile squeaking of the wryneck'd fife', abhorrent sounds made by physically contorted players. With song and instrument forbidden, no instances arise for diagetic music. The imperative in this world is silence. For the director, though, this still allows the use of music non-diagetically, as disembodied accompaniment offstage to reflect mood, mediate character, and add emotional colour. But Irving chose not to do so: with music characterising and expressing the Christian world, the focus of attention turns indirectly on Shylock as outsider; the silence of his world amplifies his isolation.

In film, music is inseparable from the visual narrative in the ways in which it intersects with images, words and sounds. It mediates other elements by speaking directly to the emotions, evoking mood, deepening identification with character and commenting on events. But this is so only because we know what certain types of musical sounds mean: we have learnt the code; particular sounds mean particular things.[7] In nineteenth-century theatre, music served a similar function to music in film and was similarly inseparable from the performance event. To appreciate as fully as possible a performance in its time, the music must be heard: hearing the music enables us not only to appreciate the aural code and its emotional and dramatic effect in performance, but also to understand the interrelationship between music and stage action. For this purpose, I have recorded the music from the piano transcription to the interpolated scene and the three other incidental pieces integrated into scenic action. The recordings were made digitally with instrumental samples and a computer sequencer. While the results lack the authenticity of a recording made by actual musicians in a studio, they are adequate for the purposes of this inquiry and were produced at a small fraction of the cost (many film scores today are created on similar digital systems).[8] Inevitably, the recording process entailed some guesswork: we cannot know exactly what instructions Irving gave to his orchestra

---

7   Anahid Kassabian, *Hearing Film* (New York, 2001), pp. 16–17.

8   Three types of software were used in the recording process: *Sibelius* for notation and scoring, *Garritan Personal Orchestra* for orchestral samples and *Cubase SX* for mixing and editing.

about tempo, volume and feel, but the musical signs in the piano transcription, and the style of the music itself, indicate how the music should be heard. All cues for starting and finishing the music are marked clearly in the promptbook.

Before examining the interpolated scene in detail, I would like briefly to look at the three other instances of incidental music in the play. In each case the recording follows the piano transcription faithfully, but replaces the human voice with an orchestral instrument in the second and third examples – the song heard while Bassanio chooses the casket (flute) and the song in the final Belmont scene with Lorenzo and Jessica (oboe) – the reason being that, while orchestral instruments can be accurately sampled for digital recording, the human voice cannot. (The reader may, of course, with the melody as guide, sing the text of the song to the accompaniment provided.)

The Prince of Morocco Chooses the Casket

Irving merged the two Prince of Morocco appearances in a single scene at the beginning of Act III. Musical accompaniment commences with Portia's invitation to the Prince, 'Now Make your Choice', and continues through his speech (from which Irving cut only four lines) to 'Here Do I Choose and Thrive as I May'. The caskets are located upstage left, Portia and Nerissa downstage just right of centre, flanked by a formal grouping of nobles, ladies and pages.

Play CD track 1.

The Prince's speech is encompassed by a single arcing melody in 2/4 time with harmonic shifts and modulations reflecting the Prince's thoughts, returning to the tonal base at the point of his choice. The feel is light, understated and ironic, in contrast to the Prince's sonorous and self-assured deliberations, suggesting that the music's purpose is to underscore the actions of Portia and Nerissa who, seated downstage, were able to engage in by-play out of the Prince's view. Ellen Terry's Portia, described by William Winter as a woman who is 'as ardent in temperament as she is fine in brain and various and splendid in personal peculiarities and feminine charm',[9] would surely have exploited the possibilities of acting with music which serves as a comment on the pompous Morocco, as well as to set mood.

Song as Bassanio Chooses the Casket

Clarke's setting of the song in Shakespeare's text is heard as Bassanio deliberates his choice.

Play CD track 2.

---

[9] In Jeffrey Richards, *Henry Irving: A Victorian Actor and His World* (London, 2005), p. 46.

Here, the mood of the song, also in 2/4 time, is more intense and romantic with no hint of ironic comment. Critics commented that Portia's anxiety could be 'seen in her face, in her eyes, in her twitching fingers',[10] and while Bassanio made his choice, she barely suppressed her surging love for him, showing a 'coming-on' disposition that was considered too forward by some critics, notably Henry James and John Ruskin. In later years Terry was influenced by an Italian article on *The Merchant of Venice*, suggesting that Portia had deliberately chosen the song in order to guide Bassanio to the right casket: 'I like this idea, and why shouldn't Portia sing the song herself? She could make the four rhymes, "bred, head, nourished, fed", set the word "lead" ringing in Bassanio's ears. A woman of Portia's sort couldn't possibly remain passive in such a crisis in her life.'[11]

Song in Act V – Belmont

As Lorenzo muses with Jessica on the 'sweet power of music', Portia's musicians perform their part. Here, Clarke introduces a new melody, but in the 6/8 time and rhythm of the barcarolle, echoing the serenade in the gondola as the lovers eloped. The text calls for instrumental music, but Irving elevates the interlude to the performance of a song to words that have no origin in Shakespeare:

> O lovely night, O hour of rarest pleasure,
> Bless'd with the glow of Luna's tend'rest light,
> Goddess of Love, thou fill'st with holiest treasure
> Each heart that throbs responsive to thy might [last 2 lines repeated].

Unlike the other music cues, there is no indication in the promptbook that the song was sung over speech, so it is likely that it was heard in its entirety between Lorenzo's call to 'wake Diana with a hymn' and Jessica's comment, 'I am never merry when I hear sweet music'. A pause after the song before she speaks would have added emphasis to her mood, suggesting deeper thoughts that Lorenzo, mystical stargazer, misreads.

Play CD track 3.

The Elopement Scene and Interpolated Episode

Irving reserved his main musical attentions for the elopement scene and its afterpiece at the end of Act II. From the entry of a gondola in the distance after Shylock leaves to dine with the Christians through to his return to his empty house, music is heard almost continuously. In this instance the limitations of the piano transcription are more apparent, for the effect of the scene in performance must have depended on a rich orchestral sound. In an attempt at a fuller realisation of the score performed at the Lyceum I have scored the piano version for theatre orchestra and used instrumental

---

10 *The Times*, 3 November 1879.
11 Terry, *Ellen Terry's Memoirs*, p. 152.

Illustration 17   *The Merchant of Venice*: Act II Scene 3: Shylock's House by a Bridge

samples in the recording. Imagining how Clarke deployed the instruments of his orchestra is, of course, even more speculative than recording the published piano transcription: variables in orchestration are endless, making the task of re-creating the original score with exactitude a fruitless task. But the piano transcription gives some indications of the original instrumentation and the constitution of the orchestra, and use of instrumental sections may be deduced from Clarke's own *Manual of Orchestration*, published in 1888, in which he discusses the specific requirements of the theatre orchestra.[12] The Lyceum regularly had 26 to 28 players in the pit, and Clarke advised that an orchestra of this size should comprise two flutes, one oboe, two clarinets, one bassoon, two horns, two cornets, one trombone, percussion, six first violins, four second violins, two violas, two cellos and two double basses. The piano transcription of music for *The Merchant of Venice* indicates the use of a harp. A special problem for the theatre orchestra, Clarke advises, is that the strings, through reduced numbers, lack the strength of sections in a large orchestra and require support from wind instruments: flute, oboe and clarinet for violins and

---

12 Hamilton Clarke, *A Manual of Orchestration: Designed Especially to Enable the Amateur to Follow Intelligently the Performance of Orchestral Music* (London, 1888).

violas; bassoon and trombone for cellos and basses. His manual also offers a clear exposition of the basic rules of traditional orchestral practice, discussing various sonorities that may be achieved through particular instrumental combinations, the merits of sparse writing, how to distribute harmonies across instrumental sections for tone and balance, and mood effects of particular instruments. Clarke also cannot resist the occasional jibe at modern composers fond of making instruments play 'out of character'. Theatre music to spoken plays of the period was not distinguished by experimental sorties into new musical territory, and Clarke's manual gives a practical insight into established methods of deploying a theatre pit orchestra. I have attempted to apply his principles in my orchestrations.

A sketch in the promptbook of the set outside Shylock's house designed by Hawes Craven bears many similarities to the layout in William Telbin's design for Charles Kean's production in 1858. The bridge, the physical focus for stage action, is placed more centrally, with Shylock's house located downstage left. Movement between house and bridge to the exit centrestage left cuts a double diagonal, with the canal beneath the bridge creating a line intersecting both diagonals between Shylock's house and the upstage stage centre right entry (Illustration 17).

The musical score in the elopement scene and interpolated episode begins not with the first notes of incidental accompaniment, but with the silence that concludes the previous scene: Shylock, outside his house, orders Jessica to lock up his doors and 'stop my house's ears'; Launcelot, in gentle mockery of his master, whispers to Jessica to keep an eye open for Lorenzo who is about to arrive with masquers. Shylock then takes his leave of Jessica in order to keep his appointment for dinner with the Christians. He slowly winds his way up the steps of the bridge, leaning heavily on his stick, lantern in hand, and murmuring to himself, 'Fast bind, fast bind...' (II.5.52). 'Pausing at the top, he glanced once more at the home he is loath to leave; then, keeping his eyes fixed on his daughter, he slowly ambled off.'[13] In her *Memoirs* Ellen Terry remembers that, in later years, Irving made one change to his dress at this point:

> He asked my daughter – whose cleverness in such things he fully recognised – to put some stage jewels on to the scarf that he wore round his head when he supped with the Christians.
>
> 'I have an idea that, when he went to supper, he'd like to flaunt his wealth in the Christian dogs' faces. It will look well, too – "like the toad, ugly and venomous", wearing precious jewels on his head!'[14]

All sound fades with the tapping of Shylock's stick in the distance, leaving Jessica, alone, to muse: 'if my fortune be not crost, I have a father, you a daughter, lost.' At this point, music, 'as a gondola crosses the stage', breaks the silence. The piano transcription indicates *sempre staccato* throughout, suggesting that it was played by *pizzicato* strings.

---

13 James C. Bulman, *The Merchant of Venice*, Shakespeare in Performance Series (Manchester, 1991), p. 37.

14 Terry, *Ellen Terry's Memoirs*, p. 147.

Play CD track 4.

The running time is one and a half minutes – short for a piece of music, yet a considerable length of time between scenes in a play, but, as the music plays, various characters populate the stage, creating the world of 'shallow fopp'ry' that Shylock has forbidden Jessica to witness. The action follows a prescribed sequence: a gondola with a lady seated in it and a noble reclining on the prow playing a zither, and rowed (in fact punted) by a gondolier, enters from behind Shylock's house front stage left. The gondola crosses, passes under the bridge and exits upstage right. While music plays, two ladies and a noble enter arm-in-arm downstage left in front of Shylock's house, followed by another noble, all of them masked and laughing. They cross over the stage to steps on the bridge and look over at the passing gondola. Gratiano, Salanio and Solarino, all masked, enter from centre left and encounter the nobles and ladies on the bridge. They step to one side, allowing the party to pass, bowing to them, the others returning the salute and moving off centre left. The concluding *pizzicato* chords are heard as Gratiano, Salanio and Solarino look across to Shylock's house from the bridge:

Gra: This is the penthouse under which Lorenzo
 Desired us to stand.
Sal: His hour is almost past.
Gra: And it is marvel he out-dwells his hour,
 For lovers ever run before the clock.

They converse for 13 lines (six of Gratiano's lines being cut). Lorenzo then enters from centre left and meets them on the bridge, and together they descend the steps. Lorenzo crosses to Shylock's house while the others remain by the bridge:

Lor: Sweet friends, your patience for my long abode
 (Not I but my affairs have made you wait): ...
 Here dwells my father Jew.

Jessica appears above and, during her exchange with Lorenzo, throws down the ducats. He then playfully pretends to lose the box and Jessica re-enters the house to 'make fast the doors':

Lor: Beshrew me but I love her heartily,
 For she is wise, if I can judge of her,
 And fair she is, if that mine eyes be true.

At this point, the gondola returns from upstage right carrying a group of serenaders holding 'coloured lanthorns'. It moves slowly under the bridge, coming to a halt in front of Jessica's window. As the gondola moves, the serenaders sing a song with the rhythm of a barcarolle, accompanied by the harp in the orchestra. The melody (given to the oboe on the recording) is sung to the first four lines of Sonnet 39:

> Oh how thy worth with manners may I sing,
> When thou art all the better part of me?
> What can mine own praise to mine own self bring?
> And what is't but mine own when I praise thee?

Then, as Jessica re-enters:

> Lor: What, art thou come? – on gentlemen away!
> Our masquing mates by this time for us stay.

Lorenzo and Jessica leave quickly across the bridge, followed by the others and disappearing centre stage left. Antonio's entrance is cut from the scene. The gondola moves away from Shylock's house towards the upstage exit, the singers repeating the serenade and gradually fading into the distance. Then a group of masquers with tabor and pipes, followed by a group of dancers with jangling bells and more tabors, enter downstage left past Shylock's house. All of them are masked, many carrying 'coloured lanthorns'. They shout and dance, crossing the stage up the steps and over the bridge. Then a group of girls rush on, screaming, pursued by another group of male masquers over the bridge and out centre left. The curtain drops.

Play CD track 5: serenade and masquers' music.

In the piano transcription the music for the 'serenade in a gondola' is followed immediately by the masquers' music. The CD recording adheres to this sequence, but in performance the 'serenade', as we have seen, was sung twice. For a correct alignment of the music cue for cue with the text, track 5 should be played on Lorenzo's 'and fair she is, if that mine eyes be true', then paused at the end of the serenade; and when Lorenzo and Jessica leave, the track should be replayed from the beginning, without pause, through to the end of the masquers' music.

As the masquers cross the bridge and disappear centre left, the curtain descends and rises quickly on the same scene, now empty and silent. There is no light, except for a pale moon. In the silence the tapping of Shylock's stick is heard – first from afar, then drawing nearer. Shylock enters (Illustration 18) carrying a lantern, preoccupied, slowly wending his way home after dinner. Wearily he crosses the bridge, descends the steps and crosses to his house. As he approaches the door, the curtain falls, signifying the end of the act. Following applause, the orchestra strikes up with the entr'acte music (*CD track 1*) that precedes the Prince of Morocco's casket scene, setting a change of mood.

Robert Hitchens, who saw Irving perform the role of Shylock, commented that:

> Irving had a remarkable power of impressing an audience in silence. He proved this in the scene of Shylock's return to his empty dwelling after his daughter had left it. It was an absolutely silent scene. One simply saw the figure of the Jew in the shadows walking slowly and alone to his house. But who that saw that figure can ever forget it? I at least cannot.[15]

---

15 Robert Hitchens, 'Irving as Shylock', in H.A. Saintsbury and Cecil Palmer, eds, *We Saw Him Act: A Symposium on the Art of Sir Henry Irving* (London, 1939), p. 168.

Illustration 18   *The Merchant of Venice*: Act II Scene 3: Shylock Returning Home

It is significant that Hitchens's memory skips over the colour and musical vitality of the elopement scene to the 'absolute' silence of Shylock's return. Silence intensifies the meaning of the simplest stage actions; it gives the audience space to think, feel and interpret what they see. The interpolated scene, though brief, is charged with meaning framed by silence.

The section from Shylock's departure for his evening with the Christians to the curtain fall on his return home forms a coherent unit within the dramatic narrative. Irving shapes the dynamic of the unit to reach its focal point in the final seconds – that is, in the afterpiece he has created, not in Shakespeare's scene. Though there is more elaborate stage business and musical interest in the elopement scene, the point of dramatic 'arrival' is Shylock's return to his empty house. It is as if Irving visualised this moment, then, thinking backwards, assembled the elements needed to give it maximum potency.

Music underscores each section of the elopement scene to Shylock's entry. From the first note, it sets a dramatic momentum: strings played *pizzicato* build a tension signalling that something is about to happen. The animated and exuberant movements of the characters contrast with the musical accompaniment set in a minor key, anticipating other business while suspending development towards it. Unity of musical form adds shape to diverse stage business: the characters' entries, their encounter on the bridge, passing and leaving, the approach of the gondola. The barcarolle, seductive and romantic, shifts the mood, the serenaders singing together, their lanterns lilting and gliding away in the half-light. The crowd of masquers cuts in with staccato dance rhythms accented by tabors, their noise and exuberant revelry filling the stage as gondola and serenade fade into the distance. Then all rhythm and melody of romance and carnival fall away to silence – a silence 'underscored' by the absence of music – and the moment is set for Shylock's return.

Irving's use of this silence changed over time. The audience watching one of the early performances saw Shylock come over the bridge and approach his house, the curtain dropping before he reaches the door. Laurence Irving, in his biography of his grandfather, remembers an adapted ending introduced in later performances:

> After the elopement of Jessica and Lorenzo, the curtain fell slowly as the maskers, sweeping across the stage, swallowed them up. After a second or two it rose again upon an empty stage. Shylock was seen returning over the bridge. He crossed to his house and, unsuspecting, knocked upon the door.
>
> A second and third knock echoed through the empty house. The curtain fell again as, without word or sign, Irving conveyed to the audience Shylock's crushing realisation of the perfidy of his daughter.[16]

In this version the audience witnesses Shylock's realisation of his betrayal. By dwelling on this moment, Irving significantly altered the meaning and effect of the interpolation:

> The *Herald*, 7 November 1883, noted how Shylock knocking at his door, finds himself robbed and deserted by his daughter, and the unrelieved simplicity of Irving's characterisation as he stands there, waiting, waiting, while the curtain slowly descends.[17]

The stillness draws compassion for a man deeply wronged:

> ... by so poignantly portraying a man betrayed by his own flesh and blood, Irving appealed to the sacred Victorian belief in the obedience of children, a belief here violated by a rebellious daughter who in the opinion of the *Spectator*, 'amply justifies his plain distrust of her, an odious, immodest, dishonest creature, than whom Shakespeare drew no more unpleasant character' (8 November 1879).[18]

The adapted version better suited Irving's purpose to portray Shylock not as the stereotypical snuffling usurer with hooked nose, malignant in his desire for revenge,

---

16 Laurence Irving, *Henry Irving: The Actor and His World* (London, 1951), p. 341.

17 Toby Lelyveld, *Shylock on the Stage* (Cleveland, 1960), p. 85.

18 Bulman, *The Merchant Of Venice*, p. 38.

but as a more rounded religious Jew, learned and Bible-read: 'the type of a persecuted race, almost the only gentleman in the play, and the most-ill used' whose 'speech is always lofty, and full of dignity'.[19] The *Examiner* described Irving's Shylock as 'a man ruled, not by one, but many passions; a man with manifold characteristics, and swayed by opposing influences, and therefore a natural man'.[20] Irving used the interpolation specifically to manipulate sympathy for Shylock, and the adapted ending tightened the screw.

It is a commonplace in modern theatre that some of the most potent moments are moments of stillness and silence. In this particular instance, Irving knew that, having established a silence, it should be held to the very end. Ruling out further musical underscoring shows remarkable restraint, given the times and tradition in which he was working. Most musical directors of the period would have seen it as an imperative of established practice, if not of principle, that the 'image of the father convulsed with grief'[21] should be accompanied by music: what more deserving cue could there be for a melody that touches the heartstrings, understated if necessary, reinforcing pathos and compassion? Clarke would certainly have been able to provide such accompaniment, but Irving's instinct was to let the silence flow naturally as a continuation of the dramatic narrative. Power to manipulate the moment was his alone.

Yet, given that the invented after-piece fitted so seamlessly into Shakespeare's text, it is puzzling that Irving insisted on a curtain drop between the exit of the masquers and the entrance of Shylock. The effect of Shylock's entry would seem to depend on continuity, but a curtain drop, like a soundless blackout, has the effect of halting the drama – everything stops. The drop also signals ending and a cue for applause, and applause breaks the audience's concentration, which, in this instance, Irving would have had to recover after the curtain rise. The point was not lost on the critic for the *Spectator* following the opening night:

> Lorenzo has fled with his stolen bride and her stolen money, and a crowd of masquers has crossed the stage and disappeared over the picturesque bridge with laughter and music. Then Shylock is seen, lantern in hand, advancing, bent in thought; and, as he comes close to his robbed and deserted house, the curtain falls. The effect, however, would, to our thinking, be doubled if the curtain had not fallen for a moment and been raised again just before this appearance of Shylock – if the masquers had disappeared in sight of the audience, and the sounds of revelry had died away in the distance. It may be conjectured that the dropping of the curtain signifies the interval of time which might naturally elapse between the elopement and Shylock's return; but this, we think, is needless.[22]

A note in the piano transcription, however, indicates that 'the curtain descends during the following music, which continues pianissimo until the curtain has risen again discovering Shylock returning across the bridge to his house, when the curtain descends again'. It is possible that the music played pianissimo held off applause

---

19 Joseph Hatton, *Irving's Impressions of America* (Boston, 1884) pp. 224–33.
20 *Examiner*, 8 November 1879.
21 William Winter in Lelyveld, *Shylock on the Stage*, p. 85.
22 *Spectator*, 8 November 1879.

long enough for the curtain to rise, though there must have been a risk that it would not. For an actor who borrowed the interpolation from Irving, this was a risk too far:

> A younger actor, producing 'The Merchant of Venice' in recent years, asked Irving if he might borrow this bit of business. 'By all means', said Henry. 'With great pleasure.'
>
> 'Then why didn't you do it?' inquired my daughter bluntly when the actor was telling us how kind and courteous Henry had been in allowing him to use his stroke of invention.
>
> 'What do you mean?' asked the astonished actor.
>
> My daughter told him that Henry had dropped the curtain on a stage full of noise, and light, and revelry. When it went up again the stage was empty, desolate, and with no light but a pale moon, and all sounds of life at a great distance – and then over the bridge came the weary figure of the Jew. This marked the passing of the time between Jessica's elopement and Shylock's return home. It created an atmosphere of silence, and the middle of the night.
>
> 'You came back without dropping the curtain', said my daughter, 'and so it wasn't a bit the same.'
>
> 'I couldn't risk dropping the curtain for the business', answered the actor, '*because it needed applause to take it up again!*'[23]

A feature of Irving the actor that won admiration from his colleagues was his willingness to consider opinion and incorporate revisions to his performance during a play's run, but, on the matter of the curtain drop between the elopement scene and its after-piece, he held firm to his view that it should remain.

---

23 Terry, *Ellen Terry's Memoirs*, pp. 146–7.

Chapter 10
Arthur Sullivan's Incidental Music to Henry Irving's Production of *Macbeth* (1888)

Kenneth DeLong

Although incidental music formed an integral part of Victorian theatrical productions, there is, as yet, only a limited body of scholarship that addresses such fundamental questions as the circumstances of its creation, what kind of music was used, how it was fitted to the stage action, or how it contributed to the total dramatic effect. While a considerable amount of Victorian theatre music survives, much of it exists in a fragmentary or incomplete form, making it a difficult, even exasperating, subject of study. This situation is exacerbated by the often makeshift circumstances that surrounded the composition of incidental music, in which ad hoc decisions had to be made at the last moment, rapid insertions and deletions fashioned, and connecting musical tissue quickly concocted. The musical scores that have survived in a form sufficiently complete that they can serve as the basis of an extended study are relatively few; and even with the complete score to hand there comes the additional problem of reconstructing the specific production for which the music was composed.[1]

---

1 Two useful articles on this subject, treating the early Victorian period, are David Mayer, 'Nineteenth Century Theatre Music', *Theatre Notebook*, **30**(3), 1976, pp. 115–22; and 'The Music of Melodrama', in David Bradby, Louis James and Bernard Sharratt, eds, *Performance and Popular Drama: Aspects of Popular Entertainment in Theatre Film and Television, 1800–1976* (Cambridge, 1980), pp. 49–63. For a more recent account of Victorian theatre music see Michael Pisani, 'Music for the Theatre: Style and Function in Incidental Music', in Kerry Powell, ed., *The Cambridge Companion to Victorian and Edwardian Theatre* (Cambridge, 2004), pp. 70–92; and Barry Yzereef, 'The Art of Gentlemanly Melodrama: Charles Kean's Production of *The Corsican Brothers*', (University of Victoria PhD dissertation, 1995). The latter contains a full score of the music for *The Corsican Brothers*, as well as a detailed account of Charles Kean's 1853 production of *Macbeth* for the Princess's Theatre. The practice of fitting music to the stage actions is discussed in the introduction to David Mayer's and Matthew Scott's *Four Bars of 'Agit': Incidental Music for Victorian and Edwardian Melodrama* (London, 1983), which includes over 50 short 'melos' composed by Alfred Edward Cooper. A description of Edwardian and post-Edwardian practice regarding theatre music can be found in Norman O'Neill, 'Music to Stage Plays', *Proceedings of the [Royal] Musical Association*, 37th Session, 1910–11, pp. 85–102. Derek Hudson's biography of O'Neill, *Norman O'Neill: A Life of Music* (London, 1945), also contains much useful information, including a reprint of the O'Neill's 'Music to Stage Plays'.

Despite these general difficulties, enough information has survived to provide at least a broad sketch of the typical kind of music that was used in Victorian theatre productions and at least anecdotal evidence of the way in which music was fitted to a production.[2] A number of the overtures, entr'actes and short set pieces composed for larger theatre productions have also survived in versions for solo piano, piano four-hands, or as band or orchestral arrangements.[3] Much of this music was composed by workaday musicians who made a living in the theatre as composers, conductors and arrangers. Only a few attained a wider reputation, and today their names are known only within a specialised community of Victorian theatre aficionados. Many of these musicians – including Robert Stoepel, Meredith Ball and Hamilton Clarke – were, in fact, thorough-going professionals, and their contribution to the world of Victorian theatre music deserves greater investigation.

Beginning around 1875 there was, however, a gradual increase in the number of productions for which incidental music was especially commissioned by composers of acknowledged rank. This change in the practice of incidental music for theatre productions was, in significant measure, the result of efforts by Henry Irving, a point stressed by Norman O'Neill, himself one of the most prominent composers of theatre music of the generation immediately after Irving.[4] The list of composers who wrote incidental music for productions at the Lyceum Theatre during Irving's time includes virtually all composers of distinction working in England during the late Victorian period: C.V. Stanford (*Queen Mary*, 1876; *Becket*, 1893), Julius Benedict (*Romeo and Juliet*, 1882), Hamilton Clarke (*Faust*, 1885), Alexander Mackenzie (*Ravenswood*, 1890; *Coriolanus*, 1901), Edward German (*Henry VIII*, 1892) and, of course, Arthur Sullivan, whose music for Shakespeare's *The Tempest* (1862) at the

---

2 In *Problems of the Actor* (New York, 1918), pp. 222–4, Louis Calvert vividly describes an encounter between a music director and Irving regarding music for a melodrama. Further comments regarding Irving's sometimes difficult working relationship with the musicians in the Lyceum orchestra are contained in Edgar Shelton, 'Victorian Memories', *Music and Letters*, **29**, 1949, pp. 7–8. This general view is corroborated by W.H. Reed, for many years the leader of the London Symphony Orchestra, who in his early years played in the Lyceum orchestra. Reed's memories of his Lyceum years were recalled in a BBC broadcast in 1939 (*Looking Back: Many Years in the Orchestra*), the typescript for which was kindly provided by the Royal College of Music. Reed's remarks on life in the Lyceum orchestra pit can be found on pp. 2–9.

3 For example, Sullivan's incidental music to *The Merchant of Venice*, composed for a production at the Prince's Theatre in Manchester in 1871, was issued not only in an orchestral version, but also as a piano duet and for solo piano. The 'Graceful Dance' from his music for *Henry VIII* was published in a variety of forms for amateur home performance.

4 O'Neill, 'Music to Stage Plays', p. 87. Referring to the practice of commissioning eminent composers to compose incidental music for specific productions, O'Neill comments: 'It is to Sir Henry Irving, who did so much to improve the artistic conditions of the theatre, that we are indebted for this. He saw the need of something better than the "hurries", "tremolos", and sentimental hymn-like tunes which were being served up again and again in our theatres to an easily imposed-upon public ... Irving gave commissions to many young composers of his day ... Sullivan's music to "Macbeth", "the Foresters" (Tennyson), and "King Arthur" was all highly successful; and the first mentioned contains some of his best work.'

Crystal Palace opened his brilliant career.[5] Sullivan's six sets of incidental music to Shakespearean plays constitute the most significant body of incidental music for the late Victorian theatre in both amount and in musical quality.[6] His scores included not only attractive interlude music, songs and orchestral preludes, but also a significant number of skilfully constructed melodramas (music over which the actors spoke) to heighten the effect of a given scene. Aside from Sullivan's music for *The Tempest*, the most extended and most important of his creations in this mode was his incidental music to Henry Irving's production of *Macbeth* at the Lyceum Theatre that opened on 29 December 1888.

In theatrical terms, Irving's *Macbeth* was, in many ways, a watershed production, one of the many climaxes in his long, celebrated career in the theatre (Illustration 19).[7] Consider the mere statistics. In addition to the presence of such acknowledged stars as Henry Irving and Ellen Terry in the two principal roles, the production featured elaborate, massive and realistically detailed sets designed by Hawes Craven with the assistance of Joseph Harker, T.W. Hall, W. Hann and the scene painting firm of Perkins & Caney, built at extraordinary expense – some 21 changes of scene in all.[8] Irving went to inordinate lengths to get the right feel of place, even taking a trip to Scotland in the summer of 1887 to get ideas for the scenes. As Ellen Terry noted in her *Memoirs*, 'Visited the "Blasted Heath". Behold a flourishing potato-field! A smooth softness everywhere. We must blast our heath when we do Macbeth.'[9] An entire month was spent searching the British Museum and South Kensington Museum to guarantee Celtic or Anglo-Saxon eleventh-century authenticity in every scenic detail, from such practical implements as swords and helmets to household utensils such as salt-cellars and Anglo-Saxon wine pots. The designer of the costumes

---

5 On C.V. Stanford's incidental music, see Kenneth DeLong and Denis Salter, 'C.V. Stanford's Incidental Music to Henry Irving's Production of Tennyson's *Becket*', *Theatre History Studies*, 3, 1983, pp. 69–86.

6 Sullivan's music to Shakespeare is surveyed by David Russell Hulme, 'Sullivan's Macbeth Music', *Sir Arthur Sullivan Society Magazine* (18), Summer 1984, pp. 11–17 and Arthur Jacobs in 'Sullivan and Shakespeare', in Richard Foulkes ed., *Shakespeare and the Victorian Stage* (Cambridge, 1986), pp. 196–205. The complete list of Sullivan's incidental music to Shakespeare is as follows: *The Tempest* (1862); *The Merchant of Venice* (1867); *The Merry Wives of Windsor* (1874, 1889); *Henry VIII* (1877); and *Macbeth* (1888).

7 The reviewer for the *Lady's Pictorial* (5 January 1889) remarked incisively: 'No production of Mr. Irving's management has excited such widespread interest as the present revival of *Macbeth*. From a histrionic, musical, scenic, and literary point of view it is the most important production that the modern stage has known.' Of the many discussions of Irving and *Macbeth*, it is necessary here to instance only Dennis Bartholomeusz, *Macbeth and the Players* (Cambridge, 1969), pp. 196–208; Nancy Lynn Simon, 'Henry Irving and Ellen Terry in *Macbeth*: Lyceum Theatre, 29 December 1888' (University of Washington dissertation, 1975); Wendy Phyllis Rouder, 'Henry Irving's *Macbeth*' (University of Illinois dissertation, 1971); Alan Hughes, *Henry Irving, Shakespearean* (Cambridge, 1981), pp. 88–116; and Marvin Rosenberg, *The Masks of Macbeth* (Berkeley, 1978), *passim*.

8 *Sporting Times*, 5 January 1889; and programme for the 135th performance, 11 June 1889 (Salter Collection).

9 Ellen Terry, *Ellen Terry's Memoirs*, ed. Edith Craig and Christopher St John (London, 1933), p. 231.

and accessories, Charles Cattermole, designed over 400 costumes, including 165 for the various soldiers and 60 for the spectacular witches' scenes in Act IV.[10] Forty workers spent five months executing the designs. The capstone of the production was Sullivan's incidental music, newly commissioned by Irving and conducted by Meredith Ball, which was performed by a larger than normal orchestra of 46 players, including two harpists, and which featured, in Act IV, a female chorus of 60 voices.[11]

Illustration 19   Henry Irving watching a rehearsal

The production was as successful as it was spectacular and ran for 150 performances, rivalling that of *Faust* some three years earlier. The opening was attended by a virtual army of journalists from newspapers all over England and from America, and reviews were published not only in all the major English newspapers but also in American newspapers, including the New York ones – *The Times*, the *Herald*, the *World* and the *Tribune* – together with *Texas Siftings* and the *Detroit Free Press*. In fact the journalistic fall-out was so great and of such perceived consequence that the *Era* collected many of the reviews and printed them together in one mammoth

---

10 M.H. Spielmann, 'Il. – A Shakespearean Revival', *Magazine of Art*, **12**, 1889, pp. 98–100.

11 *World*, 2 January 1889; interview with Cattermole in the *Pall Mall Budget*, 3 January 1889.

article a month after the opening.[12] This collection of articles and reviews, some 40 in all, discusses and evaluates the production from every conceivable angle and constitutes a veritable Anglo-American homage to Irving's production.[13]

As the critic for the *People* pointed out:

A four-fold interest has attached to this revival of *Macbeth*. First the pictorial presentment of the scene which, as promised, was to exceed in its supernatural effects with the weird sisters, even those lately seen in *Faust*; secondly, the new incidental music composed for the tragedy by Sir Arthur Sullivan in lieu of the inadequate prettiness of Locke's time-honoured harmonies; thirdly, the assumption for the first time of Lady Macbeth by Miss Ellen Terry; and fourthly, the revised reading of Macbeth by Mr. Irving upon his resumption of the character after a decade of valuable practice in his art.[14]

The scenic element was clearly spectacular and was commented upon by virtually every reviewer. The remarks of the critic for the *St. James's Gazette* on the general effect of the production are characteristic: 'As an example of the supreme art of stage-management applied to the worthiest of subjects, as a picturesque and impressive creation, harmonious in every detail, whether of music or mounting, of tableau or of concerted action, this revival of *Macbeth* is an absolute triumph.'[15] The production was not simply 'realistic' in its simulation of eleventh-century life, it also had a picturesque *figurative* dimension: as the critic for the *Illustrated London News* explained, the production 'is materially supported by the elaborate, convincing, and beautiful character of the scenic and allegorical arrangements ... Doré himself might have designed the supernatural portion of the play, and any Royal Academician might be proud to have painted such Shakespearean pictures'.[16] The production provided Irving with an opportunity, as was his custom, to experiment with highly evocative, sensuous chiaroscuro, in which the interplay of light and dark conformed, in the 'allegorical' pattern referred to by the *Illustrated London News*, to the play's continuous dramatic conflict between 'good', on the one hand, and 'evil' on the other.

Irving's interpretation of Macbeth (Illustration 20) was singled out for special comment – some of it favourable, some not. However, no one remained neutral, and a lengthy debate ensued among the critics, extending to those who wrote for the weighty, intellectual periodicals, including the *National Review*, the *Gentleman's Magazine* and the *Cornhill Magazine*, in which they not only analysed Irving's production, but

---

12 *Era*, 26 January 1889, pp. 15–26.

13 Although the New York reviews were not included in the *Era*'s collection, *The Times* deemed the production so important that it not only assigned its special correspondent, Harold Frederic, to cover the production, but it also ensured that his review appeared immediately after the opening night on 30 December 1888, ahead, in many cases, of those in the English newspapers. *The Times* sent both its drama critic, J.F. Nisbet, and its music critic, Francis Hueffer, to see the production. Both reviews appeared on 31 December 1888. Similarly, the *Daily Telegraph* sent both its drama critic, Clement Scott, and its music critic, Joseph Bennett. Scott's review appeared on 31 December 1888; Bennett's review on 3 January 1889.

14 *People*, 30 December 1888.

15 *St. James's Gazette*, 31 December 1888.

16 *Illustrated London News*, 5 January 1889.

Illustration 20   Henry Irving as Macbeth

placed it – and the great expectation for it – within the context of the play's long, complicated stage history.[17] Expanding upon and deepening his earlier 1875 reading of the role, Irving interpreted Macbeth as, in his words, 'a villain, cold-blooded, selfish, remorseless, with the true villain's nerve and callousness when braced to evil work, and the physical heroism of those who are born to kill; a moral nature with only sufficient weakness to quake momentarily before superstitious terrors; a man of sentiment and not of feeling'.[18] As acted by Irving, Macbeth was, according to Nisbet, a 'dark, malignant schemer who augurs the success of his criminal projects

---

17 See Sylvanus Urban, 'Table Talk', *Gentleman's Magazine*, **266**, 1889, pp. 206–8; John Coleman, 'Facts and Fancies about *Macbeth*', *Gentleman's Magazine*, **266**, 1889, pp. 218–32; Wyke Bayliss, '"Fears" or "Teares", *Macbeth*, Act IV, Scene 5', *National Review*, **12**, 1889, pp. 730–35; John Douglas Montegomery, 'Macbeth, Considered as a Celt', *National Review*, **12**, 1889, pp. 181–90; L[aurence] G[ifford] Holland, '"Macbeth"', *Cornhill Magazine*, NS **12**, 1889, pp. 133–54; and Francis Thompson, 'The *Macbeth* Controversy', *Dublin Review*, 3rd Series, 1889, pp. 140–56.

18 Irving, 'The Character of Macbeth', in Thomas B. Reed, ed., *Modern Eloquence: Occasional Addresses* (Philadelphia, 1900), Vol. 8, p. 735. Aside from the extensive commentary in the *Era*, 26 January 1889, on Irving's conception of Macbeth, there is also

from the oracular utterances of the weird sisters' and who 'becomes, by a natural transition, the contemptible craven whose anguish of mind is obviously inspired by dread of possible consequences to himself, and not by any shreds of honourable feeling'.[19] By the end, he 'looked', according to Ellen Terry, 'like a great famished wolf, weak with the weakness of an exhausted giant'.[20] In a letter to Irving, written shortly after the opening night, Oscar Wilde declared:

> My dear Irving, My best congratulations on your magnificent production, and your magnificent performance. The murder-scene and the banquet-scene remain in my memory as two of the finest, most imaginative bits of acting I have ever seen. They were instances of the highest *style*, and of the most subtle psychological insight; and the true temper of tragedy never left you all through the play.[21]

In Ellen Terry's reading of the role, Lady Macbeth (Illustration 21) was a loving, but by no means acquiescent, wife who helped to spur Macbeth on to murder. As the veteran critic Edward R. Russell observed:

> Captivating is not at all the word to apply to Ellen Terry's Lady Macbeth. Feminine it is; wifely it is; her character, as it were, seizes Macbeth's in a vice, and uses it and him by sheer force – all under forms of probable and life-like conjugal compulsion, pretty enough to look at, if the business in hand were less ghastly and the husband not visibly haunted by the most horrible and unnerving apprehensions.[22]

Russell elaborated his analysis of these character traits when he returned to the Lyceum to see *Macbeth* in June 1889:

> For the first time Lady Macbeth has been boldly thought out on the lines of a Saga-heroine. Now, a Saga-heroine is not, as a rule, grim, vague, and weird. She is bold, incisive, impetuous, imperious; ruddy in complexion, and red-haired; dazzling, but and for the resolute fierceness with which she uses her power.[23]

Russell recognised that Terry was *in part* seeking to resist Mrs Siddons's performance of the role – a performance marked by fierce intensity, uncanny self-absorption and terrifying authority. Although Terry's portrayal of Lady Macbeth notably differed from the Siddons tradition, it was an interpretation arrived at through considerable study and reflection that took into account Mrs Siddons's own remarks as well as her own sense of the character and physical and dramatic abilities.[24] Controversial and

---

a considerable modern commentary on the salient points, a convenient summary of which is contained in Hughes, *Henry Irving*, pp. 91–116.

19 *The Times*, 31 December 1888.
20 Ellen Terry, *The Story of My Life* (London, 1908), p. 232.
21 Oscar Wilde, *The Letters of Oscar Wilde* (2nd edn), ed. Rupert Hart-Davis (London, 1962), p. 235. The letter was probably written on 30 December 1888.
22 *Liverpool Daily Post*, 31 December 1888.
23 Edward R. Russell, 'Macbeth' Revisited, *Liverpool Daily Post*, June 1889; reprinted in the Lyceum *Macbeth* programme of 11 June 1889 (Salter Collection).
24 Terry's work in developing her portrayal of Lady Macbeth included her detailed study of George Fletcher's article on *Macbeth* published in the *Westminster Review*, **41**, March

Illustration 21   Ellen Terry as Lady Macbeth

unexpected, Terry offered a sympathetic understanding of the character of Lady Macbeth; she provided a contrasting counterpoint to Irving's portrayal of Macbeth and, in so doing, created dramatic images that also resonated in the gentler and more intimate passages in Sullivan's incidental music.

Whatever one may think of the validity of Irving's and Terry's ideas regarding *Macbeth*, it is nonetheless essential to understand their view of the play if the nature and dramatic significance of Sullivan's music is to be grasped. As conceived by Irving, and expressed not only in his acting, but also in the sets, lighting and in Sullivan's music, *Macbeth* is a psychologically informed morality play: the evil that is Macbeth is contemplated in a picturesque fashion, emotionally heightened by the music, which makes strikingly vivid the triumph of goodness at the end of the play. In this context the witches and spirits were therefore regarded as unworldly apparitions; and to enhance what Irving called their 'supernatural significance', he

---

1844, pp. [1]–72, which contains numerous annotations concerning the fundamental nature of the role. Terry's annotated copy of Fletcher's essay is in the Theatre Museum (Shattuck, *Macbeth*, No. 100).

ensured that 'in their first introduction on the stage they are represented as coming out of a thunder cloud, suggesting that their home is among the dark and tempestuous elements of nature. It could be argued that they served to reflect what was already in Macbeth's mind.'[25]

The incidental music for the 1875 production during Irving's early years at the Lyceum (before he became manager) provides a good example of the prevailing practice in larger theatres during the mid-Victorian period. The music was compiled and composed in the pastiche fashion by the company's house composer and conductor, Robert Stoepel, an efficient, if less than gifted, composer of theatre music.[26] The overture was composed by Stoepel himself, and the entr'actes consisted of selections from Mendelssohn's *Walpurgis Night*, a fantasia on what was then thought to be Matthew Locke's *Macbeth* music, and excerpts from Giuseppe Verdi's opera on *Macbeth*.[27] Presumably there was also some music to accompany certain important speeches and for special effects, but the direct relationship of most of this

---

25 Irving, 'Preface' to William Shakespeare, *Macbeth: A Tragedy by William Shakespeare as Arranged for the Stage by Henry Irving and Presented at the Lyceum Theatre* (London, 1888), pp. 6–7. The tradition of how the witches were customarily played goes back to the Restoration era, and Irving's decision sharply to depart from this tradition was central to the mood and atmosphere of his new, 'modern' production. This point was noticed in virtually every review, the comment by Clement Scott in the *Daily Telegraph*, 31 December 1888, is typical: 'The sisters are not old men dressed up as women, dancing about a theatrical cauldron, squeaking in shrill treble, and waving clothes-props in their hands, but three grey, gloomy women, dignified, mysterious, impressive, with wailing women's voices, who appropriately set the seal on the supernatural character of the play …' A similar view was expressed in the *Morning Advertiser*, 31 December 1888: 'That men – and usually a low comedian among them – should have always appeared as the weird sisters is inexplicable, and one of those stage traditions we can, nowadays, most willingly dispense with. The witches have often made a dangerously near approach to the comic, and Mr. Irving is to be thanked for the important change he has made in putting actresses into these characters.' Irving's understanding of the witches seems to have been consistent with an earlier view regarding these supernatural creatures, one stemming from the period around Shakespeare. About the conception of the fundamental nature of witches during the Elizabethan period, Daniel Albright, *Cambridge Opera Journal*, **17**(3), 2005, p. 227, writes: 'Their function is simply to open up areas of empty space, in which ugly desires can manifest themselves, in which deeds without names can take place. Theirs is not the moving finger that writes down all that will come to pass; they simply provide a blank tablet that the human characters figure with obscene scrawls.'

26 The music cues, together with notes for extra-musical effects – trumpets, for example – have been carefully marked, presumably by Stoepel, in Irving's 1874 annotated study-copy: Shattuck, *Macbeth*, No. 81.

27 These details are cited by Francis Hueffer in the article in *The Times* reproduced in the *Evening Post* on 31 December 1888. The music for *Macbeth*, then thought to be by Matthew Locke (1621/22–77), is now known to be largely the work of Richard Leveridge (1670/71–1758). See Roger Fiske, 'The Macbeth Music', *Music and Letters*, **45**(2), 1964, pp. 114–25. It should be noted that, for the 1875 production, Irving eliminated the two songs from Middleton's *The Witch* that, following the performing edition by William Davenant in the 1660s, were customarily included in performances of *Macbeth*, normally with the music thought to be by Locke. This practice continued for many years and was accepted as *de rigueur* until their elimination by Irving in his 1875 production. For the 1888 production,

music to the progress of the drama was necessarily slight, consisting merely of a parade of musical items which, ignoring vast differences in musical style, happened to share the same title or general atmosphere of the play and thereby were deemed 'appropriate'. Although not originally written with *Macbeth* in mind, Mendelssohn's *Walpurgis Night* had a clear and unmistakable function: it provided the touch of ghoulish pictorialism needed to evoke the witches. Verdi's opera probably provided the moments of more urgent human emotion.

For the 1888 production Irving determined to make a change. During the years since he had taken over the Lyceum, Irving had been trying to achieve a new, more refined seriousness of artistic purpose in his productions through the integration of all the component parts. Being a man of the theatre, he naturally first concentrated on aspects of acting, scenic design, costumes and lighting. As Oscar Wilde memorably put the matter in 'The Soul of Man under Socialism':

> With his marvellous and vivid personality, with a style that has really a true colour-element in it, with his extraordinary power, not over mere mimicry but over imaginative and intellectual creation, Mr Irving, had his sole object been to give the public what they wanted, could have produced the commonest plays in the commonest manner, and made as much success and money as a man could possibly desire.[28]

This, however, was *not* Irving's objective, for, as Wilde went on to explain, '[h]is object was to realise his own perfection as an artist, under certain conditions and in certain forms of art. At first he appealed to the few: now he has educated the many.'[29] A landmark had been reached with the fabulously successful production of *Faust* in 1885, but even here the music had been constructed on the pastiche principle by Hamilton Clarke and Meredith Ball, producing a jarring note in an otherwise brilliant production. The critic of the *Musical Times*, after praising Irving for his brave attempt to provide suitable music despite the 'absolute indifference of an English theatre audience as to what music is played', made a plea for 'one of our foremost composers' to be asked to provide a score for a Lyceum production.[30] The opportunity arose with the production of *Macbeth*, planned for Christmas of 1888.

On 2 June 1888 Bram Stoker approached Sullivan on Irving's behalf with the offer to provide the incidental music to his production of *Macbeth*.[31] The music critic Herman Klein, a friend of both Sullivan and Irving, recalled in his memoirs an incident relating to the music:

Irving restored the two songs (newly set by Arthur Sullivan) on the strength of evidence from the First Folio. See Irving, 'Preface', Shakespeare, *Macbeth: A Tragedy*, pp. [5]–6.

28 In *Collected Works of Oscar Wilde* (Ware, 1997), p. 914.

29 Ibid.

30 Cited in Arthur Jacobs, *Arthur Sullivan: A Victorian Musician* (2nd edn) (Portland, 1992), p. 282.

31 Sullivan's diary entry for this date reads: 'Bram Stoker called on behalf of Irving to ask me to write music for forthcoming production of "Macbeth" – gave conditional consent.' Access microfilms of Sullivan's diaries for these dates provided by the Pierpont Morgan Library, New York. (The original diaries are located in the Beinecke Library, Yale University.)

He [Irving] was then mounting various Shakespearean plays without incidental music other than that provided by his regular conductor, Meredith Ball. It had always seemed to me to be a great opportunity lost, and I ventured to tell him so.

'Never mind', said Irving, 'I am going to make up for it now. Before this year [1888] is out I hope to revive *Macbeth*, and *not* with Lock's [*sic*] music.'

'With whose music then?' I asked.

'With Arthur Sullivan's. He has promised me to write it during the summer, and you may look for the production at about Christmas.'

'Splendid!' I exclaimed. 'That is really doing something worth while for native music; worthy of Shakespeare and worthy of yourself.' Then an idea occurred to me ...

'Do you mind, Mr. Irving, if I make a suggestion? It is that you ask Sir Arthur to provide his *Macbeth* music with a full overture. It ought to have one, and he will not hesitate if you ask him.'

'Why not?' said the actor as he rose to obey the call-boy. 'Overtures to tragedies, I suppose have gone out of fashion a little since Beethoven wrote the *Coriolanus* and Mendelssohn *Ruy Blas*; but what they thought worth doing I am sure that Sullivan will think worth doing too. Thanks for the suggestion!'[32]

Illustration 22   Arthur Sullivan: caricature by 'Ape' (Carlo Pellegrini)

By the time Sullivan came to compose his music to *Macbeth*, he was both an experienced composer and no stranger to the task of composing incidental music

---

32 Herman Klein, *Musicians and Mummers* (London, 1925), pp. 163–4.

to Shakespeare's plays. As a young man of 20, recently back in London after three years' study in Leipzig, Sullivan had had his first major success with his music to *The Tempest* in 1862. In succeeding years he had gone on to compose incidental music to *The Merchant of Venice* (1871), *The Merry Wives of Windsor* (1874) and *Henry VIII* (1877) – the scores to which contain much delightful music but nevertheless lack the musical purpose and depth of the earlier score.[33] Since 1877 Sullivan had composed no incidental music of consequence, but the years were hardly idle. During this period, between 1877 and 1888, he composed the scores to nine of his most successful operettas with W.S. Gilbert, as well as the cantata *The Golden Legend* (1886). The score to *Macbeth* was composed at a time in Sullivan's life when his operetta phase with Gilbert was nearing its end and when he felt increasingly the need to express himself in what, for him at least, were more substantial, intellectually complex forms. The culmination of this trend was, of course, his grand historical opera *Ivanhoe* (1891), the relative failure of which was a career watershed and a setback from which he never fully recovered as a composer.

Immediately after having accepted the *Macbeth* commission, Gilbert presented Sullivan with the libretto of *The Yeomen of the Guard*, and during the summer and autumn Sullivan focused his energies on his work for the Savoy. By the end of November he was hard at work on his *Macbeth* music. Writing at lightning speed, he finished the scoring after an 11-hour stint on Boxing Day, three days before the opening.[34] At some time during the preparation of the play, Irving conveyed his wishes regarding the music to Sullivan. The undated letter from Irving to Sullivan from around this time is more than a little vague and is, as far as one can tell, what he asked of Sullivan:

---

33 Two recent recordings containing the orchestral suites extracted from these productions give an idea of the music in them. Attractive, tuneful, and apt to the atmosphere of the individual situations they are intended to support, these scores nevertheless do not strive for more than a surface-level treatment of the dramatic issues. See Marco Polo, 8.223461 (1992), *Sir Arthur Sullivan: Incidental Music* (to *The Merchant of Venice, Henry VIII,* and *The Sapphire Necklace*) and Marco Polo 8.223635 (1995), *Arthur Sullivan: Incidental Music* (to *Macbeth, King Arthur,* and *The Merry Wives of Windsor*). Both CDs with the RTE Concert Orchestra conducted by Andrew Penny.

34 Sullivan's diary entries on his composition of the music are terse, but they do give a sense of how he worked: 'Worked at "Macbeth" all day' (18 November 1888); 'working at Macbeth again' (3 December 1888); 'Working all day' (5 December 1988); 'At home all day writing' (6 December 1888); 'ditto' (7 December 1888); 'Writing all day' (8 December 1888); 'Went to rehearsal of Fourth Act Macbeth at Lyceum. Home at 3.30. Wrote all through the night' (10 December 1888); 'Scoring' (11 December 1888); 'Rehearsal at Lyceum 12.30 till 2.30' (13 December 1888); 'Rehearsed orchestra & chorus of 4th Act music at the Savoy Theatre. Licked them into good shape' (14 December 1888); 'Writing' (16 December 1888); 'Writing till 3' (17 December 1888); '11.30 Band rehearsal. 1st & 4th acts at Lyceum & home at 4. p.m.' (18 December 1888); 'Rehearsal Lyceum 11 to 5.30' (20 December 1888); Irving came at 11 to talk over cuts – easily arranged' (21 December 1888); 'Working hard at overture' (22 December 1988); 'a.m. presents & scoring all day– ...' (25 December 1888); 'Hard at work all day scoring' (26 December 1888); 'Rehearsal of all the music at Savoy 12 to 3 ... Full dress rehearsal of "Macbeth" at Lyceum at 8:15. All went smoothly over at 12.30' (28 December 1888).

Trumpets and drums are the things <u>behind scenes</u>.
Entrance of <u>Macbeth, only drum</u>
'A drum a drum Macbeth doth come'
Distant march would be good for Macbeth's exit in <u>3rd</u> scene – or drum and trumpets, as you suggest.
In the last act there will be several flourishes – trumpets –
'Make all our trumpets speak' [etc.] –
roll of drum sometimes.
Really anything you can give of x stirring sort – can easily be brought in.
As your say you can dot these down at rehearsal – but one player would be good to tootle, tootle, so we can get the exact time.[35]

Sometime in December Sullivan took his music, presumably compiled in rough, to the theatre to work it into the action.[36] Irving's assistant, Bram Stoker, records an instance of how the two men worked together on the *Macbeth* project:

As an example of the harmony of their working and of the absolute necessity in such matters for absolute candour, let me instance one scene ... Sir Arthur sat in the conductor's chair. In a pause of the rehearsal of the action on the stage he said: 'We are ready now, Irving, if you can listen.'

'All right, old man; go ahead!'

When the numbers of that particular piece of incidental music had been gone through the composer asked: 'Do you like that? Will it do?'

Irving replied at once with kindly seriousness: 'Oh, as music it's very fine; but for our purpose it is no good at all. Not in the least like it!'

Sullivan was not offended by the frankness ... He asked him if he could give any hint or clue as to what idea he had. Irving, even whilst saying in words that he did not know himself exactly what he wanted, managed by sway of body and movement of arms and hands, by changing times and undulating tones, and by vowel sounds without words to convey his inchoate thought, instinctive rather than of reason. Sullivan grasped the idea and the anxious puzzlement of his face changed to gladness.

'All right!' he said heartily. 'I think I understand. If you will go on with the rehearsal I shall have something ready by-and by.'

Sitting where he was, he began scoring, the band waiting. When some of the scenes had been rehearsed, there was some movement in the orchestra ...

'If you are ready now, Irving, we can give you an idea. It is only the theme. If you think it will do I will work it out to-night.'

The band struck up the music and Irving's face kindled as he heard.

'Splendid!' he said. 'Splendid! That is all I could wish for. It is fine!'[37]

Sullivan's score to *Macbeth* consists of an extended overture, as well as 13 musical numbers (some of considerable length) which are heard throughout the

---

35 Original in the Pierpont Morgan Library, GSC 107513.
36 Sullivan's diary entry for 10 December 1888 ('Went to rehearsal of Fourth Act of Macbeth at Lyceum') seems to mark the probable start of rehearsals.
37 Bram Stoker, *Personal Reminiscences of Henry Irving* (London, 1906), Vol. 1, pp. 111–13.

play; including the overture, the score runs to 187 pages of music.[38] The music was commented upon by virtually all the reviewers of the production, first because of its scope and perceived suitability to the atmosphere of the production, and, second, because of the breaking of the tradition of using Locke's score. Francis Hueffer, the respected music critic of *The Times*, describes the general character of the music as follows: '[Sir Arthur Sullivan's] music to *Macbeth*, if not very profound or intensely dramatic, is singularly appropriate. It is never in the way when not wanted, never out of the way when required; and the composer deserves praise for what he has left undone no less than for what he has accomplished'.[39] Hueffer elaborates this point by reference to the absence of music to accompany the Sleepwalking Scene in Act V, Scene 2, as well as the aptness of the melodramas and the atmospheric music Sullivan wrote for the opening of Act I, Scene 6, when Duncan is greeted by Lady Macbeth at Macbeth's castle. Another point Hueffer addresses is Sullivan's deliberate avoidance of any music that is composed in an antique or distinctively Scottish style. As Hueffer remarks, 'At the Lyceum, where historical accuracy and

---

38 For many years the autograph score has been in private hands and unavailable for academic study. Recently, however, the score was bequeathed to Oriel College, Oxford University, and has now been deposited on permanent loan in the Bodleian Library. The autograph score has the shelfmark: Oriel College MS. A copy of the autograph has kindly been provided by the Bodleian Library for the purposes of this study. The autograph score is also the basis of the new edition of Sullivan's *Macbeth* music by Robin Gordon-Powell, *Arthur Sullivan: Incidental Music to* Macbeth (London, 2006). This exemplary new edition also contains an extensive introduction treating both the production and the music, including salient quotations from the contemporary press and pertinent details concerning the history of the score itself. I would like to thank Robin Gordon-Powell for assistance in the preparation of this chapter, including the timely sending of the newly published score. For the final concert of the Leeds Festival in 1889, which was conducted by Sullivan, Sullivan prepared an orchestral suite, consisting of the overture, the *andante espressivo* section of the prelude to Act III, the preludes to Acts V and VI, and the introduction and two choral numbers from Act. IV. For this concert version, Sullivan expanded the scoring for the percussion and brass and revised the overture to include an extra 37 measures. It is this material that was used for the recorded performance of the suite cited in footnote note 33. The autograph of the complete orchestral score for the concert version has been lost, but the engraved orchestral parts have survived. The overture, as a separate item, and in the concert version, was published in 1893 by Chappell and Co. See Gordon-Powell, 'Introduction', *Incidental Music to* Macbeth, pp. x–xi for further details.

39 *The Times*, 31 December 1888. The reviewer for *Sporting Life*, 31 December 1888, commented: 'The overture, preludes, and incidental music, composed expressly for this production by Sir Arthur Sullivan, are eminently worthy of him. They breath and kindle with the spirit of the text, and are in melodic freshness eminently Shakespearean.' Herman Klein, the reviewer for the *Sunday Times*, wrote on 30 December 1888: 'On the whole, the *Macbeth* music is worthy alike of its theme and of the pen who wrote it. Every note is carefully considered with a view to lending colour and significance to the dramatic situation, and that air is undeniably accomplished.' The 'characterising' aspect of Sullivan's score drew the attention of William Archer in the *World*, 2 January 1889. who observed: 'The music is so descriptive that, knowing that it is written to *Macbeth*, you may guess the scenes it is meant to illustrate.'

pictorial effect are studied with the utmost care, something more elaborate, more in keeping with the spirit of the drama was required.' He goes on: 'Sir Arthur Sullivan has been intent upon giving emotional emphasis rather than a local habitation to the action by musical means; and we are inclined to think that here also he has acted wisely.'[40]

Aside from the overture, the most extended item, the incidental music includes preludes to Acts I, II, III, V and VI, as well as numbers that provide a link between scenes. There are also several extended melodramas. The most striking passage, however, is the grand choral extravaganza that occupies all of Act IV and includes two songs for female chorus.[41] The music heard during the play (summarised in Table 1) consists of three different, but related, types. First, there is the incidental music, in the sense of music played between acts or scene changes; second, there are the passages of melodrama in which the actors speak to the music; and, third, there are musical 'effects' that Sullivan thought musically insignificant enough to have omitted from his score. Many of these 'effects' seem to have been created during the rehearsal period and were probably jotted down in the conductor's score and orchestral parts; unfortunately, these last-minute insertions have not yet been located. From remarks made by the reviewers, however, there must have been a substantial amount of such music, especially for the harp, some of it involving more musically developed ideas than just simple arpeggiated chords.[42] One notable moment involving the harp appears to have been a melody that was inserted after the music for Act I, Scene 6, and was played during Lady Macbeth's welcoming of Duncan to the castle.[43] Of the other miscellaneous fanfares, drum tattoos and some of the melodrama music nothing is known at the present time.

---

40 *The Times*, 31 December 1888. There were, however, some adverse comments. The reviewer for the *Dispatch*, 30 December 1888, remarked: 'Sir Arthur's music is wholly irrelevant in character and conception to the drama. He has not used his opportunities of drawing on the rich stores of antique Northern melody. He has not caught the archaic spirit of the eleventh century, and his work might just as well be played at the Savoy as at the Lyceum.'

41 For this production of *Macbeth*, Irving altered Shakespeare's text, breaking up the original Act V into two acts and combining Act IV, Scene 1, with Act III, Scene 5, to make an Act IV of the two scenes that include the two Middleton songs, 'Black Spirits and White', and 'Come Away!'. Act III, Scene 6, was omitted. A reproduction of Irving's acting version is included in Gordon-Powell's score of Sullivan's *Incidental Music to* Macbeth, pp. xv–liii.

42 Irving's fondness for the harp as an instrument in theatre music is commented upon by Alexander Mackenzie: 'He had a great fancy for the *harp* in the orchestra, and several times suggested to me to make it prominent even when I thought it was "out of the situation".' See Alexander Mackenzie, 'Sir Henry Irving and Music: Some Reminiscences', *Musical Times*, **46**(11), 1905, p. 716.

43 Hueffer, for example, comments: 'Of the treachery underlying the words of welcome no warning note rises from the strings of the harp which accompany the dialogue to the close.' See *The Times*, 31 December 1888. Herman Klein also mentions this moment: '... the melody played on the harp as Lady Macbeth ventures forth from her castle to welcome Duncan.' See *Sunday Times*, 30 December 1888. Similar words are used in the *Sporting and Dramatic News*, 5 January 1889: '... but to the harp alone is allotted the long-drawn melody heard when Lady Macbeth issues forth from the castle to bid King Duncan welcome to Inverness'.

Table 1   Summary of Sullivan's incidental music to *Macbeth*

Musical Items (Stage Order)		Comments
1	Overture	Symphonic treatment of the main thematic ideas from the incidental music as a 'programme' overture. (See details in Table 2 and list of musical themes.)
2	Act I, Scene 1 Introduction	Eighteen bars of tempestuous introduction of stormy character (C minor, and marked by chromatic diminished-seventh chords). The curtain comes up in bar 18; the music subsides to a bass ostinato figure, and the dialogue begins in bar 39, with the music continuing (melodrama). Cornet solo at bar 72 prepares for Scene 2 and the entry of Duncan (the 'Bleeding Sergeant' scene).
3	Act I, Scene 3	Music thematically the same as Scene 1 (bass ostinato figure). Dialogue begins in bar 14 with a change to an angular, dance-like theme that anticipates and overlaps the arrival of Macbeth. This theme, heard in fragmentary form in bars 118–27 and 172–6 of the overture (Theme J), is also the theme of the witches' round dance in Act IV, Scene 1).
4	Act I, Scene 3–4	Music between Act I, Scenes 3 and 4. March to introduce Duncan at the beginning of Scene 4. Twelve-measure march tune, played three times (Theme D in the overture).
5	Act I, Scene 6	Music at the beginning of Scene 6 and the arrival of Duncan at Macbeth's castle. The softness of the evening air is conveyed by the character of the music ('The air nimbly and sweetly recommends itself unto our gentle senses'). Over soft tremolo strings, two horns – one in the pit, the other behind the scenes – play a slow, gentle melody that concludes when the dialogue begins in bar 20. The strings alone play softly underneath the dialogue until bar 34.
6	Act II, Prelude	Dotted figure in the winds prepares for the eerie, chromatic idea associated with Banquo's ghost. Following a repeat of these ideas, the music changes to undulating figures for two harps (nine measures). Following a repeat of the harp figures the music associated with Banquo's ghost returns. This leads to a brief, but powerful orchestral outburst and the return of the opening wind figure. The curtain rises nine measures before the end (Theme E in the overture).
7	Act III, Prelude	Prelude music divides into two distinct, contrasted sections: (1) a martial, chorale-style melody in two strains, fully scored, in 5/4 time (!) and of antique character. This is followed by an Andante expressivo in slow 6/8 time with a prominent clarinet solo.

8	Act III, Scene 3, 'Banquet Scene'	At the cue, 'May't please your highness sit', the music for Banquo's ghost is played (Theme E in the overture).
9	Act IV, Introduction	Opens with the powerful, suggestive music for the witches (Theme B), leading directly to the 'Spirits of the Air' figure (Theme C), clearly a paraphrase of the opening of the overture. Following a repeat of this music, the dialogue begins in bar 33. Extended melodrama continuing to bar 70.
9a	Act IV, Scene 1, Chorus: 'Black Spirits'	Repeat of the first witches' motive (Theme B) followed by choral setting of Middleton's 'Black Spirits', with accompaniment derived from Theme C.
10	Act IV, Scene 1	Extended melodrama cued to begin with the entrance of Macbeth ('How now, you secret, black and midnight hags!'). Music continues throughout the scene, with sombre march in B minor for the Show of Eight Kings at bar 52.
11	Act IV, Scene 1, 'Witches' Dance'	A grotesque-style dance in E minor, derived from theme from Act I, Scene 3 (Theme H in the overture).
12	Act IV – Scene 2, Chorus: 'Come Away'	Choral setting of Middleton's song 'Come away', introduced by Theme B. Theme G from the overture appears towards the end.
13	Act V, Prelude	Seven-measure string introduction leads to solo clarinet theme in the style of Bizet. Melody repeated in full, but soft scoring for full orchestra.
14	Act VI, Prelude	Repeat of grand march melody (Theme D) from Act I, Scene 3, with a new musical figure as melodic extension. The extension contains a transformation of Theme A (bars 52–56).

The greatest proportion of the incidental music is devoted to the entr'actes and to self-contained numbers that introduce or link scenes in the play. In the general practice of the time there was usually no specific connection between the entr'acte music and the following scene or act. With Sullivan's *Macbeth*, however, the case is quite the reverse: both the entr'acte music and the music played between scene changes are linked to some specific stage action or fashioned to set the mood for the ensuing scene. Some of this music has the function of a leitmotif and returns at different points in the play with increasingly suggestive power; other passages are merely local in their connection to the play. The melodramas are handled with great care in the relationship between music and speech, both with respect to the timing of the music and in the composition of the musical figures that support the spoken words. Some of these musical figures that are treated as leitmotifs; others merely provide a moment of local atmosphere.

An instance of melodramas that blend both types of musical figures (with and without leitmotif associations) occurs in the two scenes involving the witches in

Act I. Before the curtain rises on Scene 1, there are 18 measures of agitated storm music, which, following a clap of thunder, dies down to a mysterious rumble. As the music subsides, the curtain rises (cued to rise at bar 18), and as the music fades, the dialogue begins (cued to bar 29). During the witches' dialogue, the music plays a new idea in the strings, with an ominous tread in the 'cello. When the witches have finished, there is another thunderclap, and the witches disappear to the same music to which they entered. This leads directly to a cornet fanfare to signal the arrival of Duncan. The atmospheric music of the opening scene returns in Act I, Scene 3, where Macbeth first encounters the witches. The mysterious rumble of Scene 1 is heard again, but now the scoring is changed to evoke the passage of time between scenes. The use of similar musical ideas in these scenes helps to link them, but their significance is ultimately, only local, for these musical ideas never return.

With the witches 'round dance' that occurs Act I, Scene 3, the musical signification is quite different.[44] The music of this round dance (see theme J of the musical examples) admirably underscores the activity of the witches during the scene, but, at the entrance of Macbeth and Banquo, it is gradually transformed into something broader in character and more harmonically conventional. At its end, it is transformed into a pompous-sounding march that effects a link from the supernatural world of the witches to the 'normal' world of the two military commanders. In these two opening scenes are planted the seeds of musical ideas that gradually take on the properties of a leitmotif as the play progresses. This is particularly evident in the return of the round dance in Act IV, Scene 1, the opening music foreshadowing the later, far more extended treatment in Act IV. The music thus serves as a metaphor, the prophetic words of the witches having their musical analogue – one that reaches its own dramatic and musical fulfilment in the music to Act IV.[45]

In a similar way, the larger, musically self-contained numbers include items that have both local and wider symbolic significance. For example, between Act I, Scenes 3 and 4, Sullivan includes a brief march in G major. On first hearing, this music appears to have only a local purpose: to provide suitable exit music to Macbeth and Banquo at the end of the scene. This short march, first presented at a moderate dynamic and then very loud, conveys a certain grandeur, but is not, in

---

44 The odd quality of this 'round dance' comes not only from the irregular rhythm but also from the treatment of the harmony: beginning in C minor, it modulates first to the conventional key of E-flat major, the relative major, but from there changes to the remote, unrelated keys of E minor, F major and even D-flat major. These key relationships, so foreign to the central key, accentuate the oddness of the entire situation, especially in contrast to the blandly diatonic harmonies that conclude this passage.

45 The striking effect of these two scenes was generally noted. Hueffer comments: 'The witches declaim, they do not sing, and their voices in juxtaposition and contrast with the musical sound are of the wildest and uncanniest effect.' See *The Times*, 31 December 1888. The reviewer for *Sporting and Dramatic News*, 5 January 1889, remarks: 'In the first act we meet almost exclusively mélodrame, accompanying either the spoken dialogue or action. It is intensely appropriate, in whatever instance it is employed. The orchestra crashes with the thunder, and wails with the blast, it accompanies with subdued rhythmical sounds the utterances and movements of the witches, it suggests the martial tune and beat of drum the tread of Macbeth's soldiers as they approach and retire in the distance.'

context, a particularly notable musical moment. In the wider context of the play, however, this brief march gradually takes on the role of a musical symbol. It figures prominently in the overture (to be discussed below), but – and this is unexpected – it also constitutes the main thematic element of the prelude to Act VI and the eventual triumph of Macduff. Associated with Macbeth in its first hearing, this march melody becomes emblematic not only of regal grandeur, but also as the crown as the symbol of legitimate authority.[46] As with the previous melodramas, music heard initially as serving a local function ultimately takes on a larger dramatic resonance later in the play.

The orchestration of the music plays a significant role in the creation of mood and atmosphere. Interestingly, the use of the horns in the introductory music to Act I, Scene 6, seems originally to have been Irving's idea.[47] Following the passage with the echoing horns, there is a smooth passage for just the strings – a 'slow' in theatre music terms – that provides a delicate overlap with the beginning of the dialogue. As mentioned previously, there was also harp music in this scene, which probably began at Lady Macbeth's entrance and seems to have continued through the scene. Together with the other elements in the scene, this short scene provided a 'special moment' of reflective peace and calm in an otherwise highly charged play. This sensitivity to mood, especially moods of a delicate nature, is a striking feature of all of Sullivan's incidental music and contributed significantly to the palpable sense of immediacy that marked Irving's productions.

The prelude to Act II is a further case in point. It begins with the chromatic musical figure that in Act III is heard during the 'Banquet Scene' (Act III, Scene 3) and is associated with Banquo's ghost (see musical examples, theme E). Its presence here is, in a sense, out of place, since Banquo is very much alive during Act II. This musical idea is followed by a passage for two harps, after which Banquo's ghost music is heard again and is followed by a powerful orchestral shudder. The strong character of these musical ideas and the sudden changes in style give this prelude an operatic character, one that both sets the scene and invites programmatic interpretation. About this prelude Joseph Bennett remarks: 'The prelude for the second act ... brings before us with admirable clearness what we know to be the purpose of Macbeth, and, no less, the gentle character of the gracious Duncan.'[48] The first of the programmatic associations Bennett makes is certainly plausible, even though the initial connection is with Banquo's ghost, not 'Macbeth's purpose': the eerie tremolo figures and chromaticism are part of the musical work-in-trade devices of ghostly music, stretching back to Richard Hughes's Ghost Melody from *The Corsican Brothers* and earlier works. How this music is to be associated with

---

46 In the autograph score, this march is misplaced and is given *before* the music to Act I, Scene 3. That the music was intended to come between Scenes 3 and 4 of Act I is evident by Sullivan's marking: 'Act I, Scene 3-4.' I would like to thank Robin Gordon-Powell for his helpful communications on these and other points concerning the autograph score.

47 In Irving's annotated prompt-book, located at Harvard (Shattuck 92), there is a note opposite p. 24 that reads: 'Horns repeated distantly – Kings [*sic*] attendants enter castle come out with Lady M and others.' Sullivan's music, with its echoing horns, beautifully fulfils what Irving seems to have asked for.

48 *Daily Telegraph*, 3 January 1889.

Macbeth's state of mind is, at this point in the dramatic situation, unclear. That it becomes so later is evident only in the Banquet Scene. More likely, this is a simpler case of Sullivan's planting of a musical seed in the listener's memory that, when later encountered in the Banquet Scene, takes on specific meaning – its significance rendered more compelling through this foreshadowing of a musically pregnant idea.

The other connection Bennett makes to 'gracious Duncan' is even more curious, since any direct musical connection to Duncan would have been made in the music to Act I, Scene 6. The music here is quite different. The more probable interpretation is again simpler: this music, containing soft ripples for the harp with a string accompaniment, is simply intended to set the mood for the peaceful, nocturnal scene that opens Act II – the act in which Macbeth kills King Duncan. A similarly complex situation is found in the prelude to Act III, which opens with a march-like melody that, in its underlying rhythmic and melodic elements, resembles the 'round dance' of the witches heard briefly in Act I, Scene 3. Here, these elements are transformed into a grand-sounding march. The basic association of this music with the public scene that follows, and with Macbeth as king, was readily observed by the reviewers.[49] Significantly, the march itself is in 5/4 time, an unusual metre which in its angularity and unusually loud scoring sounds not only generically regal, but also as a musical representation of a regal status shakily founded. This march-like opening is followed by another of Sullivan's 'sweet' melodies, for which a programmatic connection is not immediately evident, although the use of harp accompaniment to a suave clarinet melody readily evokes the emotional ambience of entertainment music for the banquet. Here, as in the prelude to Act II, the music is both specifically programmatic and more generalised in its mode of expression – in both cases instances of a high level of sophistication in the treatment of entr'acte music.

The music for Act IV in Irving's acting version constitutes the most extensive and dramatically significant music that Sullivan composed for *Macbeth*. Virtually all this music involves the witches and evokes the supernatural. Moreover, most of the music has some leitmotif function, linking it to both the overture and to the music for Act I. As is well known, the First Folio version of the play contains references to two songs from Middleton's *The Witch* in the scenes involving Hecate. Rather than excising these apparently 'foreign' elements, Irving brought them together to form an Act IV that dealt entirely with the supernatural. These two scenes, each containing one of the Middleton songs, as well as the part of Scene 1 that included the witches, offered a place for genuine spectacle, and Sullivan saved his most picturesque effects for this part of the play. The amount and significance of the music for this act is quite different from anything else in the play, for here it is the music

---

49 That reviewers readily associated this music with 'Macbeth as King' is evident from their corroborating comments: the reviewer for the *Sporting and Dramatic News*, 5 January 1889, described the music as 'marked by a pompous energy and breadth evidently intended to suggest the regal state in which Macbeth now appears'; similar views were expressed by Hueffer in *The Times* on 31 December 1888 and by Bennett in the *Daily Telegraph* on 3 January 1889: 'The third act is ushered in with pageant music of ... old world character ... in association with a graceful strain full of eloquence and beauty.'

that takes the lead – a quasi-operatic, time-arresting moment inserted by Irving and Sullivan into what is otherwise a normally paced drama. The music for this scene made a great impression on the audience and the critics. The reviewer for the *Lady's Pictorial* was clearly enchanted:

> How marvellously every note told! – the rasping chords on 'Double, double toil and trouble', as the repulsive hags stalked round their fiery stew; the suggestive themes as each apparition foretold Macbeth his fate; the strangely quaint measure to which the witches danced their 'antic round'; the haunting wail of Hecate's invisible elves, singing 'Black spirits and white' in a chorus of exquisite delicacy; and, last of all, after the change of scene to that weird landscape, 'Over woods, high rocks, and mountains', the broad, suave melody sung by the two groups of veiled female figures, standing as it were in an amphitheatre on either side of the stage. No wonder the music and the scene combined brought down the house. The entire conception was in the highest degree poetic...[50]

The introduction to Act IV (Illustrations 23 and 24) opens with the same music that begins at bar 25 of the overture (Themes B and C), the section devoted to the two witches' themes. Here, these passages are now more fully developed, consisting of 32 measures of highly charged minor-key music; the version heard in the overture is, in reality, an adumbration of this remarkably effective passage. At measure 33 the witches begin to speak over atmospheric music that interjects bursts of music into the spaces in the dialogue. The opening figure (Theme B) returns at measure 72 and is immediately followed by Hecate's entrance. It now becomes clear that this motif refers specifically to Hecate. For Sullivan, she is clearly the most important of the supernatural characters – the one whose music is the most highly charged and symbolic. Following her brief speech, in which she asks the spirits to sing about the cauldron ('Like elves and fairies in a ring'), the music moves directly into the choral setting of Middleton's song 'Black Spirits', the spirits consisting – musically, at least – of an offstage female chorus who are indicated in the score as 'Spirits in the Air'. The music they sing, accompanied by rapid figures in the strings, is in the

---

50 *Lady's Pictorial*, 5 January 1889. Of the many vivid press descriptions of Act IV, the account in the *Morning Post*, 31 December 1888, concerning the witches is particularly telling: 'Upon their presentation in the fourth act the scene was a gloomy and terrible cavern in the rocks, from which the ghostly flames ascended. Hecate soared or stood above ... with a solitary star in her hair, which burned brightly, but suffered occasional eclipse as the fumes ascended. The apparitions, one and all, were in this scene admirably managed ... A magnificent spectacle was afforded in the closing scene of this act, in which, in the flooding light of a setting sun, myriads of [sic] mystically-clad figures indulged in forms of strange and unhallowed worship. It is not, perhaps, wholly a weakness in this scene that some of the designs of Blake are recalled.' Regarding Sullivan's music for this scene, the reviewer for the *Star*, 31 December 1888, commented: 'It is in the fourth act, the great act of the supernatural business, the witches' cauldron, and the flying spirits, that Sir Arthur Sullivan gets his chance. He has provided a musical accompaniment to the incantation scene that sobs and sighs like fitful gusts of wind; then comes a weird burst of melody in the "Mingle, mingle", song, and finally, when the scene changes from the witches' cave to the shores of a Scotch loch under a wild, stormy sky, the crown of Hecate's attendant spirits break forth into a magnificent Mendelssohnic chorus.'

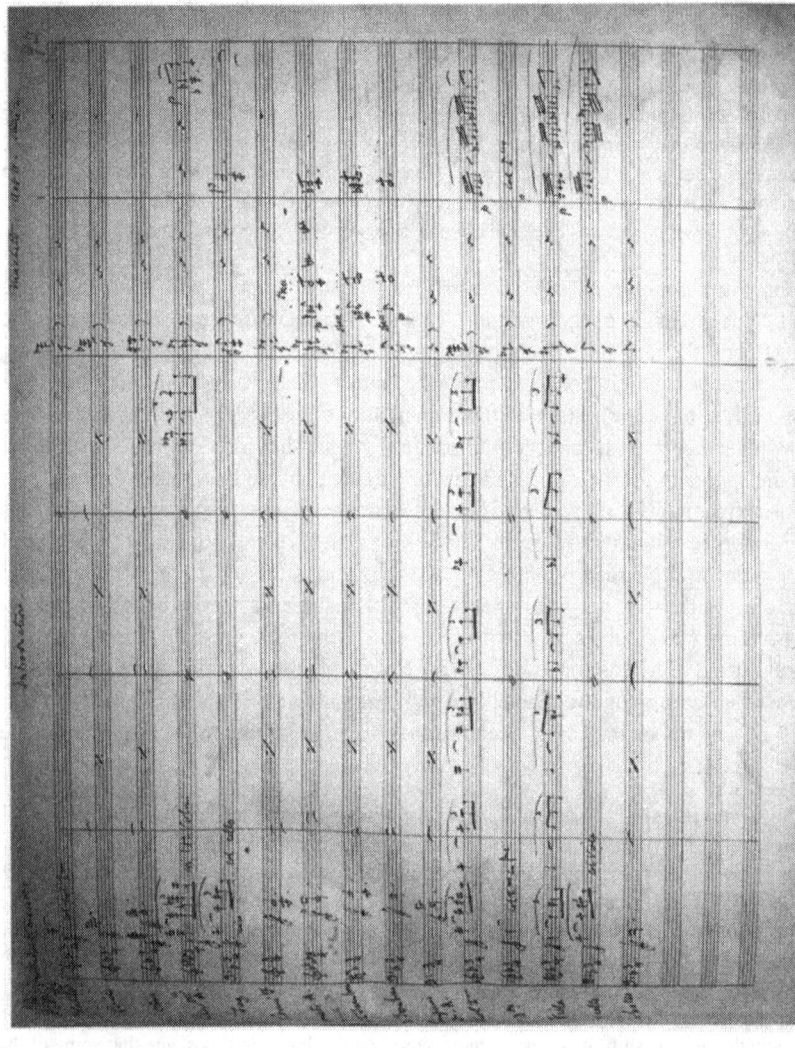

Illustration 23 Sullivan's autograph score: *Incidental Music to Macbeth: Introduction* (mm 1–6) Act IV Scene 1

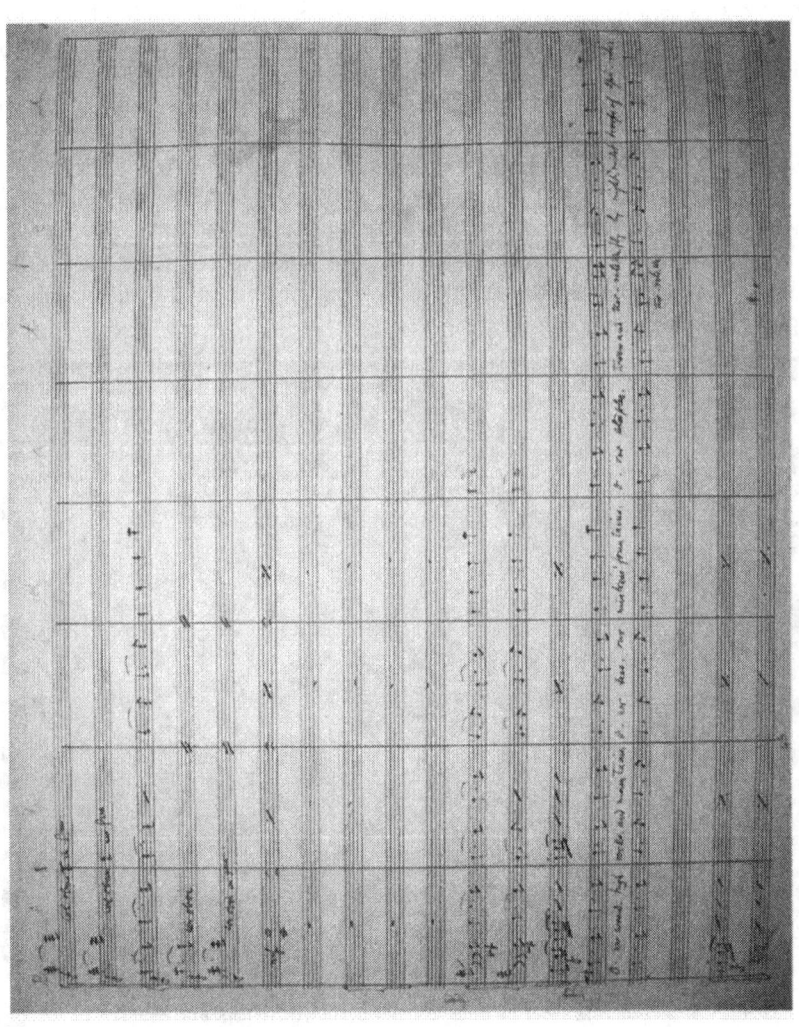

Illustration 24 Sullivan's autograph score: *Incidental Music to Macbeth* (mm 24–31) Act IV Scene 2

tradition of fairy music that goes back at least to Mendelssohn and is also found in earlier music by Sullivan.[51] In this instance, however, the musical antecedent is probably more recent, drawing its musical style from the Prologue of *The Golden Legend* (1886), a work much in vogue at the time. This point was noticed by Hueffer: 'Of the first chorus it will be sufficient to say that it is cast in the mould of the prologue to the *Golden Legend*',[52] and also by Klein: 'Anon Hecate appears, but sings not; it is her invisible familiars that sing "Black spirits and white" in a chorus of perfectly Mendelssohnian lightness and delicacy – the voices half wailing as they do in the prologue of *The Legend*, while the strings accompany with a continuous flow of staccato semiquavers.'[53] Upon the conclusion of this song, there is another melodrama for Macbeth and the witches, and for the apparitions of the eight kings (Illustration 25). The scene concludes with a short witches' dance, in which the main melody derives from Theme J, first heard in Act I, Scene 3. As with the Introduction, it is only here that the impact of the witches' music is fully encountered. What was only a shadowy reality earlier in the play is now given special force through the linking of musical ideas across the acts, reinforcing the effect of the supernatural as a significant element in the drama.

Illustration 25   *Macbeth*: Act IV Scene 1: The Weird Sisters and the Third Apparition

---

51 For example, the 'Dance of the Fairies' from The Incidental Music to *The Merry Wives of Windsor* (1874).

52 *The Times*, 31 December 1888.

53 *Sunday Times*, 30 December 1888.

Following a brief pause, the curtain rises again, now on a scene of magnificent weirdness, in which 60 choral spirits, all dressed in flowing white robes against a pale red background, sing the other Middleton song, 'Come Away, Come Away', taken from Shakespeare's Act III, Scene 5 (Illustration 26). Like the previous scene, the music opens with Theme B, but this time in D major rather than minor, and moves without delay into the tuneful melody for 'Over Woods, High Rocks and Mountains'. The continuation motif of this melody (Theme G) plays an important role in the coda section of the overture. To modern ears this entire melody has the character of an out-take from HMS *Pinafore* or *Iolanthe*, an impression which Hueffer also had, commenting: 'the composer in his final chorus becomes loud and operatic, evil-tongued persons might say "Pinaforean"'.[54] This scene, much lauded in its day, does give a good idea of what Irving's audience understood to be the appropriate musical component of spectacle – a moment, frozen in dramatic time, in which the music, in conjunction with the set and costumes, takes the audience into the emotional heart of the supernatural. The only unfortunate aspect of this spectacular and picturesque scene came at its end when, as the critic of the *Star* observed, 'in compliance with an execrable custom, Sir Arthur [was] led on by the manager, and this brief vision of a pudgy little person in swallow-tail coat shaking hands with a mail-clad warrior of the tenth-century spoiled, for some of us, all illusion of tragedy.'[55]

Illustration 26   *Macbeth*: Act IV Scene 2: Witches and Spirits in Chorus ('Come Away, Come Away...')

---

54 *The Times*, 31 December 1889.
55 *Star*, 31 December 1888.

The ensuing prelude to Act V presents a sharp contrast to the powerful effects and spectacle of Act IV. The music, quiet and serene, consists of a simple clarinet melody, accompanied by soft strings, which sets the pastoral mood that opens the act. Despite its outward simplicity, this melody, modally inflected and plaintive in tone, has a telling, inward character, one that distances the listener from the supernatural effects of the preceding act and serves to return the emotional action to the plane of 'normal life'. The style of the melody is similar to the flute melody that forms the entr'acte to Act III of Bizet's *Carmen*, the out-of-doors setting of both these scenes eliciting from their respective composers music that draws upon the long-established topos of woodwind music to evoke a sense of the pastoral. With Sullivan, the modal inflections distance the music in historical time and create an idealised sense of the 'past', appropriate in its pastoral character for the country lane in which the following scene takes place.[56] Only two minutes in length, this short number was singled out for its aptness and charm, the comment from the critic for the *World* being typical: 'The prelude to the fifth act [is], in my opinion the most interesting, with a perfectly enchanting clarionet solo; ... [it] is so original and so catching that the effect is certain'.[57]

Illustration 27   *Macbeth*: Act VI Scene 6: Macduff and Macbeth

According to the autograph score, the only music Sullivan composed for Act VI was the prelude. As indicated previously, however, the thematic material for this

---

56 It is worth noting that Sullivan chose to include this melody in the suite of pieces from the *Macbeth* music he prepared for the Leeds Festival in 1889.
57 *World*, 2 January 1889.

prelude is the same as the between-scenes music composed to link Act I, Scene 3 with Scene 4. Here the theme is extended to twice the original length. Heard as a preparation for the battle scenes for Act VI (Illustration 27), this music, essentially celebratory in character, can hardly be associated with Macbeth as villain. On one level, this music, generically march-like in character, serves to introduce the ensuing military scenes. This, at least, is the way this music was understood by Klein: 'The comparatively bright, martial prelude to the last act, founded upon the Scotch theme already heard, may be taken to indicate the coming conflict wherein right and valour will at last prevail'.[58] It is nevertheless striking that Sullivan chose to repeat (with additions) a march heard earlier in the play that is first connected to Macbeth. Since a link between this march and the image of the crown had previously been established, its musical transformation as a symbol of legitimacy is certainly a plausible interpretation.

That there was other music heard during this act is evident from comments made by several reviewers, who speak of music seemingly being 'sung' by the soldiers: 'One feature of the battle-scenes had a peculiar effect upon me. The soldiers "off" sang as they fought. Simulated distance made it a kind of hum, but there was a distinct tune in it.'[59] Similar, if more general, comments by other reviewers concerning the music heard during this act support this description: 'Much of the incidental music therein occurring is of a spirited, martial character, not untinged by certain peculiarities of Scottish tune, and essentially appropriate to the stirring incidents belonging to the final scenes of the Shakespeare's tragedy'.[60] That Irving wanted music during the final act seems clear. In a letter to Irving dated 1 December [1888], Sullivan fretted, 'I am in despair about the last Act – your idea about the wild chant or war song going on all the time is splendid in theory but at present it is impossible in practice, and I don't see any way to overcome the difficulty'.[61]

Whatever music was heard during the course of the final act remains a puzzle, for none of it is included in the extant score. One is forced, therefore, to accept a small gap between the incidental music as originally conceived by Sullivan and preserved in the formal score of the music and the music actually heard during the first production. These passages of music, including those for the harp previously mentioned, were presumably worked out during the final rehearsals and, to Sullivan, were of insufficient importance to be incorporated into his final version of the music. This approach to incidental music was by no means unique to Sullivan. He was, in fact, simply following a tradition that goes back at least to Beethoven and Mendelssohn, both of whom wrote theatre music that was at once 'practical' and 'abstract' – practical enough to work as music for a production, but also sufficiently abstract to stand on its own as an independent composition.

From a purely musical point of view, the most important item of incidental music to *Macbeth* is the overture (Illustration 28). Comprising nearly a third of the score, it is among Sullivan's most sophisticated and successful works in this genre. In style

---

58 *Sunday Times*, 30 December 1888.
59 *Liverpool Daily Post*, 31 December 1888.
60 *Sporting and Dramatic News*, 5 January 1889.
61 Sullivan's letter is in the Theatre Museum, THM 37/7/39.

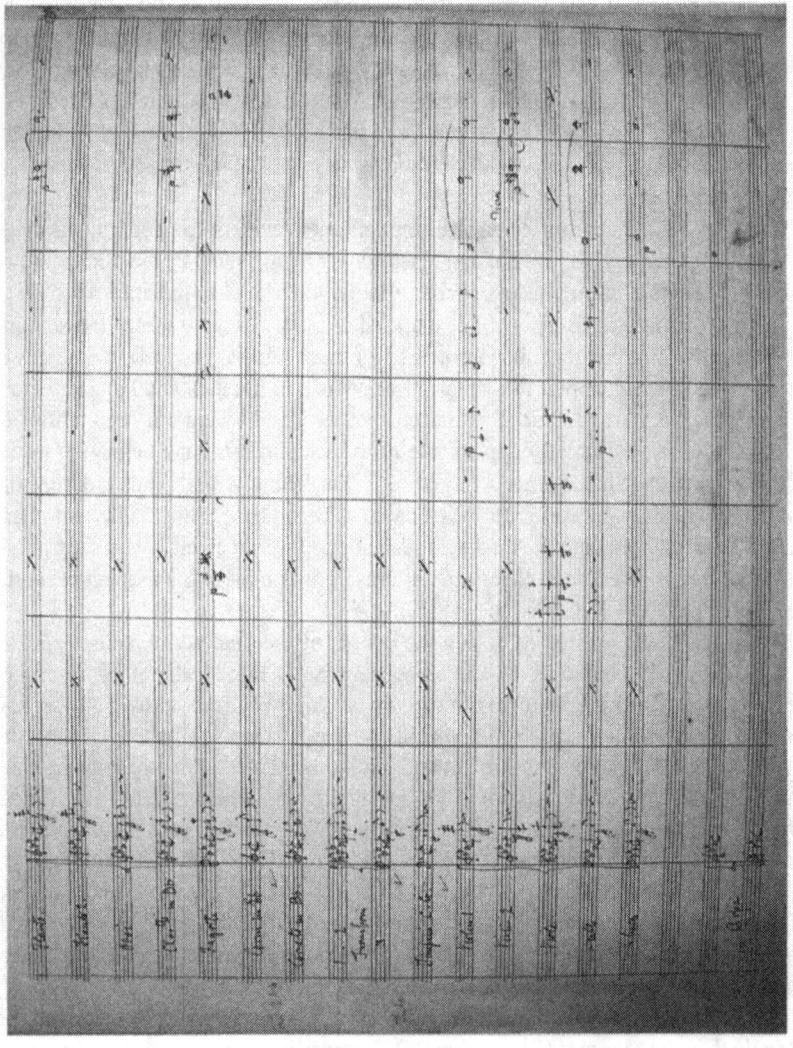

Illustration 28 Sullivan's autograph score: *Overture to Macbeth: Opening* (mm 1–7)

and structure it stands between the typical nineteenth-century orchestral overture of the Weber/Mendelssohn type, and the more modern idea of the symphonic poem as developed by Liszt in the 1850s, with its systematic transformation of a few musically pregnant motives. The overture was blithely described by most critics as appearing 'to follow the regular classical "form" with its two principal subjects and one or more episodes',[62] but the more astute reviewers were able to perceive the sophistication in Sullivan's treatment of the musical structure. Hueffer described the overture as:

> ... a finely conceived and effectively instrumented piece of music, steering a kind of middle ground between the classical form and the prelude in the modern sense of the word. For, although the themes are worked out according to rule, their dramatic significance is insisted upon, and a successful attempt at evolving a 'leit motive' for the witches and the baneful influence they represent can clearly be recognized.[63]

Bennett, writing in the *Daily Telegraph*, commented on the overture in terms of the variety of fundamental emotional states that it evokes:

> Sir Arthur's overture – in form a somewhat diminutive example of its kind – foreshadows much in the nature of the numbers to follow. It is by times suggestive of the martial, the supernatural, the purely picturesque, and the emotional; standing as a compendium for the play, so far as it comes within the province of the art.[64]

The overture thus accomplishes several things: first, on the simplest level, it provides the play with suitable music to evoke the spirit of tragedy and emotional darkness; second, it gives a parade of the main themes heard during the course of the play, allowing their significance, when heard later, to be more easily grasped; third, and most important, it provides the audience with an opportunity to contemplate the dramatic significance of the play through a working out of the themes in symphonic/dramatic fashion (see Table 2 and the accompanying table of musical themes). The overture opens with three powerful hammer strokes – chords which refer to the three witches – and are immediately followed by the gloomy, mysterious theme that symbolises Macbeth, or, perhaps more precisely, evokes the nervous, unsettled ambience of the production. This opening theme, Theme A, serves as the principal theme of the overture, but curiously it is not one of the musical leitmotifs in the incidental music to the play. This striking opening, reminiscent of Mendelssohn, is followed in rapid succession by themes associated with various characters and elements in the play: the witches (Themes B and C); the crown and the forces of justice (Theme D); and the music that accompanies the appearance of Banquo's ghost in Act III, which, with its chromatic line, is also linked to the music of the witches (Theme E). These ideas are clearly transitional in terms of their function in the musical structure and lead to Theme F – also not used in the music of the play – but which expresses with its 'musical sigh figures' an emotional character of sadness and

---

62 William Moy Thomas in the *Daily News*, 31 December 1888.
63 *The Times*, 31 December 1889.
64 *Daily Telegraph*, 31 December 1888.

longing – possibly a reference to Lady Macbeth.[65] This theme is followed in normal sonata form structure by a continuation idea, in this case a motive drawn from the second of the two Middleton songs, 'Over Woods, High Rocks and Mountains'. And the closing idea to the exposition, peaceful and calm, has the sole structural purpose to serve as closing material.

Table 2   Synoptic analysis of Sullivan's overture to *Macbeth* (1888 autograph score version)

Exposition	Measures	Comments
Theme A	1–24	Three dramatic introductory chords (three witches), followed by the opening theme (not heard in the music to the play): mysterious, gloomy, tragic/pathetic in character. (ur-Macbeth?) [Sonata form: Tonic Key Area, C minor – Principal Theme P^1]
Theme B	25–30	Principal witches' motif: weird, unworldly, illusory. Witches as agents of fate. (From Introduction to Act IV, Scene 1) [Sonata form: Tonic Key Area – P^2]
Theme C	31–42	Spirits of the Air: 'spirits in flight'. Pictorial, with running figures and 'spooky', offbeat harmonies and diminished-seventh chords. (From Act IV, Scene 1) [Sonata form: Transition T^1]
Theme D	43–48	Grand march motif: symbol of goodness, the crown, morality. (From Act I, Scene 3–4 – Duncan; and Prelude to Act VI – Macduff) [Sonata form: T^2]
Theme E	49–58	Banquo's Ghost music: also symbol of Macbeth's uneasy conscience and feelings of guilt. (From Prelude to Act II, and in Act III, Scene 3, 'Banquet Scene') [Sonata form: T^3]
Theme D	59–63	Repeat of grand march motif (Theme D).
Theme E	64–72	Repeat of Banquo's Ghost music (Theme E).
Theme F	73–90	Spacious string/woodwind melody, evoking a mood of sadness or longing, with harp/lower string accompaniment. (Not used within the music to the play: Lady Macbeth? Duncan?) [Sonata form: Second Key Area, E-flat major – Secondary Theme S^1]

---

65 It is customary in the scanty modern literature to hear this musical idea as referring to 'gracious Duncan'. At least these are the views of Percy Young, *Sir Arthur Sullivan* (New York, 1971), p. 230; and of Selwyn Tillett, Notes to *Arthur Sullivan: Incidental Music*, Marco Polo 8.223635. This is puzzling inasmuch as this melodic idea does not occur in the incidental music proper, and, compared to Lady Macbeth, Duncan is a much less important character. It may well be that this melody has only a structural purpose within the sonata structure of the overture. If, however, programmatic suggestions were to be made, this moment is more likely to be associated with Lady Macbeth, especially in the light of Terry's conception of the role.

Theme G	91–98	Second Spirits of the Air motif: spirits as benign, playful figures of the air (elves/fairies): 'Over woods, high rocks and mountains/Over seas, our mistress' fountains'. (From end of Act IV, Scene 2) [Sonata form: Secondary Theme continuation motif – S^2]
Theme H	99–108	'Peaceful theme' to conclude the Exposition [Sonata form: Closing Theme – K)
Development		
Theme B	109–14	Principal witches' motif. (In B minor!)
Themes C/J	115–24	'Spirits in flight' theme (Theme C) in alternation with second witches' motif (Theme J), the 'witches' round dance' (Act I, Scene 3, and Act IV, Scene 1)
Theme C	125–56	Long section devoted to the pictorial music of Theme C (Spirits of the Air), much in the character of Mendelssohnian fairy music. (Act IV, Scene 1)
Recapitulation		
Theme A/C	156–71	Restatement of the principal theme (Theme A) combined with the music for the Spirits of the Air (Theme C). Musical connection between Spirits of the Air and Macbeth [Sonata form: Recapitulation of thematic material in A minor – P^1]
Theme J	172–79	Restatement of second witches' motif from the Development. [Sonata form: Transition]
Theme G	180–87	Restatement of second Spirits of the Air motif in C major. [Sonata form: S^2]
Theme H	188–97	Restatement of the 'peaceful theme' in C major. [Sonata form: Closing Theme – K and conclusion of the Recapitulation (abbreviated)]
Coda		
Theme F	198–206	Restatement of Theme F. (Omitted in Recapitulation)
Theme A/D	207–33	Triplet transformation and diminution of Theme A (harmonically unstable) in combination with fragments of Theme D. Musical representation of the battle between Macbeth and Macduff, leading to a climax and a dramatic pause. Soft drum roll.
Theme D/G	234–74	Restatement and extension of Theme D (victory of Macduff) and jubilant conclusion, using final transformation of Theme G (Spirits of the Air motif) at the climax.

Example 1   Sullivan's overture to *Macbeth*: Theme A, mm 1–12 (allegro non troppo vivace)

Example 2   Sullivan's overture to *Macbeth*: Theme B, mm 25–31

Example 3   Sullivan's overture to *Macbeth*: Theme C, mm 25–27

Example 4   Sullivan's overture to *Macbeth*: Theme D, mm 43–48 (horns)

Example 5   Sullivan's overture to *Macbeth*: Theme E, mm 51–58 (strings and flute)

Example 6   Sullivan's overture to *Macbeth*: Theme F, mm 73–83 (strings, woodwind, harp)

Example 7   Sullivan's overture to *Macbeth*: Theme G, mm 91–98 (strings and clarinet)

Example 8   Sullivan's overture to *Macbeth*: Theme H, mm 99–108 (strings and clarinet)

Example 9   Sullivan's overture to *Macbeth*: Theme J, mm 118–21 (clarinet and trombones)

The development section opens with a reference to the central witches' motif and then fully develops the 'Spirits of the Air' motif (Theme C). This is followed by a passage that juxtaposes this motif with a fragment of the witches' 'round dance' before the return to a further elaboration of Theme C. Following a truncated recapitulation, the overture builds to a climax with a complex interweaving of the witches' theme and the crown theme and concludes with a peroration and transformation of the crown or 'legitimate authority' theme (Theme D). This final portion of the overture departs considerably from the 'regular form' of an overture and is clearly intended to represent the central issues of the play on a symbolic level.

The use of an overture to convey essential dramatic truths was, of course, a central feature of many nineteenth-century overtures to operas. Just how closely Sullivan was following tradition can be seen if one compares this overture with another familiar overture frequently played during the nineteenth century in opera houses and in the concert halls – Weber's Overture to *Der Freischütz*. Weber's overture contains a dramatic message similar in its essentials to *Macbeth,* at least as Sullivan and Irving viewed the play. Like *Macbeth, Der Freischütz* is the story of good versus evil, with evil ascendant throughout much of the opera; it also involves the supernatural as a significant component of the emotional and atmospheric backdrop. Sullivan's overture is similar in length and style to Weber's and, like *Der Freischütz,* contains themes which musically personify dramatic ideas. In both overtures good triumphs over evil, but only after a terrible symphonic struggle; both end with a blaze of glory. The endings of the two works are, in fact, strikingly similar in dramatic content. In both overtures the thematic material reaches a crisis, musically posing the question of which will triumph: good or evil. In both overtures, following a dramatic pause, the violins scurry from their lowest notes to their top register and in a blaze of C major glory give forth triumphant transformations of some of the main referentially coded ideas – in Sullivan's case, the witches' themes (Themes D and G). Symphonically, it appears, the witches told the truth, and, ultimately, good is indeed the victor.

Example 10   Sullivan's overture to *Macbeth*: Coda, mm 232–41

Example 11   C.M. Weber's overture to *Der Freischütz*: Coda, mm 281–95

With Sullivan the witches are, ultimately, the central element in the morality play, serving as agents of forces beyond the human domain that ultimately control human destiny. By placing the focus of the music on the witches, Sullivan – but not Irving – moves the arena of the dramatic action away from the human and concentrates, symbolically and atmospherically, on the supernatural. Thus there is no explicit thematic characterisation of either Macbeth or Lady Macbeth. Given the post-Wagnerian tendency of the time to reinforce dramatic character with musical characterisation, this is surprising.[66] While it is certainly possible to view this as admirable restraint on Sullivan's part, it is perhaps more accurate to see the *Macbeth* music as Sullivan's own conception of *Macbeth* as a play – a conception fundamentally sympathetic to Irving's, but differing slightly in emphasis. As it concerns the picturesque elements in the production and the creation of finely drawn atmosphere, Sullivan and Irving appear to have worked to a common purpose. However, the end of the play, where it was Irving's purpose to portray the moral horror that Macbeth ultimately becomes, there is no direct parallel in Sullivan. Even Lady Macbeth remains, essentially, without musical comment. Sullivan's music, marvellously atmospheric and delicately nuanced, remains, ultimately, within the intellectual and artistic framework of a decorative mode of understanding the play, its psychological dimension treated in the overture, the opening scene, and, especially, in the Act IV choral extravaganza – all of which place the emphasis upon the supernatural, not expressly Macbeth. This understanding of the significance of the play, expressed by Sullivan in musical terms, does not contradict Irving's conception; rather, it provides a dramatic counterpoint. It also may explain why there was so little music written for the end of the play. Instead of providing Macbeth with a melodrama at the end or even a celebratory fanfare for Macduff, Sullivan lets Shakespeare have the final say, the impact and symbolism of the conclusion of the play dramatically controlled by Irving without musical reinforcement of any kind.

In succeeding years Irving continued the practice, begun in earnest with *Macbeth*, of commissioning specific composers to write musical scores for his Lyceum productions. In *Macbeth* and also in other productions, Irving strived to achieve something approaching his idea of a totally integrated theatre, in which the arts of acting, costumes and scenic design, lighting and music all blended to create a total work of art or *Gesamtkunstwerk* – a kind of theatrical parallel to Wagner. Sullivan's music to *Macbeth* thus forms something of a watershed in the history of incidental music to plays through the close relationship between director and composer working towards a common purpose. In Irving's production of *Macbeth* the interpretive efforts of both director and composer coexist in a sympathetic, mutually reinforcing juxtaposition. Far from being mere 'sound and fury, signifying nothing', Sullivan's music provided an actual interpretation – a composer's interpretation – of the dramatic issues that lay at the heart of Irving's production of Shakespeare's play.

Acknowledgements

A project of this complexity incurs many debts. For help with matters minor and major, a warm thanks are extended to John H.B. Irving; Peter Ward Jones, Music Librarian, Bodleian Library; Rob Peter, College Archivist, Oriel College, Oxford; Catherine Hail of the Theatre Museum; Dr Peter Horton, Reference Librarian, Royal

---

66 Richard Strauss's tone poem, *Macbeth*, composed about the same time as Sullivan's overture, for example, concentrates almost exclusively on thematic ideas linked to Macbeth and Lady Macbeth. The supernatural element, while present, plays a lesser role. Strauss's work, written when he was still in his twenties is nevertheless more typical of its time than Sullivan's overture.

College of Music; Paul Meredith, Manager, Smallhythe Place; Dr Katharine Cockin of the University of Hull; Professor Jeffrey Richards of Lancaster University; Frances Hughes; Helen R. Thompson; Michael Kilgarriff, Editor, *First Knight*; David Eden, Editor, *Sir Arthur Sullivan Society Magazine*; the staff of Warner/Chappell Music, UK; Dr Georgianna Ziegler, Head of Reference, Folger Shakespeare Library; J. Rigbie Turner, Mary Flagler Cary Curator of Music Manuscripts and Books, The Morgan Library and Museum; Fredric Woodbridge Wilson, Curator of the Harvard Theatre Collection; Helen Adair of the Harry Ransom Center, the University of Texas at Austin; the staff of the Beinecke Rare Book and Manuscript Library, Yale University; the staff of Interlibrary Loans, McLennan Library, McGill University; and Richard Piggins of Solutions PrintPro.

I would also like to express special thanks to Professor Denis Salter of the Department of English, McGill University, for placing at my disposal his vast knowledge of Victorian theatre practices, items from his own personal collection of Victoriana, and for consultation and advice at every step of this project. The original idea for this project came from him, and, without his support and persistence, this chapter could not have been written.

Chapter 11

The Matter with Irving: Bernard Shaw and Irving Reconsidered

L.W. Conolly

It was the Austrians' fault. More specifically, it was the fault of the editor of the Vienna newspaper *Die Neue Freie Presse*. The story of the controversy arising from Shaw's response to a request from that newspaper for an obituary of Henry Irving has been told before, but it bears revisiting in light of its centrality to the received understanding of the relationship between Irving and Shaw, the relationship that is the subject of this essay – a relationship that is far more complex than one defined merely by the numerous public and private exchange of insults between them, however diverting those insults might be: 'a damned evil to the theatrical profession of Great Britain', said Irving of Shaw;[1] 'without exception absolutely the stupidest man I ever met', said Shaw of Irving.[2]

When Irving died on 13 October 1905, Shaw had written 16 plays, only one of which, however – *Arms and the Man* – had enjoyed commercial success in England. The Barker–Vedrenne seasons at the Court were on their way to establishing Shaw's reputation as a playwright, and Arnold Daly's productions in the United States – beginning with *Candida* in 1903 – were bringing Shaw's plays to the attention of American critics and audiences. (Irving died exactly two weeks before the huge public outcries about *Mrs Warren's Profession* erupted in New Haven and New York.) Shaw had flopped as a novelist, so his reputation in England at the time of Irving's death rested primarily on his work as a leading Fabian and as a music and drama critic, particularly, so far as drama was concerned, his weekly articles for the *Saturday Review* between January 1895 and May 1898. It was for the *Saturday Review* that Shaw wrote two articles about Irving that – like the obituary – feature prominently (and usually to Shaw's disrepute) in any assessment of the Shaw–Irving relationship. The articles are 'Why Not Sir Henry Irving?'[3] and 'Richard Himself Again'.[4] I shall return to both of them.

Given Shaw's prominence as a critic, it is perhaps not surprising that *Die Neue Freie Presse* should turn to him for an obituary for Irving. That no *British* paper

---

1   Edward Gordon Craig, *Henry Irving* (London, 1930), p. 24.
2   Bernard Shaw, *Collected Letters*, ed. Dan H. Laurence (New York, 1985–88), Vol. 1, p. 672.
3   Bernard Shaw, 'Why Not Sir Henry Irving?', *Saturday Review*, 9 February 1895.
4   Bernard Shaw, 'Richard Himself Again', *Saturday Review*, 26 December 1896.

asked Shaw for an obituary reflects both Shaw's known critical views of Irving and the unlikelihood of Shaw's respecting the proprieties and protocols of obituaries of the great and the good. In any event, Shaw wrote the obituary (in English) and sent it to Vienna in good faith, insisting, however, that the translation into German be done by Siegfried Trebitsch, an Austrian novelist and playwright authorised by Shaw since 1902 as his official German translator. Shaw's directive was ignored, and the unknown translator of the article that was published on 20 October 1905 made, in Shaw's words, 'a slip or two in his haste, and gave a malicious turn to some of my comments'.[5] To make matters worse, the version that was subsequently published in the British press was a clumsy translation back into English (by another unknown hand).

A good example of the mess created by all this is given by St John Ervine in his 1956 biography of Shaw. What began as a provocative, but hardly malicious, observation by Shaw that 'Irving took no interest in anything except himself ... and was not interested even in himself except as an imaginary figure in an imaginary setting' ended up in the English translation of the German translation as: 'He was a narrow-minded egoist, devoid of culture, and living on the dream of his own greatness.'[6]

In an attempt to set matters right, Shaw made available to the British press – without fee – his original essay. Of the London dailies, only the *Morning Post* took up Shaw's offer, publishing the essay on 5 December 1905.[7] But, by then, the damage – to Shaw's reputation, not Irving's – had been done. As Shaw ruefully observed some years later, 'there is no getting over the hard journalistic fact that as quarrels and vituperations make thrilling reading whilst vindications are dull and disappointing, it is much easier to get a calumny published than its refutation.'[8]

A particular bone of contention about the obituary was Shaw's alleged claim that Irving had *solicited* his knighthood (awarded in 1895). The offending verb from the German translation of Shaw's comments on the knighthood was 'verlangte' (in the phrase 'öffentlich und unmisverstandlich verlangte'), which Stephen Coleridge, descendant of Samuel Taylor and friend of Ellen Terry, read as 'importuned' or 'solicited'. Coleridge wrote to *The Times* on 24 October 1905 to refute 'on the authority of personal knowledge, Mr Shaw's statement that Irving ever solicited anybody at any time or place for a knighthood'.[9] But Shaw – with some justification – denied (in a letter to *The Times* the following day) that he had ever made such a statement. What he *had* written was that Irving 'actually compelled the Court to knight him by publicly and explicitly *demanding* [my emphasis] that he, as the head of the London stage, should be treated as the peer of the President of the Royal

---

5 Bernard Shaw, *Pen Portraits and Reviews* (London, 1932), p. 160.
6 St John Ervine, *Bernard Shaw. His Life, Work and Friends* (New York, 1956), p. 299.
7 The essay is also included in Shaw, *Pen Portraits and Reviews*, pp. 161–5.
8 Ibid., p. 160.
9 Shaw, *Collected Letters*, Vol. 2, p. 567.

Academy of Arts, who is always knighted in England as a matter of course'.[10] (Shaw is referring to a speech given by Irving at the Royal Institution on 1 February 1895.) And Shaw clarified his position still further in his letter to *The Times*, where he contrasts the implication of Coleridge's mistranslation ('a crawl up the backstairs of the palace') with the situation as Shaw saw it: 'There never was an act more publicly done by the head of a profession on its behalf, and never one more honourable to the doer.'

For those who could (or cared to) remember, Shaw had previously commended Irving for his Royal Institution speech – or at least that part of it that made the case for elevating the status of the acting profession in England. While regretting that Irving had missed an opportunity to speak sincerely and authoritatively about the art of acting, Shaw had praised Irving in his 1895 *Saturday Review* essay 'Why Not Sir Henry Irving?' (the appropriate emphasis is, I think, on *Not*) for advancing the case for official recognition 'worthily and courageously – worthily, because a title can add nothing to his personal eminence, and courageously, because many unworthy persons will wound him by seeing nothing in the act but a vain man grasping at a handle for his name'.[11] For once, I believe, there is no Shavian irony in what is simply a genuine compliment.

No matter. The 'appalling row' (as Shaw described the hullabaloo about his obituary in a letter to Trebitsch on 25 October 1905) went against Shaw. At a meeting of the London Shakespeare League attended by Shaw on 24 October 1905 there was a protest about his being allowed to speak,[12] and, even after all the facts became clear, Shaw continued to get bad press (from Gordon Craig, among many others) or no press (Shaw is entirely written out of Irving's life in the Brereton and Stoker biographies, though the relationship is amply and dispassionately discussed in Jeffrey Richards' recent biography).[13]

The problem with the reaction to the obituary is that the ensuing focus on the personal aspects of the Shaw–Irving relationship has diverted attention from other – more important – issues that Shaw addressed in the obituary and in previous essays on Irving. One of those essays – the notorious one on Irving's Richard III, published in the *Saturday Review* on 26 December 1896 – generated as much bustle and bother as the obituary, thus again clouding the real issues. In that essay Shaw was alleged to have accused Irving of being drunk on stage. Shaw was writing about the opening night of *Richard III* at the Lyceum on 19 December 1896. Irving, it seems, was not at his best – perhaps he rarely was on opening nights – and Shaw noted some shortcomings: nervousness, textual slips, lack of energy, lack of concentration. At one point, Shaw says, Irving 'electrified the house by very unexpectedly asking Miss [Maud] Milton [playing Elizabeth] to get further up the stage in the blank

---

10 Shaw, *Pen Portraits and Reviews*, p. 161.
11 Bernard Shaw, *Our Theatres in the Nineties* (London, 1932), Vol. 1, p. 33.
12 Shaw, *Collected Letters*, Vol. 2, p. 567.
13 Bram Stoker, *Personal Reminiscences of Henry Irving* (London, 1906); Austin Brereton, *The Life of Henry Irving* (London, 1908); Jeffrey Richards, *Sir Henry Irving: A Victorian Actor and His World* (London, 2005).

verse and penetrating tones of Richard'.[14] But the offending passage in Shaw's *Richard III* review was the one in which, having commented on the shortcomings of Irving's performance – particularly the ineffectiveness of the staging of the fight between Richard and Richmond – Shaw wrote: 'If Kean were to return to life and do the combat for us, we should very likely find it as absurd as his habit of lying down on a sofa when he was too tired or too drunk to keep his feet during the final scenes.'[15] It is a bit of a stretch to turn this into an accusation that Irving was drunk, but Irving thought it was such an accusation, and, more recently, Michael Holroyd concluded, on 'circumstantial evidence', both that Shaw *intended* to accuse Irving of being drunk and that indeed Irving *was* drunk. Part of the circumstantial evidence advanced by Holroyd – somewhat implausibly – is Irving's fall in his lodgings much later that night, causing a knee injury that necessitated the postponement (until February 1897) of further productions of *Richard III*.[16] Madeleine Bingham's view is also that Irving was 'neither sober nor perfect on that memorable night'.[17] Shaw made his own position clear in a letter to Irving on 29 April 1897, in which he said that he was 'sorry that the article should have caused you any uneasiness', but he denied absolutely that the comparison to Kean implied that Irving was drunk: 'If I had thought so, I'd have said so bluntly or else said nothing at all.'[18]

Irving used the occasion of Shaw's alleged accusation to inform Shaw that he did not wish to take up his option on *The Man of Destiny*, which he had held since July 1896, preferring instead a Napoleon play by Sardou, *Madame Sans-Gêne*, which opened at the Lyceum on 10 April 1897 (to which Shaw was not invited, but he forced his way in – 'Sardou's Napoleon is rather better than Madame Tussaud's, and that is all that can be said for it'[19]). Irving made the rejection of *The Man of Destiny* public, including his response to Shaw's letter, with a scathing comment almost worthy of Shaw himself: 'I had not the privilege of reading your criticism – as you call it – of Richard. I never read a criticism of yours in my life. I have read lots of your droll, amusing, irrelevant and sometimes impertinent pages, but criticism containing judgment and sympathy I have never seen by your pen.'[20]

---

14 *Our Theatres in the Nineties*, Vol. 2, p. 290. St John Ervine dismissed this as merely one of the 'trivial complaints' of 'a Dublin smartie'. 'Had GBS been more familiar with the stage and less addicted to the society of "intellectual" actresses', Ervine wrote, 'he would have known that players commonly carry on private conversations during a play.' 'It is recorded', Ervine continued, 'that Irving, while playing Othello and engaged in throttling Desdemona, asked the actress who took her part what they were having for supper that night, for he lodged with her mother, and as she breathed her last groan, she told him.' See Ervine, *Bernard Shaw*, pp. 294–5. History has not recorded, so far as I know, whether it was mutton or beef or poultry for supper.

15 Shaw, *Our Theatres in the Nineties*, Vol. 2, p. 291.

16 Michael Holroyd, *Bernard Shaw* (London, 1988–92), Vol. 1, pp. 362–3.

17 Madeleine Bingham, *Henry Irving and the Victorian Theatre* (London, 1978), p. 273.

18 Shaw, *Collected Letters*, Vol. 1, p. 751.

19 *Saturday Review*, 17 April 1897, quoted in Shaw, *Our Theatres in the Nineties*, Vol. 3, p. 110.

20 Laurence Irving, *Henry Irving. The Actor and His World* (London, 1951), p. 604.

Kerfuffle galore, then, between GBS and Henry Irving, and it is kerfuffle that illuminates as well as entertains. But it also distracts. There is more to the obituary than the translation row. It contains several – if muted – compliments: Irving was a 'public dignitary' who stood 'quite alone in his eminence'; he was 'imaginative and industrious in devising and executing stage effects'; his Mathias (*The Bells*) and Charles I (W.G. Wills, *Charles I*) were 'such miracles of finished execution that they raised a melodrama of no importance and a surpassingly bad historical play into dramatic masterpieces'; his success in the absence of 'a great national theatre with a highly trained audience and an established artistic tradition' was 'extraordinary'; and his 'greatest achievement' was 'the redemption of his profession from Bohemianism, the imposing himself on the nation as one of its most eminent men in it, and the official acknowledgment of that estimate by the accolade [of knighthood]'.[21]

Shaw is, however, also blunt and unequivocal in his criticism of Irving. Shaw was not enamoured of Irving's voice, which, when Irving spoke quickly, Shaw says, 'produced a hysterical whinnying which was ridiculous'. Moreover, Shaw charges, Irving had other technical deficiencies – deficiencies that restricted him to just one part in the dramatic repertory, Irving himself: 'His Hamlet was not Shakespear's Hamlet, nor his Lear Shakespear's Lear: they were both avatars of the imaginary Irving in whom he was so absorbingly interested.'[22] But it is in a couple of brief comments very early in the obituary that Shaw hits hardest: 'He did nothing for the living drama; and he mutilated the remains of the dying Shakespear.'[23]

Shaw does not elaborate on these charges in the obituary – apart from a brief additional comment on Irving's Lear, which, Shaw says, he 'murdered ... so horribly in cutting it down that he made it unintelligible'[24] – but few theatregoers could have been unfamiliar with Shaw's views on Irving's purported neglect of new plays and on his 'disembowelling' (Shaw's word) of Shakespeare. The 'disembowelling' accusation was made in Shaw's review of Irving's *Cymbeline* (Lyceum, 22 September 1896), a play that even Shaw acknowledged had to be cut (and Shaw, of course, did his own 'refinishing' of the play in his 1937 *Cymbeline Refinished*, which contains a new last act). But Irving, says Shaw, 'quite surpassed himself' in the way he 'defaced' the play 'with Cromwellian ruthlessness'.[25] This criticism of Irving's approach to Shakespeare – not just what Shaw saw as his cavalier attitude to text, but also his allegedly distorted interpretation of text – runs through all of Shaw's commentaries on Irving's productions and performances of Shakespeare. Shaw's earliest surviving theatre review, written when he was 23,[26] was of Irving's Shylock, and it sets the tone for much of his subsequent criticism. '[I]n despite of the testimony of every line of his part,' Shaw said, '[Irving] presented Shylock as a noble and mournful

---

21 Shaw, *Pen Portraits and Reviews*, pp. 161–5.
22 Ibid., p. 163.
23 Ibid., p. 161.
24 Ibid., p. 162.
25 Shaw, *Our Theatres in the Nineties*, Vol. 2, p. 198.
26 The essay was not published, however, until 1993 *Bernard Shaw: The Drama Observed*, ed. Bernard F. Dukore (University Park, 1993), Vol. 1, pp. 3–11.

man perverted by a sensational dramatist.' It was clear to Shaw, at least, that Irving's intention was 'to improve Shakespeare's delineation of the qualities indicated in the text', an 'error' caused by Irving's 'vanity', which 'blinded him to the comparatively abysmal depth of his own artistic ignorance'.[27] Fifteen years later Shaw put it this way: 'Sir Henry Irving has never thought much of the immortal William, and has given him more than one notable lesson – for instance, in *The Merchant of Venice*, where he gave us, not 'the Jew that Shakespear drew', but the one he ought to have drawn if he had been up to the Lyceum mark.'[28] Shaw was outraged by 'the Lyceum mutilation of *Lear*',[29] and perhaps even more so by Irving's treatment of *Much Ado About Nothing*, the curtailment of Dogberry's role counting as 'the most audacious' of Irving's 'manifold treasons against Shakespear'.[30] Shaw also judged Irving's Hamlet 'spurious', especially in comparison with Johnston Forbes-Robertson's. Hamlet came to Forbes-Robertson 'quite easily and spontaneously' because, unlike Irving, Forbes-Robertson 'wants to play Hamlet, and not to slip into his inky cloak a changeling of quite another race'.[31]

Such criticisms need to be set against Shaw's occasional – yet sincere – appreciation of some of Irving's Shakespearean endeavours, including his 'fine and genuine' Macbeth,[32] and his 'fresh and novel' Iachimo (despite what he did to the text of *Cymbeline*).[33] The problem, Shaw always believed, was that Irving considered *himself* the most important element of any of his productions. 'The truth is that he has never in his life conceived or interpreted the characters of any other author except himself', Shaw wrote in the *Saturday Review* on 26 September 1896. 'He is really as incapable of acting another man's play as Wagner was of setting another man's libretto; and he should, like Wagner, have written his plays for himself.' Failing this, Irving was simply 'compelled to use other men's plays as the framework for his own creations'. When, as with Shylock, Irving's 'own creation came into conflict with Shakespear's ... he simply played in flat contradiction of the lines, and positively acted Shakespear off the stage.'[34] The same was true of his *Hamlet* production, in which he 'achieved the celebrated feat of performing Hamlet with the part of Hamlet omitted and all the other parts as well, substituting for it and for them the fascinating figure of Henry Irving'.[35]

---

27 Ibid., Vol. 1, pp. 3–4.
28 *Saturday Review*, 14 December 1895; Shaw, *Our Theatres in the Nineties*, Vol. 1, p. 272.
29 *Sunday Times*, 9 December 1894; Shaw, *Bernard Shaw: The Drama Observed*, Vol. 1, p. 223.
30 *Saturday Review*, 26 February 1898; Shaw, *Our Theatres in the Nineties*, Vol. 3, p. 325.
31 *Saturday Review*, 2 October 1897; Shaw, *Our Theatres in the Nineties*, Vol. 3, p. 203.
32 *Saturday Review*, 1 December 1895; Shaw, *Our Theatres in the Nineties*, Vol. 1, p. 273.
33 *Saturday Review*, 26 September 1896; Shaw, *Our Theatres in the Nineties*, Vol. 2, p. 199.
34 Shaw, *Our Theatres in the Nineties*, Vol. 2, p. 198.
35 Ellen Terry and Bernard Shaw, *Ellen Terry and Bernard Shaw. A Correspondence*, ed. Christopher St John (New York, 1932), p. xxii.

It followed that, if Irving could treat even Shakespeare with such disrespect, other playwrights, including living playwrights, could expect little better – which takes us back to the second major charge made by Shaw against Irving in his obituary: Irving 'did nothing for the living drama'. Shaw, still a teenager, had first seen Irving act in Dublin as Digby Grant in *Two Roses*, a new comedy by James Albery. He had been enthralled, sensing then that 'a new drama inhered in this man',[36] and reflecting later that, if only Irving would apply to Ibsen the talents revealed in creating the 'modern realistic character' of Digby Grant, he 'would astonish us as much as Miss Achurch's Nora astonished us'.[37] At its best, Shaw believed, Irving's work was characterised by 'finish, dignity, and grace, and ... exactitude of ... expression of ... thoughts and feeling'.[38] What a pity that such talent 'was not applied to a new author'. It sometimes *was*, of course, but, Shaw continues, Irving 'owes it to literature to connect his name with some greater modern dramatists than the late Wills [e.g. *Charles I*, *Eugene Aram*, *Olivia*, *King Arthur*], or Tennyson [e.g. *Queen Mary*, *Becket*], who was not really a dramatist at all'.[39] Elsewhere Shaw added J. Comyns Carr to the list of living playwrights on whom Irving had wasted his talents, describing him in a review of his *King Arthur* as 'a jobber and nothing else'. 'I do not suppose that Mr Irving said to Mr Comyns Carr in so many words "Write what trash you like: I'll play the real King Arthur over the head of your stuff"; but that was what it came to. And the end of it was that Mr Comyns Carr was too much for Mr Irving.'[40] When Shaw wrote 'Sir Henry Irving is completely independent of the dramatist, and only approaches him in moments of aberration',[41] he was exaggerating, of course, just as he was (and this time he admitted it) when he said that Irving 'regarded an author as a person whose business it was to provide plays at five shillings an act, and, in emergencies, to write the fifth act whilst the fourth was being performed'[42] – relegating the playwright to much the same professional status as the five-shilling dentist in *You Never Can Tell*. For Shaw, Irving abandoned 'a fundamentally serious social function for a fundamentally nonsensical theatrical accomplishment'. He could have helped 'create a new drama instead of galvanizing an old one and cutting himself off from all contact with the dramatic vitality of his time'.[43]

What prompted Irving to take this path? In his more cynical moments Shaw saw it as a matter of ego, of power. Shakespeare was not there to argue with Irving, and when the '[living] dramatist's business is the merest trash', the actor's 'creative activity is unhampered and uncontradicted; and the author's futility is the opportunity

---

36 Ibid., p. 20.

37 Shaw, *Our Theatres in the Nineties*, Vol. 3, p. 145. Shaw is referring to Janet Achurch's success as Nora in Ibsen's *A Doll's House* at the Novelty Theatre, London, in June 1889 (which Shaw reviewed in the *Manchester Guardian* on 8 June 1889; see Shaw, *Bernard Shaw: The Drama Observed*, Vol. 1, pp. 106–7).

38 *Saturday Review*, 14 December 1895; Shaw, *Our Theatres in the Nineties*, Vol. 1, p. 271.

39 Shaw, *Our Theatres in the Nineties*, Vol. 1, p. 273.

40 *Saturday Review*, 19 January 1895; Shaw, *Our Theatres in the Nineties*, Vol. 1, p. 15.

41 *Saturday Review*, 10 July 1897; Shaw, *Our Theatres in the Nineties*, Vol. 3, p. 185.

42 Terry and Shaw, *Ellen Terry and Bernard Shaw: A Correspondence*, p. xxii.

43 *Saturday Review*, 29 May 1897; Shaw, *Our Theatres in the Nineties*, Vol. 3, p. 146.

for the actor's masterpiece'.[44] In more sanguine (and forgiving) moods Shaw simply came to the conclusion that it was pointless to criticise Irving for not serving the needs of the drama. Irving's artistic sensibilities were unsuited to the task. '[H]ow *can* [my emphasis] he bring his transfigurations and fantasies to bear on the realties of the modern school? They have no more to do with Ibsen than with Shakespear or any other author save only Henry Irving himself.'[45]

Thus it is that, although Shaw says in his preface to the Terry–Shaw correspondence that he was 'enraged' by the direction that Irving's (and Terry's) career took, the tone of this retrospective (written in June 1929) is more one of sorrow than of anger: sorrow that the Irving–Terry partnership, one 'apparently marked out by Nature to make a clean break with an outworn past and create a new stage world',[46] had not fulfilled its potential; sorrow that Irving's 30 years at the Lyceum, though 'a most imposing episode in the history of the English theatre', represented, in the end, 'an exasperating waste of talent'.[47] It had hardly been a waste, but one can understand Shaw's disappointment. Was Shaw's view of Irving driven by jealousy (of his success) and ignorance (of the art of acting) as Laurence Irving supposes?[48] I think not. Shaw was not given to jealousy, and in any case he was not likely to be jealous of what he could not respect. And expressing distaste for Irving's acting is not quite the same as being ignorant of the art itself – which Shaw certainly was not. 'Grudge' was the word that Shaw used – a 'grudge against the old Lyceum Theatre, against Irving, and even against Ellen herself'.[49] The grudge applied especially strongly to Terry's relationship with Irving – a relationship that, in Shaw's view, destroyed her career. The frustration is palpable when Shaw speaks of this: 'When I think of the originality and modernity of the talent she revealed twenty years ago, and of its remorseless waste ever since in "supporting" an actor who prefers *The Iron Chest* [by George Colman the Younger] to Ibsen', he wrote in the *Saturday Review* on 6 February 1897, 'my regard for Sir Henry Irving cannot blind me to the fact that it would have been better for us twenty-five years ago to have tied him up in a sack with every existing copy of the works of Shakespear, and dropped him into the crater of the nearest volcano.'[50] The 'us' in this context is on one level (perhaps the subconscious level) Shaw and Ellen Terry, but its surface referent at least is the world

---

44 *Saturday Review*, 26 September 1896; Shaw, *Our Theatres in the Nineties*, Vol. 2, p. 199.

45 *Saturday Review*, 30 January 1897; Shaw, *Our Theatres in the Nineties*, Vol. 3, p. 31.

46 Terry and Shaw, *Ellen Terry and Bernard Shaw: A Correspondence*, p. xxi.

47 Ibid., p. xxiii.

48 Irving, *Henry Irving*, p. 577. In a letter to *The Times Literary Supplement*, 7 July 1966, Laurence Irving spoke of Shaw's 'implacable sense of grievance' against Henry Irving, a feeling that caused him 'to make Irving the target of his ridicule, pursuing his quarry beyond the grave until 1937'. As a condition for agreeing to design the film version of *Pygmalion* (released in 1938), Irving insisted on Shaw's 'recantation or the cessation of his hostilities'. Thereafter, 'Shaw held his fire and let Irving rest in peace'. Laurence Irving also says in the letter that Shaw told him that 'I was never really fair' to Irving.

49 Terry and Shaw, *Ellen Terry and Bernard Shaw: A Correspondence*, p. xiv.

50 Shaw, *Our Theatres in the Nineties*, Vol. 3, p. 37–8.

of theatre. And no doubt Shaw did dream from time to time what a Shakespeare-less and Irving-free theatre might have been like.

Shaw learned to come to terms with Shakespeare, but never with Irving. In 1952, two years after Shaw's death and nearly 50 years after Irving's, Gordon Craig was invited by Val Gielgud, Director of BBC Radio and Television Drama, to reflect on what divided Shaw and Irving. In his talk on the BBC's Third Programme Craig said that 'it was all too petty', that 'there is no reason why any playwright and any great actor should not get along famously'. He talked then about 'some of the minor reasons why a partnership between Irving and Shaw was impossible', but concluded – as if analysing a Shakespearean tragedy – that they quarrelled 'because they were alike in one thing – and that the most wicked thing on earth. Each was possessed by the same demon ambition: overwhelming and awful personal ambition.'[51]

Well, yes, it doesn't do to be modest in the theatre business, and while Craig chose not to refer at all to the spats about the knighthood, Irving's Richard or *The Man of Destiny*, he was right to look for a bigger cause. Putting it all down to ambition, however, begs too many questions. What divided Irving and Shaw in the final analysis was the great gulf between their views of what theatre could and should be and do, the gulf between the actor's theatre and the playwright's theatre – a theatre that, in Shaw's view, should be 'a factory of thought, a prompter of conscience, an elucidator of social conduct, an armoury against despair and dullness, and a temple of the Ascent of Man'.[52] The rhetoric and vision of such statements are definitively Shavian, not Irvingesque. They bespeak a fundamental difference of principles and practices that Shaw defined and debated more eloquently and vigorously than Irving – it was, after all, not just his job but his vocation to do so – a difference that both men recognised, but only one of whom regretted.

---

51 Craig's talk was broadcast in July 1952 and published in The *Listener*, 17 July 1952. I am indebted to Denis Salter for bringing this to my attention.

52 Bernard Shaw, *Dramatic Opinions and Essays* (London, 1909), Vol. 1, p. xxiii.

Bibliography

Ahmad, Raffiüddin, Letter to the Editor, *The Times,* 26 September 1890.
Allen, Vivien, *Hall Caine: Portrait of a Victorian Romancer*, Sheffield, 1997.
Antoine, André, *Mes Souvenirs sur le Théâtre-Libre*, Paris, 1921.
Archer, William, *Henry Irving Actor and Manager: A Critical Study*, London, 1883.
——, *The Theatrical 'World' of 1895*, London, 1896.
——, and R.W. Lowe, *The Fashionable Tragedian*, London, 1877.
Ashwell, Lena, *Myself a Player*, London, 1936.
Auerbach, Nina, *Ellen Terry: Player in Her Time*, London, 1987.
Bablet, Denis, *The Theatre of Edward Gordon Craig*, London, 1981.
Bancroft, Squire, *Empty Chairs*, London, 1925.
Barrows, Susan, *Distorting Mirrors*, New Haven, 1981.
Batholomeusz, Dennis, *Macbeth and the Players*, Cambridge, 1969.
Bayliss, Wyke, '"Fears" or "Teares", *Macbeth*, Act IV, Scene 5', *National Review*, 12, 1889, pp. 730–35.
Beaugé, Gilbert and Jean-François Clément, *L'image dans le monde arabe*, Paris, 1995.
Beerbohm, Max, *And Even Now*, New York, 1921.
——, *Around Theatres*, London, 1953.
——, *More Theatres 1898–1903*, London, 1969.
Besançon, Alain, *The Forbidden Image: An Intellectual History of Iconoclasm*, trans. Jean Marie Todd, Chicago, 2000.
Bingham, Madeleine, *Henry Irving and the Victorian Theatre*, London, 1978.
Bland, Lucy, *Banishing the Beast*, London, 1995.
Bond, R. Warwick, '"King Arthur" on the Stage', *The Fortnightly Review*, CCCXLI, New Series, 1 May 1895, p. 720.
Borowitz, Helen, '*King Lear* in the Art of Ford Madox Brown', *Victorian Studies*, **21**, 1978, pp. 309–34.
Bradby, David, Louis James and Bernard Sharratt, eds, *Performance and Popular Drama: Aspects of Popular Entertainment in Theatre Film and Television 1800–1976,* Cambridge, 1980.
Braun, Edward, ed., *Meyerhold on Theatre*, London, 1968.
Brereton, Austin, *The Life of Henry Irving*, 2 vols, London, 1908.
Brereton, Austin, 'Laurence Irving. Life in Russia', *The Times*, 31 August 1921.
——, *'H.B.' and Laurence Irving*, London, 1922.
Brook, Peter, *The Shifting Point: Forty Years of Theatrical Exploration 1946–1987*, London, 1988.
——, *The Empty Space*, Harmondsworth, 1990.
Bulman, James C., *'The Merchant of Venice'*, Manchester, 1991.
Burne-Jones, Georgiana, *Memorials of Edward Burne-Jones*, London, 1912.

Caine, Hall, *Richard III and Macbeth: The Spirit of Romantic Play in Relationship to the Principles of Greek and of Gothic Art, and to the Picturesque Interpretations of Mr. Henry Irving: A Dramatic Study*, London and Liverpool, 1877.
Caine, Hall 'A Literary Causerie', *Speaker*, 4 October 1890.
——, *My Story*, New York, 1909.
——, *The White Prophet*, London: Heinemann, 1909.
——, 'Why I Wrote *The White Prophet*', pamphlet, London 1909.
Calvert, Louis, *Problems of the Actor*, London, 1919.
Carr, Alice, *Mrs. J. Comyns Carr's Reminiscences* (2nd edn), ed. Eve Adam, London, 1926.
Carr, J. Comyns, *King Arthur; A Drama in a Prologue and Four Acts*, New York and London, 1895.
——, *Some Eminent Victorians*, London, 1908.
Chothia, Jean, *André Antoine*, Cambridge, 1992.
Clarke, Hamilton, *A Manual of Orchestration: Designed Especially to Enable the Amateur To Follow Intelligently the Performance of Orchestral Music*, London, 1888.
Cockin, Katherine, *Edith Craig (1869–1947): Dramatic Lives*, London, 1998.
——, *Women and Theatre in the Age of Suffrage: The Pioneer Players 1911–25*, London, 2001.
Coleman, John, 'Facts and Fancies about *Macbeth*', *Gentleman's Magazine*, 266, 1889, pp. 218–32.
Compact Edition of the Dictionary of National Biography, 2 vols (Oxford, 1995).
Craig, Edward Gordon, *Henry Irving*, London, 1930.
——, *Ellen Terry and Her Secret Self*, London, 1931.
Daly, Frederic, *Henry Irving in England and America 1838–44*, London, 1884.
Darbyshire, Alfred, *The Art of the Victorian Stage*, New York, 1969.
Davis, Tracy C., *Actresses as Working Women: Their Social Identity in Victorian Culture*, London, 1991.
——, *The Economics of the British Stage, 1800–1914*, Cambridge, 2000.
de Bornier, Henri, *Mahomet, drame en cinque actes, en vers*, Paris, 1890.
DeLong, Kenneth and Denis Salter, 'C.V. Stanford's Incidental Music to Henry Irving's Production of Tennyson's *Becket*', *Theatre History Studies*, **3**, 1983, pp. 69–86.
Denny, Colleen, *At the Temple of Art: The Grosvenor Gallery, 1877–1890*, Madison, 1996.
Eaton, Walter Pritchard, 'Of Justifiable Homicide', *Sunday New York Sun*, 15 March 1908.
Ellmann, Richard, *Oscar Wilde*, New York, 1988.
Ervine, St John, *Bernard Shaw. His Life, Work and Friends*, New York, 1956.
Farfan, Penny, *Women, Modernism, and Performance*, Cambridge, 2004.
Fenster, Thelma S., ed., *Arthurian Women: A Casebook*, New York, 1996.
Finck, Herman, *My Melodious Memories*, London, 1937.
Fiske, Roger 'The Macbeth Music', *Music and Letters*, **45**(2), 1964, pp. 114–25.
Fitzgerald, Percy, *Henry Irving: Twenty Years at the Lyceum*, London, 1893.
——, *Sir Henry Irving: A Biography*, London, 1906.

Foulkes, Richard, ed., *Shakespeare and the Victorian Stage*, Cambridge, 1986.
——, ed., *British Theatre in the 1890s*, Cambridge, 1992.
——, *Church and Stage in Victorian England*, Cambridge, 1997.
Funck-Brentano, Frantz, *Legends of the Bastille*, trans. George Maidment, London, 1899.
Gabriel, Gilbert W. 'Dostoievsky to the Contrary', *New York Sun*, 14 October 1926
Galdemar, Ange, *Robespierre*, London, 1899.
Gardner, Joseph T. Jr, 'Hawes Craven, William Telbin and Joseph Harker: An Analysis of the Scenographic Practices of Henry Irving's Principal Scene Painters at the Lyceum', Florida State University PhD dissertation, 1977.
Gilbert, Sandra M. and Susan Gubar, *The Madwoman in the Attic: The Woman Writer and the Nineteenth-Century Literary Imagination*, New Haven, 1979.
Girouard, Marc, *The Return to Camelot: Chivalry and the English Gentleman*, New Haven, 1981.
Gordon-Powell, Robin, *Arthur Sullivan: Incidental Music to* Macbeth, London, 2006.
Hall, Philip, 'The Theatre', *Boston Herald*, 20 December 1931.
Hammond, Mary, 'Hall Caine and the Melodrama on Page, Stage, and Screen', *Nineteenth Century Theatre and Film,* **31**, June 2004.
Hammond, Percy, 'The Theaters', *New York Tribune*, 15 October 1926.
Harker, Joseph, *Studio and Stage*, London, 1924.
Hatton, Joseph, *Irving's Impressions of America*, Boston, 1884.
——, *Reminiscences of J L Toole*, London, 1889.
Haydon, Colin and William Doyle, eds, *Robespierre*, Cambridge, 1999.
Heilbrun, Carolyn G., *The Garnett Family*, New York, 1961.
Hemmings, F.W.J. *The Theatre Industry in Nineteenth Century France*, Cambridge, 1993.
Hiatt, Charles, *Henry Irving: A Record and Review*, London, 1899.
Hicks, Seymour, *Between Ourselves*, London, 1930.
Hime, H.W.L., *Wagnerism: A Protest*, London, 1882.
Holland, L[aurence] G[ifford], '"Macbeth"', *Cornhill Magazine*, NS 12, 1889, pp. 133–54.
Hollingshead, John, *Gaiety Chronicles*, London, 1898.
Holroyd, Michael, *Bernard Shaw*, London, 1988–92.
Hosek, Chaviva and Patricia Parker, eds, *Lyric Poetry: Beyond New Criticism*, Ithaca, 1985.
Hudson, Derek, *Norman O'Neill: A Life of Music*, London, 1945.
Hughes, Alan, *Henry Irving, Shakespearean*, Cambridge, 1981.
Hughes, Frances, 'The End of a Quest: Letters of Stephen Coleridge and E.T.', *First Knight: The Journal of the Irving Society,* **IX**(1), June 2005, pp. 13–26.
Hulme, David Russell, 'Sullivan's *Macbeth* Music', *Sir Arthur Sullivan Society Magazine*, (18), Summer 1984, pp. 11–17
Innes, Christopher, *Edward Gordon Craig*, Cambridge, 1983.
Irving, Henry, *The Drama: Addresses*, London, 1893.
Irving, H.B., *Occasional Papers, Dramatic and Historical*, Boston, 1907.
——, *A Book of Remarkable Criminals*, New York, 1918.

Irving, John H.B, 'Quest For Missing Ellen Terry Letters', *First Knight: The Journal of the Irving Society*, **2**, December 2001, pp. 44–51.
Irving, Laurence, *Henry Irving: The Actor and His World*, London, 1951.
——, *The Successors*, London, 1967.
Jacobs, Arthur, *Arthur Sullivan: A Victorian Musician*, Portland, 1992.
Jameson, Fredric, *Postmodernism, or, The Cultural Logic of Late Capitalism*, Durham, 1991.
Jones, Henry A., *The Shadow of Henry Irving*, London, 1931.
Kassabian, Anahid, *Hearing Film*, New York, 2001.
King, W.D., *Henry Irving's Waterloo*, Berkeley, 1993.
Klein, Herman, *Musicians and Mummers*, London 1925.
Large, David C. and William Weber, eds, *Wagnerism in European Culture and Politics*, Ithaca and London, 1984.
Leatherbarrow, W.J., ed., *Dostoevskii and Britain*, Oxford and Providence, 1995.
Le Bon, Gustave, *Psychologie des foules*, Paris 1895.
Leighton, Robert, Letter to the Editor, *Speaker*, 1 November 1890.
Lelyveld, Toby, *Shylock on the Stage*, Cleveland, 1960.
Llewellyn Smith, H. and Vaughan Nash, *The Story of the Dockers' Strike, Told by Two East Enders*, London, 1890.
Lupack, Alan, *Arthurian Drama: An Anthology*, New York, 1991.
Lyotard, Jean-François, *The Postmodern Condition: A Report on Knowledge*, trans. Régis Durand, Manchester, 1984.
'M. de Bornier's "Mahomet"', *Spectator*, 21 June 1890.
Mackail, J.W., *Life of William Morris*, 2 vols, London, 1899.
Mackenzie, Alexander, 'Sir Henry Irving and Music: Some Reminiscences', *Musical Times*, 46(11), 1905, pp. 714–16.
MacKenzie John M., *Orientalism: History, Theory, and the Arts*, Manchester, 1995.
McClelland, J., *The Crowd and the Mob, from Plato to Canetti*, London, 1989.
Mancoff, Debra N., ed., *The Athurian Revival*, New York, 1992.
——, ed., *The Return of King Arthur*, New York, 1995.
Marbury, Elizabeth, *My Crystal Ball: Reminiscences*, London, 1924.
Mayer, David, 'Nineteenth Century Theatre Music', *Theatre Notebook*, **30**(3), 1976, pp. 115–22.
—— and Mathew Scott, *Four Bars of 'Agit': Incidental Music for Victorian and Edwardian Melodrama*, London, 1983.
—— et al., eds, *Henry Irving and 'The Bells': Irving's Personal Script of the Play*, Manchester, 1987.
Meisel, Martin, *Realizations: Narrative, Pictorial and Theatrical Arts in Nineteenth-Century England*, Princeton, 1983.
Michelet, Jules, *Histoire de la révolution française*, Paris, 1847–52.
Montegomery, John Douglas, 'Macbeth, Considered as a Celt', *National Review*, 12, 1889, pp. 181–90.
'Mr. Irving as "Mahomet": New Schemes at the Lyceum', *Pall Mall Gazette*, 27 June 1890.
Murray, Paul, *From the Shadow of Dracula: A Life of Bram Stoker*, London, 2004.
Newton, H. Chance, *Cues and Curtain Calls*, London, 1927.

——, *Crime in the Drama*, London, 1927.

Ninova, A.A., ed., *Dostoevskiy i teatr. Sbornik statey*, Leningrad, 1983.

Odell, George C., *Shakespeare from Betterton to Irving*, 2 vols, New York, 1920.

O'Neill, Norman, 'Music to Stage Plays', *Proceedings of the [Royal] Musical Association*, 37th Session, 1910–11, pp. 85–102.

Osborne, John, *The Meiningen Court Theatre 1866–1890*, Cambridge, 1988.

Palmer, John, 'Laurence Irving', *Saturday Review*, 6 June 1914.

Pemberton, T. Edgar, *Sir Charles Wyndham: A Biography*, London, 1904.

Phelps, Gilbert, *The Russian Novel in English Fiction*, London, 1956.

Phené-Spiers, Richard, 'The Architecture of *Coriolanus* at the Lyceum Theatre', *Architectural Review*, **10**, 1901, pp. 2–21.

Poulson, Christine, 'Costume Designs by Burne-Jones for Irving's Production of *King Arthur*', *The Burlington Magazine*, 128, 1986, pp. 18–24.

Powell, Kerry, ed., *The Cambridge Companion to Victorian and Edwardian Theatre*, Cambridge, 2004.

Raysor, T.M., ed., *Miscellaneous Criticism of Samuel Taylor Coleridge*, London, 1936.

Reed, Thomas B., ed., *Modern Eloquence: Occasional Addresses*, Philadelphia, 1900.

Richards, Jeffrey, *Sir Henry Irving: A Victorian Actor and His World*, London, 2005.

——, ed., *Sir Henry Irving, Theatre, Culture and Society: Essays, Addresses and Lectures*, Keele, 1994.

Robertson, W. Graham, *Time Was*, London, 1931.

Rosenberg, Marvin, *The Masks of Macbeth*, Berkeley, 1978.

Rosenfeld, Sybil, *A Short History of Scene Design in Great Britain*, Oxford, 1973.

Rouder, Wendy Phyllis, 'Henry Irving's *Macbeth*', University of Illinois dissertation, 1971.

Rowell, George, ed., *Nineteenth Century Plays*, London, 1953.

Russell, Edward R., '*Romeo and Juliet* at the Lyceum', *Macmillans Magazine*, 46, 1882, p. 326.

St John, Christopher, *Henry Irving*, London, 1905.

Saintsbury, H.A. and Cecil Palmer, eds, *We Saw Him Act. A Symposium on the Art of Sir Henry Irving*, New York, 1939 and 1969.

Sardou, Jean, *La Maison de Robespierre, réponse à M.E. Hamel*, Paris, 1895.

——, ed., *Théâtre Complet*, Paris, 1935.

Sayler, Oliver M., *the Russian Theatre*, New York, 1922.

'Scene Painters and Scene Painting: A Talk with Mr. Hawes Craven', *Sala's Journal*, 4 March 1893, pp. 208–9.

Scott, Clement, Review of *Romeo and Juliet*, *Theatre*, 5, 1882, pp. 230–3.

——, 'Death of Mr. Pigott, Examiner of Stage Plays', *Daily Telegraph*, 25 February 1895

——, *From 'The Bells' to 'King Arthur'*, London, 1896.

Senelick, Laurence, *The Prestige of Evil. The Murderer as Romantic Hero from Sade to Lacenaire*, New York, 1987.

Shakespeare, William, *Macbeth A Tragedy by William Shakespeare as Arranged for the Stage by Henry Irving and Presented at the Lyceum Theatre*, London, 1888.

Shattuck, Charles H., *The Shakespeare Promptbooks: A Descriptive Catalogue*, Urbana and London, 1965.

Shaw, Bernard 'Down with the Censorship!', *Saturday Review*, 2 March 1895.

——, 'King Arthur', *Saturday Review*, **79**, 19 January 1895.

——, *Dramatic Opinions and Essays*, London, 1909.

——, 'The Critics of *The White Prophet*', pamphlet, London, 1909.

——, *Our Theatres in the Nineties*, 3 vols, London, 1932.

——, *Pen Portraits and Reviews*, London, 1932.

——, *Collected Letters*, ed. Dan H. Laurence, 4 vols, New York, 1985–88.

——, *Bernard Shaw: The Drama Observed*, ed. Bernard F. Dukore, 4 vols, University Park, 1993.

Shelton, Edgar 'Victorian Memories', *Music and Letters*, **29**, 1949, pp. 7–8.

Sherard, Robert Harborough, 'Hall Caine: Story of His Life and Work, Derived from Conversations', *McClure's Magazine*, **6**, December 1895.

Showalter, Elaine, *The Female Malady*, London, 1987.

Simon, Nancy Lynn, 'Henry Irving and Ellen Terry in *Macbeth*: Lyceum Theatre, 29 December 1888', University of Washington dissertation, 1975.

Sinden, Donald, *A Touch of the Memoirs*, London, 1982.

Spielmann, M.H 'll. – A Shakespearean Revival', *Magazine of Art*, **12**, 1889, pp. 98–100.

Stefane-Pol, Paul, *Autour de Robespierre*, Paris, 1901.

Steiner, George, *Tolstoy or Dostoevsky*, New York, 1959.

Stephens, John Russell, *The Censorship of English Drama, 1824–1901*, Cambridge, 1980.

Stoker, Bram, *Personal Reminiscences of Henry Irving*, 2 vols, London, 1906.

——, 'Irving and Stage Lighting', *Nineteenth Century*, **69**, May 1911.

Stottlar, James F., 'The Theatre Magazine under Clement Scott', Chicago University PhD dissertation, 1966.

Swanson, Vern, *Sir Lawrence Alma-Tadema*, London, 1977.

Swinnerton, Frank, *The Georgian Literary Scene. A Panorama*, London, 1935.

Taine, Hippolyte, *Origines de la France contemporaine*, 6 vols, Paris, 1876–94.

Taylor, George, *Players and Performances in the Victorian Theatre*, Manchester, 1989.

Telbin, William, 'Art in the Theatre', *Magazine of Art*, **12**, 1889.

Tennyson, Sir Alfred, *The Poems of Tennyson*, ed. Christopher Ricks, London, 1969.

——, *The Letters of Alfred Lord Tennyson*, ed. Cecil Y. Lang and Edgar F. Shannon, 3 vols, New York, 1981–90.

Terry, Ellen, *The Story of My Life*, London, 1908.

——, *Four Lectures on Shakespeare*, ed. Christopher St John, London, 1932.

——, *Ellen Terry's Memoirs*, ed. Edith Craig and Christopher St John, London, 1933.

—— and Bernard Shaw, *Ellen Terry and Bernard Shaw: A Correspondence*, ed. Christopher St John, London, 1931.

Tetens, Kristan, 'Commemorating the French Revolution on the Victorian Stage: Henry Irving's *The Dead Heart*', *Nineteenth Century Theatre and Film*, 32, 2005, pp. 36–69.
'Théâtres et Concerts', *Journal des débats*, 20 June 1890.
Thompson, Francis, 'The *Macbeth* Controversy', *Dublin Review*, 3rd. Series, 1889, pp. 140–56.
Thomson, Peter, *On Actors and Acting*, Exeter, 2000.
Tillotson, Geoffrey and Kathleen, *Mid-Victorian Studies*, London, 1965.
Urban, Sylvanus, 'Table Talk', *Gentleman's Magazine*, 266, 1889, pp. 206–8.
van Ginneken, Jaap, *Crowds, Psychology and Politics, 1871–1899*, Cambridge, 1992.
Wade, Alan, ed., *The Scenic Art*, London, 1949.
Wearing, J.P., *The London Stage, 1890–1899: A Calendar of Plays and Players*, Metuchen, 1976.
White, Andrew D., *Autobiography*, 2 vols, London, 1905.
Wilde, Oscar, *The Letters of Oscar Wilde* (2nd edn), ed. Rupert Hart-Davies, London, 1962.
——, *Collected Works of Oscar Wilde*, Ware, 1997.
Wills, Freeman, *W.G. Wills, Dramatist and Painter*, London, 1898.
Wilson, A.E., *The Lyceum*, London, 1952.
Woollcott, Alexander, '"Crime and Punishment" Again', *New York World*, 14 October 1926.
Young, Percy, *Sir Arthur Sullivan*, New York, 1971.
Yzereef, Barry, 'The Art of Gentlemanly Melodrama: Charles Kean's Production of *The Corsican Brothers*', University of Victoria PhD dissertation, 1995.
Ziter Edward, *The Orient on the Victorian Stage*, Cambridge, 2003.

Journals, Magazines and Newspapers

Architectural Review
Ayrshire Post
Boston Herald
Burlington Magazine
Caledonian Mercury
Cambridge Opera Journal
Christian World
Conferencia
Daily Telegraph
Dispatch
Dramatic Mirror
Era
Evening Journal
Evening Post
First Knight: The Journal of the Irving Society
Fortnightly Review

Graphic
Great Thoughts
Homeland Mail
Illustrated London News
Indian Daily News
Indian Mirror
Journal des débats
Lady's Pictorial
L'Aurore
Leicester Journal
Le Temps
Listener
London Quarterly Review
Macmillans Magazine
Magazine of Art
Manchester Guardian
McClure's Magazine
Morning Advertiser
Morning Post
Musical Times
Music and Letters
New Penny Magazine
New York Globe
New York Herald
New York Post
New York Sun
New York Times
New York Tribune
New York World
Nineteenth Century
Nineteenth Century Theatre and Film
Observer
Overland Mail
Pall Mall Gazette
Penny Illustrated Newspaper
People
Proceedings of the Royal Musical Association
St John's Gazette
Sala's Journal
Saturday Review
Sir Arthur Sullivan Society Magazine
Sketch
Speaker
Spectator
Sporting and Dramatic News
Sporting Life

Star
Sunday Times
Telegraph
Theatre
Theatre History Studies
Theatre Notebook
The Times
The Times Literary Supplement
Today
Victorian Studies
Westminster Budget
Westminster Review
Windsor Magazine
World

Index

References to illustrations are in **bold**

Abbey, Edwin 131
Abdülhamid II, Ottoman sultan 53, 59
acting
    Irving on 30, 35
    Terry on 34–5
actors, hierarchy 13–14
Ahmad, Raffiüddin 58
Albert, Prince 67
Albery, James, *Two Roses* 191
Alma-Tadema, Sir Lawrence, designer,
    Coriolanus 108–9
Antoine, André 5, 7, 28
    bankruptcy 133
    on Irving's stage management 33–4, 123
    works
        La Patrie en Danger, crowd scenes
            123, 124
        Quatre-Vingt-Treize (film) 133
Appia, Adolphe 27
Aram, Eugene 93–4, 95–6
Archer, William, Irving, critique of 29–30,
    32, 135
Architectural Review 109
Arthurania
    frescoes, Palace of Westminster 67–8
    publications 68
    satirised 69
    Victorian revival 66–8
    see also Carr, J. Comyns
artistic freedom, Caine on 60
Ashwell, Lena 103
    King Arthur, Elaine 80, **81**
Aveling, Edward 50

Ball, Meredith 8, 150, 152, 158
Barker, Granville 132, 133
Barrett, Wilson 51, 52
Barrie, J.M.
    Ibsen's Ghost 20
    Walker, London 20
Bateman, Col Hezekiah Linthicum 105
Beardsley, Aubrey 68

Beerbohm, Max 132
    'Kolniyatsch' 87
Bellew, Kyrle
    Charlotte Corday 125
    Robespierre, Olivier **129**, 130
Benedict, Sir Julius 108, 150
Bennett, Arnold 87
Bennett, Joseph 167, 168, 177
Benson, Frank 88
Bernhardt, Sarah 7, 119
Bingham, Madeleine 188
Bizet, Georges, *Carmen* 174
Boulanger, Gen Georges 118
Bourchier, Arthur, *The Arm of the Law* 89
Brecht, Bertold, *Galileo* 132
Brereton, Austin 92, 112
Bright, Arthur 45
Brook, Peter
    on Craig 28
    on memorable theatre 117
    The Empty Space 117
Brown, Ford Madox 108, 111
    paintings
        Cordelia's Portion 109
        King Lear 109
Buchanan, Robert, *The Sixth Commandment*
    88
Büchner, Georg, *Danton's Death* 132
Bulwer Lytton, Edward, *Eugene Aram* 94,
    96
Burdett-Coutts, Angela 49
Burnand, F.C., *Faust and Loose* 22
Burne-Jones, Sir Edward 6, 34, 65, 67, 71,
    108, 111
    King Arthur
        costumes 73, 110
        Great Hall at Camelot **75**
        The Queen's Maying 105
        Whitethorn Wood **78**
    Stoker on 109–10
Burne-Jones, Sir Philip 111
Burton, Sir Richard, *Arabian Nights* 49, 52

Caine, Hall 49–51
  on artistic freedom 60
  on Irving's temperament 62
  works
    Good Old Times 51–2
    The Bondman 51
    The Deemster 51
    The Prophet 5–6, 52
      adaptation 61–2
      Lord Chamberlain's intervention 58–9
      Muslim protests 57–9
      narrative 55–6
      plot 56–7
      sale to US 61
      writing of 52–4
    The White Prophet 61 n42
Calvert, Charles 17
Calvert, Louis 125
Cameron, Julia Margaret 68
Carew, James 38
Carlyle, Thomas, *French Revolution* 117
Carr, J. Comyns, *King Arthur* 6, 65–85, 191
  adultery 81, 82
  anachronisms 81–2
  Arthur 82–3
  Arthurania, culmination of 85
  Elaine 79–80
  ephemerality of 84–5
  Excalibur scene **73**, 74
  Grail Quest scene 75–6, **75**
  Guinevere 75–7, 78–9, **78**, 82, 83
  The Magic Mere scene **72**
  performances 66
  power ideology 74
  The Queen's Maying **78**
  reception 66
  Scott's review 72, 83
  Shaw's review 66, 71, 83–4, 191
  structure 71
  success 74–5, 84
  Tower Above the River at Camelot **81**
Cattermole, Charles 152
chivalry, Victorian age 68
Clarke, Hamilton 7, 8, 150, 158
  Manual of Orchestration 141–2
  The Merchant of Venice music 136–8
    Bassanio chooses casket 139–40
    Belmont 140
    elopement scene and aftermath 140–48
    piano transcription 136, 137, 141, 147
    Prince of Morocco chooses casket 139
Coleridge, Samuel Taylor 66
Coleridge, Stephen 186
Colman Smith, Pamela 41
Copeau, Jacques 27
Coquelin, Benoît Constant 93, 119
Cornhill Magazine 153
Craig, Edith 38, 48
  acting roles 41
  costume design 41
  director 41
Craig, Edward Gordon 38, 39, 41, 131
  Brook on 28
  on Irving 27, 28–9, 30, 32, 35, 42, 44, 104
  Shaw, relationship 193
Craven, Hawes 7, 71, 111
  on Irving 107
  King Arthur
    Great Hall at Camelot **75**
    The Magic Mere **72**
    The Queen's Maying 105
    reputation 104–5
  Romeo and Juliet, scenery 114
crowd scenes
  Faust 126
  Julius Caesar 133–4
  La Patrie en Danger 123, 124
  Richard II 126
  Robespierre 123, 126–9, 130
    Convention Scene **129**
  Romeo and Juliet 114–15, 122
  The Dead Heart 126
crowds
  concern about 122–3
  revolutionary
    in films 133
    on stage 114–15, 122–8, 132–3
  The Crowd (Le Bon) 125

Daily Telegraph 177
Daly, Frederic 94
Darbyshire, Alfred 109
  Art of the Victorian Stage 99
Daumier, Honoré 104, 131
David, Jacques-Louis, *Tennis Court Oath* 130–31, **131**
de Bornier, Henri 5

Mahomet 49, 52, 55
  suppression 53
Diaghileff, Serge 27
Dickens, Charles
  on Irving 18
  Tale of Two Cities 117
Diderot 30, 31
Doré, Gustave 68, 104, 131
Dostoevsky, Fyodor
  true crime, interest in 96
  works
    Crime and Punishment 6
      dramatizations 88
    The Brothers Karamazov 87
drama, role of music 136, 138, 149–50
Dramatic Notes 112
Dreyfus case 132
Duncan, Isadora 27
Duse, Eleonora 119
Dyce, William 67

Eaton, Walter Pritchard 89, 92
Era 3, 113, 152
Examiner 147

Fielding, Henry, *Tom Thumb* 66
Forbes-Robertson, Johnston 104–5, 190
  King Arthur, Lancelot 65, **81**, 82
Fouquier, Armand, *Causes célèbres de tous les peuples* 96
Freie Bühne theatre 125
French Revolution, stage melodramas 117, 118
Froude, J.A. 123

Gardner, Joseph T. Jr 101, 105
Garnett, Constance, translation, *The Brothers Karamazov* 87, 88
Gentleman's Magazine 153
German, Edward 150
Gesamtkunstwerk 7, 34, 110, 183
Gielgud, Val 193
Gilbert, John 104, 131
Girouard, Marc 68
Gissing, George 87
Godwin, Edward 37, 41, 44, 99
Griffiths, D.W., *Intolerance* 133
Grotowski, Jerzy 28, 32
Guzzoni, Enrico, *Quo Vadis?* 133

Hackney, Mabel, Sonia, *The Unwritten Law* 90, **91**
Hall, T.W. 151
Hamel, Ernest 119
Hann, W. 151
Harker, Joseph 7, 71, 104, 151
  on Irving 107
  on professional painters 110–11
  Ravenswood, Ravenswood-A Room **106**
Harvey, John Martin, *The Only Way* 125, 129
Hauptmann, Gerhart, *The Weavers* 125
Herkomer, Sir Hubert von 111, 115–16
Herman, Henry 104
Hiatt, Charles 121–2
Hicks, Seymour 23
Hitchens, Robert, on Irving's use of silence 144–5
Holroyd, Michael 188
Hood, Thomas, 'The Dream of Eugene Aram' 4, 94
Hopkins, Tighe, on Irving's stage management 100–101
Hueffer, Francis 162–3, 172, 173, 177
Hughes, Alan 131
Hughes, Richard, *The Corsican Brothers* 167
Hugo, Victor, *Quatre-Vingt-Treize* 133
Hunt, William Holman 67
  The Light of the World 76

Ibsen, Henrik
  A Doll's House, Shaw's review 84
  Irving's aversion to 33
illness, gendered discourse on 43–4
Illustrated London News 120, 153
illustrators, Irving's use of 104
Innes, Christopher 31, 33
Irving, H.B., *Book of Remarkable Criminals* 95–6
Irving, Henry
  on acting 30, 35
  acting ability, views on 29–32
  biographies 187
  burial, Westminster Abbey 2
  caricatures of 29
  cartoons/illustrations 121–2
  'Chief' designation 20, 37
  Craig on 27, 28–9, 30, 32, 35, 42, 44, 104
  Craven on 107
  criticism of 29–30

Shaw's 32, 189–90, 191
debut 2
Dickens on 18
dominance 4, 7, 9
drunkenness allegations 188
early life 2
financial problems 121, 133
funeral 3
Garrick Club membership 19
Harker on 107
health 3
honorary degrees 2
Ibsen, aversion to 33
illustrators, use of 104, 131
James on 29
Jones on 29
knighthood 2
    soliciting allegations 186–7
last of Victorian actors 27–8
leadership 20
Lyceum Theatre, manager 1, 2, 19, 65
marriage 2
masonic connections 19
modernity of 5, 27, 28, 35
music, use of 7–8, 136–8
new drama, encouragement of 20
obituary, Shaw's 186, 189
perfectionism 103, 107
performance style 5
performances
    Becket, Becket 3, 29
    Charles I, Charles I 189
    Eugene Aram, Eugene Aram 4, 5, 9, 16–17, 94–5
        critical reception 95
        Scott on 95
    Hamlet, Hamlet 50, 190
    King Arthur, King Arthur 6, 65, 68, 72, **73**, **81**, 82, 84, 110
    Macbeth, Macbeth **124**, 153–5, **154**
        interpretation 156–7
        Wilde on 155
    Robespierre, Robespierre **129**
    The Bells, Mathias 2, 24, 30, 92, **93**, 189
    The Merchant of Venice, Shylock 189–90
    Two Roses, Digby Grant 191
    Uncle Dick's Darling, Reginald Chevenix 17–18
portrait **21**
productions
    Cymbeline, Shaw's review 189
    Dante 103
    Faust 102, 103, 126, 152, 158
    King Arthur 34, 65–85
    King Lear 109
    Macbeth 8
        costumes 151–2
        critical reception 153–4
        lighting 153
        Macduff and Macbeth **174**
        research for 151
        scenery 151, 153
        success 152–3
        Sullivan's music 8, 149–83; *see also under* Sullivan
        The Weird Sisters **172**
        Witches and Spirits in Chorus **173**
    Richard III 131
        Shaw's review 187–8
    Richard Lovelace 88
    Robespierre 117, 125
        Convention Scene **129**
        criticism of 120–21
        crowd scenes 123, 126–30
        music 120
        set design 119–20
        success factors 121
        Terry on 121, 122
    Romeo and Juliet
        critical reception 113
        crowd scenes 114–15, 122
        lighting 115
        scenery 112–15
        Scott's review 101, 104, 112
        Terry on 112–13
    The Cup 109
    The Dead Heart 118, 123, 126
    The Merchant of Venice 7–8
        added elopement scene 135
        cuts 135
        music 136–48
        Shylock Returning Home 144, **145**
        Shylock's House by a Bridge **141**, 142
rehearsals, observing **152**
role designer 29
scenic artists, use of 104–5, 107–11
Scott on 29, 32

Index

Shaw, relationship 185–93
silence, use of 144–5, 146–7
stage lighting, skill 107–8
stage management
    Antoine on 123
    views on 100–101
as stage manager 33–4
on stagecraft 100, 101–2
stagecraft, Stoker on 102, 103
temperament, Caine on 62
Terry
    correspondence 38
    working relationship 37–48, 192
Toole
    acting with 15–16, 17–18
    in conversation **23**
    correspondence 15
    friendship 14–25
as übermarionette 28–9
Wilde on 158
Irving, Laurence 2, 6, 7, 38, 146, 192
    on Irving-Terry relationship 39
    performances, *Robespierre* Tallien **129**, 130
    works
        Crime and Punishment
            forward to 96–7
            stage adaptation 88
        Margaret Catchpole 90
        The Fool Hath Said... 88
            criticism of 89–90
            reception 90
        The Unwritten Law (prev *The Fool Hath Said*) 90
            as Raskolnikoff 90, **91**
        Time, Hunger; and the Law 88

Jacobi, George, music
    Robespierre 120
    The Dead Heart 120
James, Henry 140
    on Irving 29
Jones, Henry Arthur, on Irving 29

Kappes, Alfred 68
Kean, Charles 34, 99, 142
    crowd scenes, *Richard II* 126
Kean, Edmund 12, 13
King Arthur
    Lyceum production *see* Carr, J. Comyns
    Purcell/Dryden opera (1691) 66
King, W.D. 27, 32
Klein, Herman 8, 158–9

Labouchère, Henry 95
Lady's Pictorial 169
Lanier, Sidney, *The Boy's King Arthur* 68
Le Bon, Gustave, *The Crowd* 125
Leeds Art Theatre 41
Leighton, Robert 56, 60
Lewis, Leopold 92
Locke, Matthew, *Macbeth* music (attrib) 153, 157
London Quarterly Review 69
London Shakespeare League 187
Loveday, George 19
Loveday, Harry 11, 20
Loveday, H.J. 127
Luteef, Abdul 57–8
Lyceum Theatre 37, 192
    Irving's management 1, 2, 19, 65

Mackenzie, Sir Alexander 108, 150
Macready, William Charles 12
Malory, Sir Thomas, *Le Morte Darthur* 67, 68, 81
Mansfield, Richard 88
Marbury, Elizabeth 125
Mathews, Charles 17
Meltzer, Charles Henry, *Rodion the Student* 88
Mendelssohn, Felix, *Walpurgis Night* 157, 158
Meyerhold, V.E. 27, 28, 31, 32
Michelet, Jules 118
Middleton, Thomas, *The Witch* 168
Millais, Sir John Everett 110
    Ophelia 80
Mohammedan Literary Society 61
Moore, George 88
Moore, Nellie 4
Morning Post 186
Morris, William 67, 68
music
    in drama 136, 138, 149–50
        composers 150–51
    in films 138
    Irving's use of 7–8, 136–48
Musical Times 158

Nash, Percy, stage manager, *Robespierre* 108
National Review 153

Die Neue Freie Presse 185, 186
New Penny Magazine 127
New York Dramatic Mirror 128

O'Callaghan, Florence 2
O'Neill, Norman 136, 150
Orlenev, Pavel 88
Oxenford, John 96–7

Pall Mall Gazette 55, 57, 59, 90
Paris Commune (1871) 117
Partridge, Bernard 121
    'Excalibur', *King Arthur* **73**
People 153
Perkins & Caney, scene painters 151
Phelps, Samuel 2
Phillips, Watts, *The Dead Heart* 118
Pigott, Edward Frederick Smyth 58
Pinero, Arthur Wing 20
Pioneer Players 41
Piscator, Erwin 27
Pocock, Isaac 69
Ponsonby-Fane, Sir Spencer 58
Poynter, Sir Edward 111
Przybyszewska, Stanislawa, *The Danton Case* 132

Reinhardt, Max 132
Réjane, Gabrielle 7
Rendell, Ruth 92
Richards, Jeffrey 42
    Sir Henry Irving 2, 187
Robertson, Graham 109
Robertson, Tom 99
Robins, Elizabeth, *Votes for Women* 132
Rossetti, Dante Gabriel 51, 67
Ruskin, John 140
Russell, Edward R. 115
    on Terry's Lady Macbeth 155

St. James's Gazette 153
St John, Christopher 42
Saintsbury, H.A., on Irving's stage lighting 108
Sardou, Victorien
    reputation 119
    works
        Fédora 119
        Madame Sans-Gêne 118, 188
        Robespierre 6, 7, 117
        Thermidor 118, 119, 122, 126, 129

Sargent, John Singer 111
The Saturday Review 84, 135, 187, 190, 192
Saxe-Meiningen Company 7, 33, 114, 122
Saxe-Meiningen, Duke 28, 34
scenic artists
    Irving's use of 104–5, 107–11
    recognition 111–12
Scenic Artists Association 112
scenic designers 6–7
Scott, Clement 69
    on Irving 29, 32
    review
        Eugene Aram 95
        King Arthur 72, 83
        Romeo and Juliet 101, 112
            costumes 104
Scott, Sir Walter, *Ivanhoe* 66–7
Shaw, Bernard 43
    Irving
        criticism 32, 189–90, 191–2
        drunkenness, allegations 188
        obituary 186, 189
        praise 190, 191
        relationship 185–93
        Terry relationship 192
    review
        A Doll's House 84
        Cymbeline 189
        King Arthur 66, 71, 83–4, 191
        Richard III 8, 187–8
    The Saturday Review articles 185, 190, 192
    on Terry 37
    works
        Arms and the Man 185
        Candida 185
        Cymbeline Refinished 189
        Mrs Warren's Profession 90, 185
        St Joan 132
        The Man of Destiny 119, 188, 193
        You Never Can Tell 191
Siddons, Sarah 155
Smallhythe Place 39, 48
Sothern, E.H. 88, 89–90, 92
Spectator 53, 87, 95, 146, 147
Spiers, Richard Phené 109
Stage 3
stage lighting
    Irving's skill 107–8
    Saintsbury on 108
    Telbin on 107

stagecraft
    developments 99–100
    Irving on 100, 101–2
Stanford, Sir Charles 108, 150
Stanislavski, Constantin 27, 28, 30, 31, 32
Stevenson, Robert Louis 88
Stoepel, Robert 8, 150, 157
Stoker, Bram 7, 8, 19, 25, 52–3, 59, 66, 70, 158
    on Burne-Jones 109–10, 111
    on Irving's stagecraft 102, 103
    Personal Reminiscences of Henry Irving 49
Stone, Marcus 111
Sullivan, Sir Arthur 6, 34, 108
    caricature **159**
    Ivanhoe 160
    King Arthur 65
    Macbeth 8, 151, 152, 153, 156, 158–9, 161–2
        autograph score **170–71**
        critical success 162–3, 169
        harp 163
        Irving's input 160–61
        overture 159, 164, 175
            autograph score **176**
            music examples **180–81**
            synoptic analysis 177–9
            Weber's *Der Freischütz*, comparison **182**
        summary table 164–5
    operettas 160
    Shakespeare plays 151, 160
    The Golden Legend 160, 172
    The Tempest 150, 151, 160
Symonds, J.A. 87

Taine, Hippolyte 118
Tairov, Alexander 27
Taylor, George 30–31
Taylor, Tom, drama, *Tale of Two Cities* 120
Telbin, William 7, 103, 104, 142
    Faust, Summit of the Brocken **106**
    on Irving's stage lighting 107
    Much Ado about Nothing, church 105
    Romeo and Juliet, Capulet tomb 105
Tennyson, Hallam 70
Tennyson, Lord Alfred
    King Arthur, ambivalence towards 69–70
    works

Becket 29
'The Day-Dream' 78
The Idylls of the King 67, 68, 70, 74, 79
Terry, Ellen 2–3, 5, 15, 22, 32, 54, 103, 135, 155
    on acting 34–5
    health 43–4, 44–5
    Irving
        correspondence 38
        working relationship 37–48
    Memoirs 142, 151
    performances
        Hamlet, Ophelia 50
        King Arthur, Guinevere 6, 65, 72, 77–8, **78**, **81**, 83
        Macbeth, Lady Macbeth 42, **124**, 155–6, **156**
        Peter the Great, Catherine 45
        preparation 42–3
        Ravenswood, Lucy Ashton 45
        Robespierre, Clarisse **129**, 130
        The Amber Heart, Ellaline 45
        The Lyons Mail, Jeanette 45
        The Merchant of Venice, Portia 43, 45, 139
    public image, awareness of 46
    on *Robespierre* 121, 122
    on *Romeo and Juliet* 112–13, 114
    Shaw, correspondence 38–9
    Shaw on 37
    sketch **40**
Théâtre Français 118
Théâtre Libre 33, 118, 123, 125, 126, 133
Theatre Regulation Act (1843) 1
Thompson, Alfred 104
The Times 58, 65, 75, 81, 113, 114, 186, 187
Today 120, 130, 132
Tolstoy, Leo, *Power of Darkness* 126
Toole, J.L. 4, 88
    appearance 12
    Edinburgh performances 12–13
    illness 24
    Irving
        acting with 15–16, 17–18
        in conversation **23**
        correspondence 15
        friendship 14–25
    manager, Toole's Theatre 19
    mimicry 12
    new drama, encouragement of 20

portrait **21**
Trebitsch, Siegfried 186, 187
Tree, Herbert Beerbohm 20, 88, 119, 133
   Julius Caesar 125

Verdi, Giuseppe, *Macbeth* 157
Vestris, Madame Lucia Elizabeth 99
Victoria, Queen, theatre enthusiast 1

Wajda, Andrez, *Danton* 132
Wales, Prince (Edward VII), theatre
   enthusiast 1
Warner, Deborah, *Julius Caesar*, crowd
   scenes 133–4
Waterhouse, John William 67
Webb, Sir Aston 110
Weber, Carl Maria von, *Der Freischütz*
   181–2

Sullivan's *Macbeth*, comparison **182**
Westminster Budget 132
Westminster Gazette 100
Wilde, Oscar 65
   on Irving 158
   on Irving's Macbeth 155
Willard, E.S. 61
Wills, W.G. 6, 70, 94
   Charles I 189
Windsor Theatricals 1
Winter, William 139
Wyndham, R.H. 12

Yeats, W.B. 41

Zola, Emile
   Germinal 118
   'J'accuse' 132

For Product Safety Concerns and Information please contact our EU
representative GPSR@taylorandfrancis.com
Taylor & Francis Verlag GmbH, Kaufingerstraße 24, 80331 München, Germany

www.ingramcontent.com/pod-product-compliance
Lightning Source LLC
Chambersburg PA
CBHW070254230426
43664CB00014B/2530